Marketing Professional Services

Marketing Professional Services

Dr. Sushma, Nalla

AKANSHA PUBLISHING HOUSE
NEW DELHI • GUWAHATI • VISAKHAPATNAM

AKANSHA PUBLISHING HOUSE
4649-B/21, Ansari Road
Daryaganj, New Delhi-110002
Phones: 23268193, 09435116718
Email: ektabooks@yahoo.com
visit us: www.akanshapublishinghouse.com

Marketing Professional Services

First Published 2011

ISBN 978-81-8370-286-7

PRINTED IN INDIA

Published by Akansha Publishing House, New Delhi-110002 and printed at Harmain Offset Printers, Delhi.

Contents

Foreword

India's service sector contributes more than 55 per cent of GDP, making in the most formidable component of the country's economy. The changing environmental and legal conditions across the world are giving ample opportunities to India's professionals to expand their operations and services globally. As service sector continues to develop at an unprecedented rate, there is a short supply of talent pool to meet to the rising demands of the industry. With knowledge and professional skill set standing out as a unique selling proposition for this industry, it is becoming increasingly important to market professional services to reach a larger client base and create a successful professional firm.

The field of marketing is undergoing a huge transformation with the concepts gaining seamless application and integration. Gone are the days when Marketing is perceived to be "sales" or just "advertising". It is emerging indeed as a powerful tool which can turn around the fate of firms and give soaring profits to them. A professional service is one such fascinating area for which marketing can be applied.

Be it doctors, lawyers or chartered accountants, marketing makes them handle the company, customers and competitors with a powerful insight and foresight which will enable them to attract and retain customers/clients in the long run. This book on Professional services is a well articulated and constructed research on the applications of wide marketing concepts to Chartered Accountants and elaborates on the doe's and don'ts for those who are in the professional services industry. Yet, it gives a Bird's eye-view on how marketing can be helpful in rendering quality services by various other services which are professional in nature as well.

It is imperative that even professional services firms need to think about how to grow their revenues and manage their clients for creating ongoing business. Above all, it is largely important for a professional services firm to understand how "Perceptions" of quality differ from a professional to a customer/client. Various dimensions of services like "differences in perception of service quality" and how "moments of truth" can be created to the clients are researched and well explained in the chapters that follow in this Book.

Many of the concepts of marketing and processes which are aptly relevant for services are researched and validated through this book which will prove helpful to the professional services industry. As competitive landscape keeps dynamically changing each year in the macro-environmental setup of India and professional services continue to stay under the scan of legal regulation, it is increasingly important to market professional services. The leaders of professional firms have to strategically combine a set of tools to attract and retain their clients through creating such services which suit to the tailored needs of them.

It is a Sincere and honest piece of research which will be useful to not just chartered accounts but also to all those who render professional services with an aspiration to create a long standing mark in their field of business.

(Shri Pydah Krishna Prasad)
Chairman
Pydah Educational Institutions

Preface

Services' marketing now faces a challenge that confronts many maturing fields of study. Specifically as the domain of services has expanded, the boundaries that define it have become more obscure. The direction in which services marketing is headed is unclear. Issues regarding the scope and future of services persist. In short, as the field has grown, it has become more diffuse. In our information based economy, where new business models are constantly emerging and disappearing, and the struggle to develop successful new frameworks raises questions regarding existing paradigms. New paradigms must evolve (Grove, Fisk and John (2003)). The relevance of Marketing to Professional services rests in the increased emphasis on service quality in customer-oriented professions. Customers no longer simply purchase products; they co-produce in service organizations (Prahalad & Ramaswamy, 2000). The co-production occurs through the front-line employees and the customer at the time of transaction, therefore, the customer buying experience must be understood from both the firms and customer perspective (Iacobucci & Nordhielm, 2000). This study examines professional Services from the customer orientation within Accountancy Profession. The purpose of this study is to determine relationships of professionals with clients and their perceptions towards the use of Marketing. The relationships between involvement on perceptions of service quality and feedback from professionals, and expectations and perceptions of professionals impact on service quality. Two distinct groups were examined: Professionals (150) and Clients (200 users and 200 non-users of Individual, Institutional and other professionals). The examination of professionals was simple random sampling and the examination of clients was done on the basis of simple and stratified random sampling. A total of 150 professionals (Chartered Accountants (100%) and 400 (100%) participants completed the survey instrument. Two instruments were utilized for this study: the participant instrument contained two sections (Personal Data and Experimental Data) and the instrument for all subjects was given through personal meetings and discussions. The results indicated similarities exist on perceptions of service quality and feedback based upon involvement of the professional with the client (Individual, Institutional and other professionals). The correlation results demonstrated that the dimensions of Professional performance greatly impacted service quality. The thesis will prove helpful to small, and medium sized professional services and is left to the imagination of the user to apply his own levels of creativity into marketing effort. Knowingly or unknowingly, professional chartered accountants are involved in using marketing efforts in their practice. But in the wake of competitive challenges and globalization clubbed with changing legal framework of India, marketing becomes a necessary principle for being successful both in the market place and in the market space.

With utmost humility and respect I am deeply indebted to my research Guide, Guru and Mentor Prof. V. Bala Mohana Das, former Vice-Chancellor, Acharya Nagarjuna University. Without his continuous guidance this work wouldn't have been possible. I am soulfully thankful to Padmasri Prof. Yaralagadda Lakshmi Prasad, Chairman Lok Nayak Foundation, I convey my gratitude to Prof. G. Satyanarayana, Department of Commerce and Management Studies, Andhra University for being a constant support in completion of my research work.

All my love and affection goes to my family, my parents Prof. Shyamala Devi Dasari, Prof. Babayya Nalla, my sister Sunitha Peyyala, my brother-in-law Srinivasa Varma Peyyala and my nephews Akshith and Akhil. Without them, I would not be what I am today. I also convey my sincere thanks to all my teachers who have taught me the wings of wisdom and my colleagues, relatives Suseela, Anand and my friends who have always supported me in my endeavour. I also thank all those who have directly or indirectly helped me in making this book possible.

Dr. Sushma, Nalla

1

Marketing Professional Services: Prologue

Service markets have never been larger, competition in services has probably never been more intense, and net employment growth within developed economies is almost exclusively derived from services. Indian service sector contributes to more than 55% of its GDP. A rare characteristic of service research is that it originated simultaneously in several European countries and the United States. The service sector is a growing part of the economy in many countries to be able to survive in this sector; it is necessary to offer the market, services that are perceived as having quality. Interviews with both providers and customer stated the importance of cooperation between the two parties. The perspective on cooperation in this chapter was from the providers' side. The question was, "What characteristics should a customer have?" Research on professional services will give a much deeper insight into the Marketing of Professional services and will erode the myopic vision of the professionals towards their perception of Marketing. Not only will Marketing help at attracting new clients but it also has the ability to induce customer loyalty. It is evident from the literature that professional services belong to High Touch-services. Before getting into the concept of professional services, let's see what is marketing?

Marketing

The marketing mix was developed throughout the 1950's and 1960's (Borden, 1964; McCarthy, 1964; Gronroos, 2002) as a method to optimize profit and act as guidelines in marketing decisions. The intentions of the marketing mix i.e. product, price, promotion and physical distribution was to create ideas on how to solve marketing problems not as a method to fix them. This creates a situation where service organizations focus on "to whom something is done" (p. 132) instead of "for whom" (p. 132). The "to whom" mentality demonstrates a product-oriented not service oriented approach, where the seller has an active role and the consumer is passive (Gronroos, 2002). Current marketing techniques attempt to focus downstream through service-based advantages and customer allegiances. It is no longer simply the product but the intangibles that are associated with the product that create additional revenue (Wise & Baumgartner, 1999) and customer expectations must be met. Expectations affect satisfaction levels, which significantly impact the customer defect rate and this, occurs through the fulfillment of basic customer needs: (1) security, (2) justice, and (3) self-esteem (Schneider & Bowen, 1999). In order to meet these needs organizations must exceed customer expectations through responsiveness, assurance, and empathy. These expectations rise and customers grow in loyalty and knowledge, therefore companies must take a customer first approach. Difficulties develop from employees who fail to fix problems and this is resolved through the creation of relationships (Parasuraman et al., 1991). Current methods in service marketing research create these relationships and include understanding customer expectations, service encounters, servicescapes, service failures, service recovery, and relationship marketing and trust-based selling. Let us trace the various definitions of marketing that evolved over a period of time. There is a time when the definition of marketing did not change for nearly 35 years.

Definition

It's interesting once in a while to step back and observe change ... You can almost hear the conversations evolve as marketing has evolved from mass marketing to segment marketing to target marketing to relationship marketing:

> "Consumers don't know what they want until someone tells them."

The pre 60s rise of branded products and advertising agencies.

Focus: mass communication

The American Marketing Association (194 & 1960) definition of Marketing:

> "The performance of business activities that direct the flow of goods and services from producers to consumers."

The 70s and 80s beginning of direct marketing.

Focus: identification of the target group

The American Marketing Association (1985) definition of Marketing:

> "The process of planning and executing the conception, pricing, promotion, and distribution of ideas, goods, and services to create exchanges that satisfy individual and organizational objectives".

The 90s rise of loyalty programs.

Focus: databases, analysis systems

The 2000s evolution of marketing.

Focus: creating value for the customer

The American Marketing Association (2004) definition of Marketing:

> "Marketing is an organizational function and a set of processes for creating, communicating, and delivering value to customers and for managing customer relationships in ways that benefit the organization and its stakeholders."

Evolution of Marketing

The academic field of marketing formally began shortly after the turn of the last century and is now about 100 years old. Both the real world of marketing and the real world of society have undergone massive changes during this time. The 4 era's of Marketing thought are as mentioned in Table 1.1 in the next page.

Table 1.1 The "4 Eras" of Marketing Thought

Era Distinctive Characteristics
"Pre-Marketing"
(Before 1900)

No distinguishing field of study; issues are embedded within the field of economics.

I. "Founding the Field" (1900-1920)

Development of first courses with "marketing" in title.

Emphasis on defining purview of marketing's activities as Economic institution.

Focus on marketing as distribution.

II. "Formalizing the Field" (1920-1950)

Development of generally accepted foundations or "principles of marketing."

Establishment of knowledge development infrastructure for the field: professional association (AMA), conferences, journals (Journal of Retailing and Journal of Marketing).

III. "A Paradigm Shift-Marketing, Management, and the Sciences" (1950-1980)

Growth boom in U.S. mass market and marketing body of thought.

Two perspectives emerge to dominate the marketing mainstream: (1) the managerial viewpoint and (2) the behavioral and quantitative sciences as keys to future knowledge development.

Knowledge infrastructure undergoes major expansion and evolution.

IV. "The Shift Intensifies—A Fragmentation of the Mainstream" (1980-present)

New challenges arise in business world: short-term financial focus, downsizing, globalization, and reengineering.

Dominant perspectives are questioned in philosophy of science debates.

Publish-or-perish pressure intensifies on academics.

Knowledge infrastructure expands and diversifies into specialized interest areas.

Concept of Marketing

Marketing is the company function charged with defining customer targets and the best way to satisfy their needs and wants competitively and profitably. Since consumers and business buyers face an abundance of suppliers seeking to satisfy their every need, companies cannot survive today by simply doing a good job. They must do an excellent job if they are to remain in the increasingly competitive global marketplace. Recent studies have demonstrated that the key to profitable company performance is knowing and satisfying target customers with competitively superior offers. This process takes place today in an increasingly global, technical and competitive environment.

Marketing has its origins in the fact that humans have needs and wants. Needs and wants create a state of discomfort in people, which is relieved through acquiring products to satisfy these needs and wants. Since many products can satisfy a given need, product choice is guided by the concepts of value, cost, and satisfaction. These products are obtainable in several ways: self-production, coercion, begging and exchange. Most modern societies work on the principle of exchange, which means that people specialize in producing particular products and trade them for the other things they need. They engage in transactions and relationship building. A market is a group of people who share a similar need. Marketing encompasses those activities that represent working with markets and attempting to actualize potential exchanges.

Marketing management is the conscious effort to achieve desired exchange outcomes with target markets. The marketer's basic skill lies in influencing the level, timing, and composition of demand for a product, service, organization, place, person, idea or some form of information.

There are five alternative philosophies that can guide organizations in their efforts to carry out their marketing goal(s). The production concept holds that consumers will favor products that are affordable and available, and therefore management's major task is to improve production and distribution efficiency and bring down prices. The product concept holds that consumers favor quality products that are reasonably priced, and therefore little promotional effort is required. The selling concept holds that consumers will not buy enough of the company's products unless they are stimulated through a substantial selling and promotion effort.

Heading towards more enlightened views of the role of marketing, the marketing concept holds that the main task of the company is to determine the needs, wants, and preferences of a target group of customers and to deliver the desired satisfactions. Its four principles are target market, customer needs, integrated marketing, and profitability. The marketing concept places primary focus on the needs and wants of customers who comprise the target market for a particular product. Rather than coax customers into purchasing a product they may not find satisfying, the emphasis is on determining the types of markets to be satisfied, and creating the product that achieves this satisfaction objective. Choosing target markets and identifying customer needs is no small task; a marketer must dig beyond a customer's stated needs. Once this is accomplished, a marketer can offer for sale the products that will lead to the highest satisfaction. This encourages customer retention and profit, which is best achieved when all areas/departments of a company become "customer-focused".

Moving beyond the marketing concept, the societal marketing concept holds that the main task of the company is to generate customer satisfaction and long-run consumer and societal well being as the key to satisfying organizational goals and responsibilities.

Interest in marketing is intensifying as more organizations in the business sector, the nonprofit sector, and the global sector recognize how marketing contributes to improved performance in the marketplace. The result is that marketers are re-evaluating various marketing concepts and tools; focus on relationships, databases, communications and channels of distribution, as well as marketing outside and inside the organization.

Building Profitable Businesses Through World-Class Marketing

> "There are three kinds of companies: those who make things happen; those who watch things happen; and those who wonder what's happened."—Anonymous

If we do not change our direction, we are likely to end up where we are headed.- Old Chinese proverb

As the world spins into the next millennium, both citizens and businesses wonder what is ahead. There is not only change, but the rate of change is accelerating. A twelve-year-old girl said of her nine-year-old sister, "She is of a different generation." Her younger sister listens to different music, plays different video games, knows different movie stars, has different heroes.

Companies often fail to recognize that their marketplace changes every few years. The book *Value Migration* documents how customer requirements and competitive forces have changed significantly every few years in such industries as steel, telecommunications, health care, and entertainment.' Last year's winning strategy may become today's losing strategy. As someone observed, there are two kinds of companies: those who change and those who disappear.

Today's economic landscape is being shaped by two powerful forces—technology and globalization. The technological landscape today is dotted with new products that President John Kennedy in the early 1960s would not have seen, such as satellites, VCRs, camcorders, photocopiers, fax machines, answering machines, digital watches, e-mail, cellular phones, and laptop computers. Technology is the ultimate shaper not only of the material substructure of society but also of human thought patterns. As Marshall McLuhan observed, "The medium is the message."

One revolutionary technological force is digitalization, where information is being encoded in "bits," namely series of zeros and ones. The bits are massaged by computers, encoded into music and videos, and sent over phone lines at incredible speed. Nicholas Negro Ponte, leader of MIT's famous Media Lab, sees "bits" as replacing "atoms."[3] No longer does a software company need to manufacture a set of floppies, put them into a printed package, and ship them on a truck to various outlets, where consumers would have to go to buy them. Sending the software over the Internet to be downloaded on the customer's computer can save all this work.

Technology drives the second major force, globalization.

McLuhan vision of a "global village" is now a reality. A Bangkok executive who wants to buy this book can type "www.amazon.com" on his keyboard, enter his credit card number, and receive it in a few days thanks to Federal Express. A Cologne, Germany, florist wholesaler who is short of red roses can order and receive a planeload of red roses the next morning from Tel Aviv. Besides technology and globalization, other forces are reshaping the economy. Deregulation is occurring in many economies. Protected companies, often monopolies, suddenly confront new competitors. In the United States, long distance telephone companies such as AT&T can now enter local markets; and regional Bell telephone companies have the corresponding right to enter long distance markets. And electrical utilities can now sell and ship their electricity into other communities.

Another strong force is privatization, where former publicly held companies and agencies have been turned over to private ownership and management, in the belief that they would be better managed and more efficient. This happened when British Airways and British Telecom were privatized. Today many public goods and services are being outsourced to private companies, including the building and management of prisons, school systems, and the like.

As the pace of change accelerates, companies can no longer rely on their former business practices to sustain prosperity.

Are There Winning Marketing Practices?

Besides winning business practices, is there a set of winning marketing practices? One frequently hears of one-liner formulas that promise marketing success. Here are nine of the more prominent one-liners:

1. Win Through Higher Quality

Everyone agrees that poor quality is bad for business. Customers who have been burned with bad quality won't return and will bad-mouth the company. But what about winning through good quality? There are four problems.

First, quality has a lot of meanings. If an automobile company claims good quality, what does it mean? Do its cars have more starting reliability? Do they accelerate faster? Do the car bodies wear better over time? Customers care about different things, so a quality claim without further definition doesn't mean much.

Second, people often can't tell a product's quality by looking at it. Consider buying a television receiver. You go into Circuit City and see a hundred different sets with the picture on and the sound blaring. The picture quality is similar with most receivers. The casings may differ but hardly tell you any-thing about the set's reliability. You don't ask the salesperson to open the back of the set to inspect the quality of the components. In the end, you have at best an image of quality without any evidence.

Third, most companies are catching up to each other in quality in most markets. When that happens, quality is no longer a determinant of brand choice.

Fourth, some companies are known to have the highest quality, such as Motorola when it touts its 6-sigma quality. But are there enough customers who need that quality level and will pay for it? And what were Motorola's costs of getting to 6-sigma quality? It is possible that getting to the highest quality level costs too much.

2. Win Through Better Service

We all want good service. But customers define it in different ways. Take, service in a restaurant. Some customers would like the waiter to appear quickly, take the order accurately, and deliver the food soon. Other customers would feel that this is rushing them on what otherwise should be a leisurely evening out. Every service break down into a list of attributes: speed, cordiality, knowledge, problem solving, and so on. Each person places different weights at different times in different contexts on each of the service attributes. Claiming better service isn't enough.

3. Win Through Lower Prices

A low price strategy has worked for a number of companies, including the world's largest furniture retailer, IKEA; the world's largest general merchandise retailer, Wal-Mart; and one of America's most profitable airlines, Southwest. Yet low-price leaders must be a lower-price firm might suddenly enter the market. Sears practiced low prices for years, until WalMart beat it on prices.

Low price alone is not enough to build a viable business enterprise. The Yugo automobile was low in price; it was also lowest in quality and disappeared. A measure of quality and service must also be present, so that customers feel they are buying on value, not price alone.

Table 1.2: Business Firms in Transition

Then	*Now*
Make everything inside the company	Buy more things outside (outsource)
Improve on one's own	Improve by benchmarking with others
Go it alone	Network with other firms,
Operate with functional	Manage business processes
Focus domestically	Focus globally and locally
Be product-centered	Be market- and customer- centered
Make a standard product	Make adapted and/or Customized products
Focus on the product	Focus on the value chain
Practice mass marketing	Practice target marketing
Find a sustainable competitive	Keep inventing new
Develop new products slowly	advantages advantage Speed up the new product development and carefully meant process cycle
Use many suppliers	Use few suppliers
Manage from the top	Manage up and down and across
Operate in the marketplace	Operate also in the market space

Source: Kotler on Marketing by Philip Kotler(2001), p. 6.

4. Win Through High Market Share

Generally speaking, market share leaders make more money than their lamer competitors. They enjoy scale economies and higher brand recognition. There is a "bandwagon effect," and first-time buyers have more confidence in choosing the company's products. But many high market share leaders are not that profitable. A & P was America's largest supermarket chain for many years and yet made pathetic profits. Consider the condition of such giant companies as IBM, Sears, and General Motors in the 1980s, a time when they were doing more poorly than many of their smaller competitors.

5. Win Through Adaptation and Customization

Many buyers will want the seller to modify his offering to contain special features or services they need. A business firm might want Federal Express to pick up its daily mail at 7 p.m., not 5 p.m. A hotel guest might want to rent a room for only part of the day. Such needs can represent opportunities for the seller. However, for many sellers, the cost may be too high to adapt the offering to each customer. Mass customization is working for some companies, but many others would find it to be an unprofitable strategy.

6. Win Through Continuous Product Improvement

Continuous product improvement is a sound strategy, especially if the company can lead the pack in product improvements. But not all product improvements are valued. How much more would customers pay if they are told about a better detergent, a sharper razor blade, a faster automobile? Some products reach the limit of their improvement possibilities, and the last improvement doesn't matter very much.

7. Win Through Product Innovation

A frequent exhortation is "Innovate or Evaporate." True, some great in-novative companies, such as Sony and 3M, have earned substantial profits by introducing superb new products. But the average company has not fared well in its new product introductions. The new product failure in branded consumer packaged goods is still around 80 percent; in the industrial goods world, it is around 30 percent. A company's dilemma is that if it doesn't introduce new products, it will probably "evaporate"; if it does introduce new products, it may lose a lot of money.

8. Win Through Entering High-Growth Markets

High growth markets such as solid-state electronics, biotechnology, robotics, and telecommunications have the glamour. Some market leaders have made fortunes in those industries. But the average firm entering a high-growth market fails. One hundred new software firms start up in an area, such as computer graphics, and only a few survive. Once the market accepts some firm's brand as the standard, that firm begins to enjoy increasing volume and returns. Microsoft's Office has become the standard, and other good alternatives have been shuttled aside. An added problem is that products become obsolete very fast in these fast-growing industries, and each company must invest continually to keep up. They hardly recoup their profits from their last offering before they have to invest in developing its replacement.

9. Win Through Exceeding Customer Expectations

One of the most popular marketing clichés today is that a winning company is one that consistently exceeds customer expectations. Meeting customer expectations will only satisfy customers; exceeding their expectations will delight them. Customers who are delighted with a supplier have a much higher probability of remaining a customer.

The problem is that when a customer's expectations are exceeded, he has higher expectations next time. The task of exceeding the higher expectations gets more difficult and more costly. Ultimately, the company must settle for just meeting the latest expectations.

Put another way, many of today's customers want the highest quality,Added services, great convenience, customization, return privileges, guarantees-all at the lowest price. Clearly each company has to decide which of these many customers wants it can meet profitably.

What Constitutes a Winning Marketing Strategy?

Clearly there is no one marketing road to riches. Instead of relying on one major differentiation or thrust, a company. Needs to weave its own unique tapestry of marketing qualities and activities. It is not enough to do most things a little better than the competitors. Professor Michael Porter of Harvard argues that a company doesn't really have a strategy if it performs the same activities as its competitors, only a little better.5 It is simply operationally more effective. Being operationally excellent is not the same as having a robust strategy. Operational excellence might help the firm win for a while, but other firms will soon catch up or pass up the firm.

Porter sees a business as having a robust strategy when it

has strong points of difference from competitors' strategies. Thus Dell Computer developed a robust strategy by choosing to sell computers over the telephone instead of through retailers. It developed a mastery of direct and database marketing and could convince customers of its superior value and service. Then Dell created a subsequent strategy breakthrough by adding the Internet as a sales channel. Today Dell is selling more than $3 million dollars' worth of computers daily on the Internet.

Other companies have created unique strategies. Ikea created a new way to make and sell furniture that stood in stark contrast to typical furniture retailers. The Saturn division of General Motors sells cars in an entirely different way from the typical auto manufacturer. Enterprise Rent-A-Car carved out a unique niche in the rental car market by renting older cars in cheaper locations and tying in with referrals from insurance companies.

But don't these successful new strategies get imitated very quickly, only to settle into being ordinary? Yes, imitators come along, as Southwest Airlines and IKEA have learned. However, it is one thing to copy some aspects of a new strategy, but quite another for an imitator to copy all aspects of the strategic architecture. The great strategies consist of a unique configuration of many reinforcing activities that defy easy imitation. The imitator not only has to incur great costs in trying to duplicate all the activities of the leader, but at best he ends up as only a pale imitation with average returns.

What Marketing Challege Do most Companies Face?

Kotler has asked many managers in his seminars to describe how they see today's customers. Here are their answers:

Customers are growing more sophisticated and price sensitive

They are short of time and want more convenience

They see growing product parity among the suppliers

They are less manufacturer brand sensitive and are more accepting of reseller brands and generics

They have high service expectations

They have decreasing supplier loyalty.

Marketing Approaches to Services

In marketing there have been a number of approaches used to clarify what are services. Some of these varying approaches are:

- Definition of services.
- Classification of services.
- Reasons for growth of services.
- Characteristics of services.
- Functional differences between services and products.
- Bases for competition in marketing of services.
- Special considerations in the marketing of services.
- Status of Marketing in the services sector.

Services Defined

1. According to the American Marketing Association (1960), "Services are activities, benefit or satisfactions which are offered for sale, or are provided in connection with the sale of goods".
2. Stanton (1978) defined services as, "Services are those separately identifiable, essentially intangible activities which provide want-satisfaction, and that are not necessarily tied to the sale of product or another service. To produce a service may or may not require the use of tangible goods. However, when such a use is required, there is no transfer of title (Permanent Ownership) to these tangible goods".
3. Gronroos on the other hand, define services as, "The service is the object of marketing i.e. the company is selling the service as the Core of its market offering".
4. According to Kotler, Armstrong, Saunders and Wong (1999) "A service is any activity or benefit that one party can offer to another that is essentially intangible and does not result in the ownership of any thing, its production may or may not be tied, to a physical products."
5. According to Gronroos (1990), " A service is an activity or series of activities of a more or less intangible nature that normally, but not necessarily, take place in interaction

between the customer and service employees and / or physical resources or goods and /or systems of the service provider, which are provided as solutions to customer problems"

6. According to Christopher Lovelock (2001) Services are economic activities that create value and provide benefits for customers at specific times and places as a result of bringing about a desired change in or on behalf of the recipient of the service.

What all the above definitions share in common is the intangible nature of a service.

Characteristics of Services (Kotler, Bloom 2002)

1. Intangibility
2. Variability
3. Perishability.
4. Customer Participation.

A brief explanation of the above-mentioned characteristics is given below:

Intangibility

Services are often intangible. It is often not possible to taste, feel, see, hear or smell services before they are purchased. Repeated purchase may rely upon previous experience. So the customer may be given something tangible to represent the service but ultimately the purchase of service is the purchase or something intangible. Kotler, Bloom (2000) Service intangibility means that services cannot be seen, tasted, felt, heard, or smelled before they are bought. For example, people undergoing cosmetic surgery cannot fully see the results before the purchase and an individual involved in a lawsuit cannot know the outcome before the end of a trial. An individual hiring an architect doesn't have the completed plans before agreeing to the transaction. As a result, the clients attempt to reduce uncertainty by looking for "signals" of service quality. They draw conclusions about service quality from the physical evidence, equipment used, people involved, or the communications they have been exposed to. The service professional needs to provide a tangible representation that communicates the likely service process and outcome.

Services that are essential intangible (Exp. Museum, Entertainment, Education, Travel Services, Security, valuation etc.)

Services providing added value to a tangible product (Eg. Insurance, maintenance, advertising, packaging, repairs, personal care etc.)

Services that make available a tangible products (e.g. financial services, transport, warehousing, hire purchase, mortgage, mail order etc.)

Between (1977) suggests that intangibility mean both (a) Palpable Tangible (i.e. the service cannot be touched by the consumer) and Mental Intangibility (i.e. the service is difficult for the consumer to grasp mentally.)

Andrew Gustafsson and Michael D Johnson (2006) illustrates that the goods-services can be represented on the tangible-intangible dominant continuum as mentioned in fig 1.1 below

Figure 1.1 Goods-to-Services Continuum

Pure Goods (Food product, Chemical Book)	Core Goods Appliance, Data Storages System	Core Services Airfine, Hotel, ISP	Pure-Services Professional Services

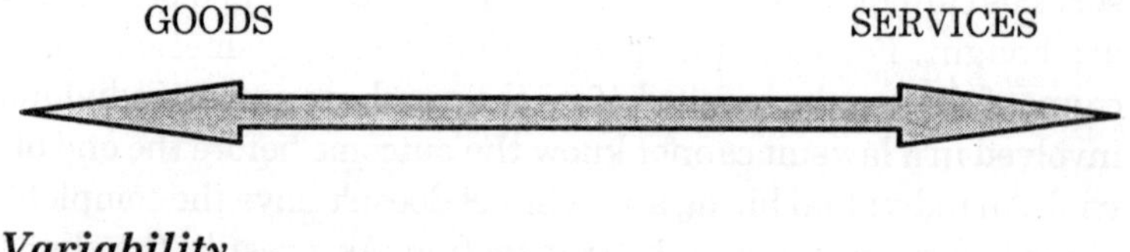

Variability

Because service is inseparable from people, the quality of the services delivered to clients can vary. The best lawyer can make a mistake; the best accountant can miss a number; the best doctor can have a bad day. The implications of variability in services are twofold. Because we know that mistakes can happen, we can develop processes that attempt to minimize these mistakes. For example, accountants can use software packages that minimize the potential mistakes in tallying income returns and architects can use computer simulations to test for structural problems before a building is built. However, even with the best preventive systems, mistakes can occur. Thus, the professional service provider should anticipate where mistakes are most likely to occur and have recovery measures in place to maintain the trust of the client who experiences the mistake.

Inseparability

Because the service cannot be separated from the service provider, how that individual is perceived—his or her professionalism, appearance, and demeanor—will all be used in judging the quality of the service firm. This inseparability carries over to those individuals who answer the phones for the organization or occupy the receptionist's desk. They often provide the first impressions prospective clients get of the service organization.

Perishability

Perishability of services means that they cannot be stored for later sale or use. Some doctors charge patients for missed appointments because the service value existed only at that time and disappeared when the patient did not show up. The perishability of services also has certain implications. One of these is that the service provider is basically selling performance. For example, although knowing that your physician has performed one thousand open-heart surgeries is reassuring, what's really essential is the physician's ability to safely perform yours. Another implication of perishability is the fluctuation of demand. When demand is steady, it may be relatively easy to perform on a consistent basis; when demand fluctuates wildly, it may become more difficult to maintain consistency. In the case of a physician, for example, it may be difficult to give every patient time and personal attention in the middle of a flu epidemic. Criterion for satisfaction is different before buying a product, a customer can assess what he or she is buying. For example, before purchasing an automobile, a customer can test drive it. But services are different. They are first sold, then produced and consumed at the same time. One cannot be sure that an architect grasps a client's needs until the construction drawings come back. In some cases, the client will never know how good the service he or she received really was. For example, a person who hurts his or her knee in a skiing accident and has surgery will not know whether physical rehabilitation would have been a better solution. Similarly, if a lawyer suggests settling out of court versus going to trial, the client will never know what results the other option would have yielded.

The Customer Participates in the Process

When customers purchase a physical product, they don't take into account the factory in which it was produced, nor the individuals working in that factory. However, when purchasing services, customers are "in the factory," observing the entire process. Each experience creates an impression about the service, known as a "moment of truth." A service provider must properly manage each moment of truth to provide a consistent message about the quality of the service.

Table 1.3 gives the implications of characteristics of services and the design of a marketing strategy to overcome these. These are only illustrative in nature and there are also other factors involved.

Table 1.3
Implications of Service Characteristics and Ways of Overcoming Them

Service characteristics	*Implications*	*Marketing Strategy*
Intangibility	Sampling difficult. Difficult to judge quality and value in advance. Not possible to patent or have copyright Retatively difficult to promote	Focus on benefits. Use brand names. personalize service. Develop reputation. Increase tangibility
Inseparability	Requires presence of performer or	Learn to work in Larger groups Work much faster

	producer. Direct sale. Limited scale of operations. Geographically limited market.	Train more service providers
Heterogeneity	Difficult to Standaridse.	Careful selection. And trainign quality of behaviour norms. Reduce role of human element.
Perishability	Cannot be stored. Fluctuations in demand and supply	Better match demand and supply with prices reductions during seasonal changes
Ownership	Customer has access to but not ownership of facility or activity	Stress advantages of non-ownershpi such as easier payment scheme.

Classification Scheme for Services

Services are categorized by market, degree of tangibility, and skill of the service provider, goal of the service provider, degree of regulation, labor intensiveness, and the amount of customer contact. The classification system is a useful way of showing the diversity of service marketing. Services can be classified based on service operations, level of tangibility customer employee presence, and customization/empowerment. According to "Silvestro6 et al., the dimensions of services can be based on service operations, level of tangibility, customer-employee presence and customization/ empowerment. These are now discussed.

Service Operations

Whether the service has a people focus (e.g., banker) or equipment focus (e.g., ATM)

Extent of customization (e.g., professional services tailored to meet the needs of individual clients)

Source of value added, i.e., is it front office (e.g., a beautician) or back office (e.g., a bank)?

Whether the service has a product focus (e.g., a Maruti Car Service Centre) or a process focus (e.g., a higher education course).

Table 1.4 gives a classification based on the class of service process in three broad categories: professional, service shop, and mass services.

Table 1.4

Classification of Service Categories

Class of Service	*Volume of Customers*	*Characteristics process*
Professional, e.g., accountant	Low	• People focus • High contact time • High customization • High level of Employment • Front office value added • Process focus
Service shop, e.g., accountant	Medium	• People and equipment focus • Medium contact time • medium customization • medium level of employment • Front and back office valume added
Mass service	High	• Process and product Focus • Equipment focus • Low contact Time • Low customization • Low level of Empowerment • Back office value added • Product focus.

Source: Adapted from Silvestro, R., Fitzgerald, L., Johnston and Voss, C., Towards a Classification of Service Processes, International Journal of Service Industry Management, 3, 1992, pp. 62-75.

Level of Tangibility

According to Shostack*, services can be classified on goods-services spectrum. If a product is more tangible, it is easier to evaluate in terms of quality, suitability, etc. If it is more intangible, then the evaluation becomes that much difficult.

---

* G. Lynn Shostack, Breaking Free from Product Marketing, *The Journal of Marketing*, April 1977, p. 77.

Empowerment of Employees	*Level of customization of service* *Low*	*High*
Low	Food retailing superstore	Telephone banking
High	National health dental	Accountant

Source: Christopher, H. Lovelock, Classifying Services to Gain Strategic Marketing Insights, *Journal of Marketing*, 47 Summar 1983, pp. 9-20.

Marketing researchers have classified services based on differnet yardstics right from 1964. Table 1.5 gives a summary of these classifications for theperiods 1964-80 and 1983-89.

Table 1.5: **Summary of Proposed Schemes for Classifying Services (1964-80)**

Author	*Proposal Classification*	*Comment*
Judd (1964)	1. Rented goods services (right to own and use for a defined time period) 2. Owned goods services (custom creation, repair or improvement of goods owned by the 3. Non goods service (personal, Experience or "experiental possession")	First two are fairly specific, but third category is very broad and ignores services such as insurance, banking, legal advice and accounting.
Rathmelt (1974)	1. Type of seller 2. Type of buyer 3. Buying motives 4. Buying practice 5. Degree of regulation	No specific application to services could apply equality well to goods
Shostack (1977)	Proportion of physical goods and each product "package"	Offers opportunities for multiattribute modeling.
Sasser et el. (1978)		Emphasise that there are very few pure goods or pure services.

Hill	1. Services affecting persons vs. those affectign goods	Emphasizes nature of service benefis and (in 5) variation in the service
	2. Permanent vs. temporary effects of the service 3. Reversibility vs. non-reversibility of these effects. 4. Physical effects vs. mental effects 5. Individual vs. collective services.	Delivery/

Summary of Proposed Schemes for Classifying Services (1964-80) (cont)

Author	Proposed classification	Comment
Thomas (1978)	1. Primarily based (a) Automated (e.g., car wash) (b) Monitored by unskilled Operators Product attributes. (c) Operated by skilled personnel (e.g., airlines)	although operational Rather than marketing Orientation, provides a useful way.
Chase (1978)	Primarily people-based (a) Unskilled labour (e.g.) lawn care (b) Skilled labour (e.g., repair work) (c) Professional staff (e.g., lawer	Recognizes that Product variability is control in high contrast services because customers exert more influenceon timign of demand and Service features due to greater involvement in service process.
Kotler (1980)	Extent of custoemr contact required in service delivery (a) High contact (e.g., health care, hotels, Restaurants) (b) Low contact (e.g., postal service, Wholestating)	Synthesises previous Work, recognises differences in purpose of service Organization.
Lovelock (1980)	1. People-based vs. equipment based 2. Extent to which client's presence Necessary 3. Meets personal needs as	Synthesises previous classification and adds several new schemes. Proposes several categories within each

	against Business Needs	classification. Concludes that defining
	4. Public vs. private, for profit vs. Nonporofit classification	object served is the most Fundamental Classification
	5. Basic demand characterisitcs	scheme. Suggests that valuable
	• Object served (persons vs. Property) • extent of demand/supp • discrete vs. continuous relationships betweencustomers and providers	marketing insights would come from combining to or more classificaiton schemes in a matrix.
	6. Service content and benefits	
	• multisite vs. single site delivery • allocation of capacity (reservations vs. first come, first served basis) • Independent vs. collective consumption • time defined vs. task defined transactions • extent to which costomers must be present during service delivery	

Source: Christopher H. Lovelock, classifying Services to Gain Strategic Marketing insights, *Journal of Marketing*, 47, Summer 1983, pp. 11-12.

Summary of Proposed Schemes for Classifying Services (1983-89) (cont)

Author	*Proposed classification Scheme*	*Comment*
Lovelock (1983)	1. The nature of the service act (a) Tangible actions to people of things	Provides a series of Provides a series of classificaitons, which together illustrate the complete nature of
	(b) Intagible actions to people or things 2. Relationshps with customer Continuous delivery (c) "Membership" relationshps (d) No formal relationships	services and provide useful background Information. for managerial purposes.
	3. Customization and judgement/ in service delivery	
	(a) Judgment exercised by cusomer contact persons	

	(b) Customization of services 4. Nature of demand in relation to supply (a) Extent to which supply is constrained (b) extent of demand fluctuations 5. Methods of service delivery (a) Single or multisite delivery (b) Service delivered on provider's or customer's premises	
Schmenner (1986)	1. Degree of interaction and customization (a) Low (b) High 2. Degree of labour intensity (a) Low (b) High	Reconizes that some services may be more customized and involve a higher degree of labor intensity and may help the reader to understand the strategic and tactical options available.
Vandemerwe & Chadwick (1989)	1 Degree of consumer/ producer interaction (a) Lower (b) Higher 2. Relative involvement of goods (a) "Pure" services (b) Services with some goods or delivered through goods services embodied in goods	Recognises that some services and role of goods components in service business.

Source: Christian Gronroos, Service Management and Marketing, Massachusetts: Lexingon Books, 1990, pp. 33-34.

Customer-Employee Presence

According to Booms and Bitner[7], service organizations can be classified as:

Self-service (customer only), e.g., playing squash

Interpersonal services (customer and employee), e.g., dry cleaning services

Remote services (employees only), e.g., insurance providers

Based on the type of service being provided, organizations can emphasize on front office or back office design.

Customization/Empowerment

A comprehensive classification suggested by Lovelock (see Table 1.4) suggests five different two-dimensional classifications of services. It combines two dimensions identified by Silvestro et alb with three additional dimensions.

Applying Marketing to Services

Special considerations in applying marketing to services are eleven as discussed below:

- Services cannot be stockpiled.
- The entire service mix is usually not visible to the Consumer.
- The intangibility of services make's pricing and Promotion difficult.
- The existence of a direct service organization - consumer relationship makes, employee-public relations skills important.
- Services often have high cost and low reliability.
- Peripheral services are frequently needed to supplement the basic service offering.
- Production and consumption are simultaneous so they cannot be stored and direct sales are possible.
- Tangible products are assets, while services products are expenses.
- Services are expressed in terms of rates, fees etc.

Services cannot be stored for later sales; therefore, demand must be carefully matched with the supply

Services cannot be stockpiled, e.g. if a movie theater has 500 seats, it can admit more than 500 customers to a Sunday night showing, even though a Wednesday matinee might had 400 empty seats. It is clear that the empty seats during the Wednesday movie cannot be used to increase theater capacity during the Saturday peak demand period. Therefore, in order, to match demand and supply, a service firm must alter the timings of demand and/or exert better control over the supply of services offering. It should avoid excess demand that goes unsatisfied as well as excess capacity that results in an unproductive use of the resources.

Methods for balancing the Timing of Demand

- Adding attractive services in off-peak periods, such as hotel providing convention-meeting room at reduced prices.
- Utilizing a reservation system to spread out demand.
- Employing price discrimination, with lower prices for off-Peak periods. Providing customers with peripheral services while they are Waiting, such as a cocktail lounge in a restaurant.

Methods for balancing supply

- Using part time employees at peak periods.
- Training employees in different skills so they can be shifted to whatever task has the greatest demand at any point of time, thus avoiding battlement.
- Increasing consumer participation in the completion of services, such as direct dialing for long distance calls.
- Sharing capacity with other service provider, Such as hospitals sharing expensive, but seldom used, diagnostic equipment.

[*Source:* W.Earl Sasser. "Match Supply and Demand in service industries." *HBR,* Vol. 54, (Nov. - Dec.) 1976, pp. 133-140.]

Customer sees only a small portion of the service mix for some services

For some services, only a small portion of the service mix is visible to the consumer, e.g. repairs are normally not seen by the consumers. Although the repairperson may spend 3 hours on a TV set and insert two parts priced only at Rs.16/- the consumer gets a bill for Rs.200/- and does not realize the amount of service involved. Therefore, service time and function must be explained to the consumer.

The Intangibility of service makes pricing and promotion decisions more difficult

The intangibility of service makes pricing difficult. How

should the price be broken down into problem analysis and service components? Should the prices vary among repairs performed by the head-mechanic and regular mechanics? Services that are equipment based and routine in nature may be suited to cost-oriented pricing. Other services should rely on the competitive pricing.

The intangibility of services also makes promotion difficult. Unlike product promotion, which may stress tangible attributes and consumer analysis prior to a purchase of service attributes can only be measured after a purchase is made. Therefore the seller must appeal to the consumers' imagination in describing its benefits. A seller of service must appeal to the prospect's ability to visualize a better state of being or a better future because of the service, being purchased. In marketing life Insurance, for example, the seller may try to create an image in the prospect's mind of the happiness security provides or the financial difficulties that family may encounter or should the consumer die with inadequate coverage. All these appeals are designed to help the consumer see not what can be, if the services are purchased. Word of mouth is more important means of promotion in case of services.

Interpersonal skills are often important because of the close relationship between the consumer and the service provider

Inseparability in case of services makes interpersonal skills important. The workforce be trained to interact well with consumers, and employee appearance and mannerism have a greater impact on services firms. All employee-customer contact should be performed properly, including sales, credit, delivery and repair.

Services often have high costs and low reliability

Inseparability in case of services makes interpersonal skills important. The workforce be trained to interact well with consumers, and employee appearance and mannerism have a greater impact on services firms. All employee-customer contact should be performed properly, including sales, credit, delivery and repair.

Services often have high costs and low reliability

As competition increases and the cost rises, professional

service firms are to increase their productivity. There are five approaches to this (a) to have service providers work harder and skillfully, (b) by increasing the quantity of service by surrendering some quality, (c) to add equipment to increase services capabilities as Levitt recommended "manufacturing attitude" towards producing services, (d) to make obsolete the need for a service by inventing a product solution and (e) to design a more effective (Kotler and Bloom, 1983).

Many services have high costs and low reliability. One solution to this problem is the industrialization of services using Hard, Soft and Hugh bird tegnologs. (Levitt, 1976)

Hard Technologies

Substitute machinery for people such as implementation of electronic teller system instead of manual teller. "Hard technologies cannot be applied to service requiring extensive personal skili and contact such as medical, legal and accounting services."

Soft Technologies

Substitute preplanned systems for individual services e.g. many travel agents sell prepackaged vacation tours. This standardizes the transportation, accommodation, food and sightseeing.

Hybrid Technologies

Combine hard and soft technologies, e.g., in case of automobile repair computer X-Ray of the total automobile combined with low-priced repair facilities of mechanics. The industrialization of service cuts high costs and increases reliability. Service reliability can also be improved through higher service level standards by setting of higher employee standard of performance levels.

Peripheral services are complimentary and supplement the basic service

Peripheral services are complementary services that are needed to supplement the basic service offering. For example, when a tourist hotel markets rooms for travelers, it will also need an adequate reservation system, clearing, personnel, parking facilities etc. Peripheral services increase a service firm investment, require additional employee and management skills, and may be time-consuming. But they enable the company to create and sustain a competitive advantage.

Production and Consumption are simultaneous

In case of service, production and consumption takes place at the same time. We consume a lot of services at the same time, like a football games, a telephone call or a college education services. Therefore skills of services provider are very important.

Tangible products are Assets, while services are expenses

Consumer products have resale value; long after the initial purchase is made. Services, usually depreciate fully upon purchase. Moreover, there is no market for used services. One cannot obviously resell a movie seen yesterday. In accounting language tangible products are listed as assets, while services are considered expenses.

Services are expressed in terms of rates, fees etc.

Unlike a good, where monetary values are stated in terms of a price, services are more likely to be expressed as rates, fees, admissions, charges, contributions, interests and the like. In many types of service transactions, the buyer is a client rather than a customer of the seller; the client when buying a service literally places himself in the hands of the seller.

The Status of Marketing in Service Firms

Although spending for services has increased substantially, the development of marketing as a major business activity has come slowly to most service industries. It has also been suggested through research studies that service dominant organizations are less market oriented than manufacturing firms; and the growth in services has not been due to marketing developments (professional firms in United Kingdom and India are perhaps better known for their lack of market-orientation than for their zeal to meet customer needs. (George and Barkedele, 1974).

(a) The dominant intangible nature of service products may cause more difficult marketing problems as compared with physical items (e.g. display, selling service product benefits.)

(b) Some services business (e.g. Professional firms are opposed to the idea of marketing. They consider it unprofessional to use certain marketing practices associated with goods marketing (e.g. advertising is still prohibited or forbidden by many professional services.) Also they tend to think themselves as producers of services not as marketers of services.

(c) Many service organizations are small and in direct contact with their customers. They therefore consider many marketing techniques as irrelevant (e.g. hairdressers, repair shops).

A Theoretical Framework for Marketing Professional Services

In this new millennium, the concept of "survival of the existing" no longer applies to professional services. Major transformations in the environments of all the professions are leading many professional service organizations down new paths. Traditional professions are facing major competition not only from within, but among one another as well.(Kotler, Bloom 2002). Before looking at the importance of professional services marketing, let us look at the various definitions of what professional services are:

Professional Services Defined

There is no generally accepted definition of what constitutes a professional or a professional service. The word professional is so loosely used in marketplace that it is difficult to find any occupation that has not added the term professional to their title.

1. There is one excellent definition given by Gummesson. The definition states:

> "A professional service is qualified, it is advisory and problem solving even though it may encompass some routine work for clients. The professionals involved have a common

identity like physicians, lawyer's, accountants or engineers and are regulated by traditions and code of ethics. The service offered if accepted involves the professional in taking on those assignments for the client and those are themselves the limits of the professional's involvement. Such assignments are not undertaken to merely sell hardware or other services (1981, p.108)

The key operational concepts of this definition are the problems solving and advisory roles that must be played by professional service marketers. Many marketers believe that the marketing of services may be completely different from the marketing of goods. However marketing as a process and as a functional area can be applied to both.

2. Professional services are infrequent, technical, or unique functions performed by independent contractors or consultants whose occupation is the rendering of such services. While not limited to licentiates (individuals holding professional licences), the services are considered "professional" and the contract may run to partnerships, firms, or corporations as well as to individuals" www.wikipedia.org(Last updated on Feb, 2007)

3. Simon (2005) defines professional services as "those services that are provided by people who have maintained a minimum 4-year degree in their area of expertise and have been licensed by completing a state administered test and/or by fulfilling other requirements that may be imposed by peer groups and regulatory bodies."

Need for the Study on Professional Services

The professional services industry deserves serious study for two reasons.

First, Nearly every market segment of the modern economy - manufacturing, technology, transportation, energy, etc. - intersects on a routine basis with the professional services industry - lawyers, accountants, engineers, etc. - at multiple levels. In this sense, professional services can be likened to a DNA strand within the overall economic picture - a smaller, often un-noticed element that nevertheless exists within and influences every cell of the organism.

Second, The professional services industry is a powerful economic force in and of Itself. At the dawn of the new millennium, the professional services industry accounted for some 17 percent of all employment in the United States and Western Europe(Laura Empson, Lessons from professional services firms, Financial Times, Nov. 8, 1999. It has grown more than 10 percent annually over the past 25 years and generates over $1 trillion in global revenues(Laura Empson, Professional Services Firm, in Stewart Clegg and James Bailey (eds.)).

The largest professional services firms rival other industry sectors in both revenues and global reach. For example, "the world's largest accounting firm, PricewaterhouseCoopers, currently employs 130,000 people in almost 150 countries, with a 2005 gross revenue of US $20 billion, making it larger than Fortune 500 companies such as Oracle, McDonald's and Sears Holdings. The largest consulting firm, Accenture, is a Fortune 500 firm in its own right. The investment bank Goldman Sachs makes it into the top 100 of the Fortune rankings."

The Indian service sectors story is not quite different from the global scale; India's service sector has matured considerably during the last few years and has been globally recognized for its high growth and development. This sector has been growing at an annual growth rate of about 28% during the last 5 years. Services exports amounted to a meager US$ 8.9 billion in 1997 but over the years services exports have grown substantially. There has been rapid growth in the services exports from the year 2002. The exports have grown up from US $ 19.1 billion to US $ 73 billion in 2006. Presently services sector account for about 55% of India's GDP. India's service sector contributes more than 55 per cent of GDP, making it the most formidable component of the country's economy. An extrapolation of Reserve Bank data by India Brand Equity Foundation in fact shows that service exports could topple merchandise exports in the medium term. The Government of India is taking up most care to uplift this potential sector, which contributes heavily in India's Foreign exchange.

The professional services industry thus is important not only as an inherent component of the inner business workings of all other aspects of the economy, but also as a major economic power in and of itself that plays an increasingly important role in the global economy.

At the outset, it is important to note that there is no common definition of "professional" services or universal understanding of how they differentiate from "Services" in general. Some limit the term "profession" narrowly to the traditional fields of law, accountancy, medicine, architecture and engineering, whereas others adopt a broader conception that includes such diverse occupations such as "advertising, the clergy, consulting, education, investment banking, and nursing." It is not necessary to engage in that wider debate here. For present purposes, it suffices simply to set out the general traits that tend to characterize professional services and the manner in which they are delivered.

Three key characteristics fit this broad description. The first distinguishes "professional" services based upon barriers to entry. Many segments of the professional services industry have specialized requirements in education, training, and accreditation that must be satisfied before an individual can work in that specialty. Examples include law, accounting, medicine, architecture and engineering, each of which requires many years of formal higher education. The educational requirements do not themselves entitle a person to practice, however. They simply qualify an individual to progress into a further phase of testing, accreditation and training before the appropriate licensing and practice qualifications are achieved. In India, Institute of Chartered Accountants of India (ICAI) is the concerned body for regulating the accounting profession, similarly the Bar Council of India for Legal profession and Medical Council of India for Medical Profession.

A second characteristic of professional services is a high degree of self-regulation.

This typically includes control over initial qualification and accreditation, as well as the creation and enforcement of a code of ethics or practice standards against which a professional's ongoing work is measured. Such regulatory power often involves legal authority delegated to the profession by a government body or agency.

In India, for example, the regulation of Accountants and the practice of accountancy fall within the purview of Institute of chartered accountants of India.

A third characteristic of professional service providers is their ability to use specialized knowledge or training in a customized way to solve problems that their Clients cannot solve for themselves. This distinguishes the professional service industry from other knowledge-based industries (such as pharmaceutical manufacturers, computer software companies, and the like). The "deliverable" for a professional service provider is the solution to a particular type of problem. The industry creates value through its ability to customize and apply specialized expertise to unique sets of factual circumstances.

As noted above, these characteristics are by no means exhaustive. Rather, they are offered simply to illustrate some of the ways in which the professional services industry is characteristically different from the other "service" segments of the Indian economy. With this general backdrop in mind, the Research now focuses on one particular segment of the professional service industry - the Accountancy profession.

The Accounting services industry was selected for detailed review here for three principal reasons

First, the practice of Accounting falls within even the most restrictive definition of "professional services," as it requires a high degree of specialized education, training and accreditation.

Second, being a Chartered Accountant is a well-known and visible profession, and the practice of accounting is generally accompanied by a high degree of earning power and social prestige.

Third, the Accounting profession faces many trends and challenges that are common to all aspects of the professional services industry. As such, it serves as a useful context in which to discuss such issues as Client needs, service quality, client expectations, perception, Importance of experience, segmentation of clients etc.

Ten Distinctive Problems in Marketing of Professional Services

Following are the distinctive problems in marketing of professional services, which have also been mentioned by Kotler, Thomas Hayes, Bloom (2002).

Problem No.1: Third Party Accountability: Marketers of Professional services must given substantial considerations to how third parties (e.g. Government Regulatory Agencies, Stockholders, employees etc.) other than their clients will react to their marketing programs, e.g. a CA cannot offer to over look a client's financial irregularities; and accede to pressures while auditing because while servicing their own clients, they are also serving third party clients like-investors, insurance companies, Government agencies and members of their own profession.

Problem No. 2 Client uncertainty:- Wilson (1972) proposed that, "uncertainty is high for buyers of professional services." These stem from difficulty in evaluating the performance characteristics of the offering prior to purchase or use, or even after purchase. e.g. a patient may not be convinced that he should have had surgery for a certain ailment.

High level of client uncertainty creates a unique challenge for professional service marketers i.e. of client education, about the criteria's they may use in evaluating professionals, and thc need to seek the services of a professional.

Problem No. 3 Prior Experience is Essential:- Prior experience with similar situation is one of the frequently used criteria in selecting a professional. People prefer to use accountants who have worked in their industry before. The need to have this kind of experience to obtain clients produces problems for many professional service organizations. So inexperienced accountants often find it difficult to find any work at all. Firms with limited experience find it difficult to diversity into new lines of work. Therefore, professionals specialized services, which they can offer to clients to gain business.

Problem No. 4: Limited Differentiability:- In case of Professional services, differentiability is often limited. It is hard to differentiate an accounting audit, a little search and an eye examination because of intangibility of services.

Problem No. 5: Maintaining Quality Control:- Keeping high quality control levels is a challenging task for professional service marketers. Sampling in case of services is difficult. People-intensive service organizations (Professional firms) must emphasize finding good people and making them to work conscientiously. Quality of their service depends on performer, and behaviors of clients. Uncooperative clients do not follow the advice of accountants and thus leads to bad reputation for professionals.

Problem No. 6: Making "Doers" into "Sellers":- Before "buying" professional services, the client will like to meet and get acquainted with the professionals who will be serving them. The professionals who will be 'Doers' of certain kind of work needs to be sellers of that work and need to be oriented towards better selling skills. But the problem is that these Doers are opposed to selling-like Accountants, Dentists, and Lawyers etc. And so do not have anything to do with selling.

Problem No. 7 Allocating Professionals time to Marketing:- Many professionals are opposed to the idea of marketing but show their zeal to meet customer/clients needs. But in the age of competition, rapid changing technology, changes in the way of business life etc, the need for professionals to be both doers and marketers, cannot be overlooked. So these professionals have to devote some of their time in marketing their services.

Problem No. 8 Pressure to React rather than Proactive: Clients are some time fussy and wants their work done by them "immediately", and this frequently cut into time that has been set aside for marketing planning. So, they cannot be proactive when clients are putting time pressure on them.

Problem No. 9 The effect of advertising is unknown: The use of Advertising is still prohibited in the profession by their Institute. So direct Advertising and its effect/advantages have not so for been realized in case of professional services marketing.

Problem No.10 A Limited Marketing Knowledge Base: This has already been discussed in preceding discussions. This limited Marketing knowledge, in case of professional services, has restricted the applicability of marketing in the area of professional services. In the absence of theoretical knowledge, no rules or concept can be applied and be put to use. After having identified the problems in marketing of professional services the various marketing styles that can be adopted by professional firms as identified by Kotler, 1977 are being presented below:

What Styles of Marketing are possible for a Professional Firm

Professional firms are having three major objectives 1. Sufficient Demand, 2. Sustained Growth, 3. And Profitable volume. So they must turn to some form of marketing to achieve these objectives. Three styles of marketing suggested by Kotler and Connor (1977) are:

(i) Minimal Marketing

(ii) Hard Sell Marketing

(ii) Professional Marketing.

(i) *Minimal Marketing*:- Most professional firms in India practice minimal marketing (Gulvarjani, 1987). They avoid or minimize conscious development of a marketing program. They believe that by rendering high quality services they will satisfy their clients and these satisfied clients will recommend them to others and bring in more new clients. By doing so they feel they are adhering to ethical cannons probhiting direct selling activity. But now-a-days acceptance of this philosophy is being questioned on account of the following:

"It is reactive rather than proactive approach to marketing opportunities. The firm does little to shape its future clients or services.

"It assumes that the firm will deliver distinctively better quality than its competitors. But several firms may be using the same philosophy and therefore, no firm may strike the client as particularly exceptional in this respect.

"It assumes that competitors are not practicing the stronger forms of marketing which can lead them to disaster.

(i) *Minimal Marketing* means that client choose the firm rather than the firm choosing the client.

(ii) *Hard-Sell Marketing*: A few professionals firms practice hard-sell marketing. However often it reflects a sales orientation rather than a marketing orientation. The professional engage in sharp price-cuttings, discounting, brochures preparations, some direct solicitation and possible referral commissions. So this hustling for business violates the profession's code of Ethics. Therefore, majority of practitioners consider it distasteful and predatory in nature.

(iii) *Professional Marketing*: This has been discussed in the foregoing discussions above. Its major attributes are:-

Stating long-term marketing objectives and strategies

Being market-oriented i.e. client or user oriented.

Organizing regular, training seminars to improve the professional person's effectiveness at marketing.

Ensuring that quality of professional works does not suffer as marketing activity is increased.

Using only those marketing tools and procedures that are consonant with the industry's code of professional ethics.

Based on these styles the effective marketing strategies for a professional firm can be suggested as:-

(a) *Expanding Service to existing Clients*: Cross selling of services accountant while doing auditing may identify some of the areas of deficient performance and suggest the client to utilize the firm's management services division.

(b) *Identifying and Cultivating High*-Potential Prospective Clients: Use of referral sources be there for identifying eligible and attractive potential clients and laying plans for their cultivation. All clients should not be accepted and they need to be evaluated in terms of one's offering high growth and profit potential.

(c) *Widening and Deepening Personal Referral Sources*: Steps be taken by professional firms to cultivate key referral sources. They need to recognize that their growth is dependent on the growth of referral sources i.e. existing clients, other professionals, friends, relatives, other business houses like bank and insurance companies etc.

(d) *Service and Market Specialization*: One of the major marketing errors of professional firms is to strike out in all directions for possible new clients. They accept all clients. This "total service" philosophy is inferior strategy to that of service and market specialization. Specialization offers two distinct advantages to professional firms.-

1. It gives the firm a preferred position, placing it favorably to potential clients seeking that kind of expertise.
2. Specialization permits a greater profit on volume of business because the firm develops "Cutting edge" expertise and low cost expertise in handling recurrent positions.

(e) *Replacing Clients*: The client review be carried out and some of the clients who are small with little potential be dropped without hurting the reputation of the firm. This will enable the professional firm in building a strong potential and profitable client base. Thus professional firms need to be involved in marketing of their service to prosper and grow. They need not be opposed to the idea of marketing. In fact, marketing and selling are not synonymous words or identical functions. Selling is merely the tip of the marketing iceberg. "To market One's Services, or Sell without learning how to develop a true marketing program, is like learning how to sail but not how to navigate. Your expertise would be sufficient for a while, but once out of sight of land, watch out, (Bachner and Khosla, 1977).

Thus, the last we can say that some key aspects of service marketing where attention is needed are: -

1. *People*: The key to services is not that they are provided by people (they may be performed by equipment) but that they are to be provided for people. Service Organisations must obtain greater under understanding of why customer behave the way they do, how they make their choices, what role intangibility plays in these choices.
2. *Process*: There are opportunities in service performance and marketing to reduce the barriers that exist between the

operation side of an organization and the marketing side of an organization. Service performance and delivery cannot be separated. Service marketers should encourage and develop closer relationships with their operational management colleagues.

3. *Physical Evidence*: Physical evidence and atmospherics (office location, layout, décor, sound and light level, costuming i.e. dress etc.) have always been important in marketing. There is a need for a better understanding of how this element of the marketing mix influences customer choices, satisfaction and response for service organization.

The Changing Self Image of the Accountant Today:

Denney (1983) has projected five ways in which the modern accountant sees himself/herself:-

a) *The Dedicated Professional*: for him work is work. He derives satisfaction through work.

b) *The Antimarketing Accountant*: One who considers marketing unprofessional and unethical, basically, found in developing countries context.

c) *The anxious but insecure professional*: Many firms are of this type today. They do realize that time has changed and something should probably be done in the way of marketing their practice, but their lack of knowledge keeps them pondering over the subject without applying it.

d) *The Go-Go-Man*: He welcomes the idea of marketing and is at the other extreme of one who is Anti-marketing accountant.

e) *The Secure Professional*: One who appreciates that there are three essential ingredients of success in public accounting today-technical marketing, and management.

Recognizing this, the secure professional attempts to understand what is required in each of these areas.

The beauty in marketing of accounting services is that a firm doesn't have to push square pegs into round holes. There are such a broad range of activities that a person can adopt to contribute to the marketing success of the firm and thereby help the firm to grow, as enumerated below:

1. Client Review Program.
2. Client Profile.
3. Seminars/Webinars
4. Articles.
5. Talks & Speeches.
6. Membership in Professional Groups.
7. Community Activities.
8. Clubs.
9. Client's Board & Stock Holders.
10. Sources-Development & Retaining (Referrals).
11. Social Functions.
12. Business Functions.
13. Contributions.
14. Membership in Trade Groups.
15. Industry Specialization.
16. Personal Letters, Notes etc.
17. Publicity & Public Relations/ Communication Mix.
18. Sales Promotion/Firm Brochure.
19. Billing.
20. Routine Firm Operations.
21. Fees.
22. Integrated Marketing.
23. web-based Marketing
24. Quality service

The present study is an exploratory work, to explore the status of marketing in professional accounting through empirical survey of practicing Chartered Accountant in India, restricted to Visakhapatnam (Andhra Pradesh, South India).

Gulvarjani (1987), in his study has observed that Accounting in India is 40 years behind the United States and Western Europe.

So in order to see practically what is the real position of Chartered Accounting profession and to what extent they have accepted and applied the concept of "Marketing" the present study has been undertaken.

Objectives of the Study

1. To find out if the CA's can be identified as having a production, sales or consumer oriented marketing management orientation. To see whether services businesses (i.e. professional firms of CA) were opposed/or opposed to the idea of marketing, and whether they perceive themselves as producer of services Vs marketers of services.
2. To know whether the "Satisfaction of Client" was "Central" goal of CA. and to suggest a viable marketing strategy to practice development.
3. To identify the professional tactics used by most of the professionals while interacting with client and determine what were the potential areas for the CA in which they could do practice, to change over, or to diversify to what new areas of service product offerings.
4. Which types of service product offerings constituted the major chunk of Business in case of professional services of practicing accountants? And to bring about if location, design and timing of service availability were considered important in marketing of professional service of CA's.
5. To find out the factors those are considered as important in practice development and client attraction, and the type of communication mix being used to inform prospective customers about the service and promote its use.
6. To know which information sources contributed maximum share of clienteles for the practicing CAs and to study the importance and type of referrals as a source of business.
7. To determine if these professionals feel change in the practicing environment: Change in what respect, and their valuable suggestions for improvement.

8. To find out the type of client groups using CA services-their relationship with income, and category to which belonged and to know how the users and the non-users perceived, the different factors while choosing the CA firm.
9. To study how the user and non-users perceived, the necessity of a CA in different cases/service product offerings and to study among users, their sources of information about CA.
10. To find out the differences in service quality expectations between users and non-users of all the categories of clients and service quality perceptions of the professionals.

On the basis of the above, attempts have to be made to arrive at certain conclusions with a view to suggesting

a) Improvements in package of services, modification in the existing methods of practice, expansion of market etc. with complete consonance with consumer needs.
b) Modifications in the thinking of professionals as regards marketing, suggesting modification in government policies towards restrictions on marketing in case of professionals, recommending the institute on CA's India its greater role in improving the practicing environment and the like.

Propositions

In view of the (later on amenable to hypothesis formulation) objectives of the study, and sound theoretical base build up during review of literature stage, following propositions have been framed for the present study:-

Proposition 1. Minimal marketing strategy is used to market professional accounting services, where gradually the CAs are experiencing a change in the practicing environment; are worried about the future; and think of diversifying their service packages and scope of operations.

Proposition 2. The marketing of accountancy services is limited to the study of service product offerings; constant review of clients, charging valued fees. They are opposed to advertising and do not use it for promotion of their practice.

Proposition 3. Accounting firms to larger extent are client centered and in their zeal to meet customer needs lack marketing orientation.

Proposition 4. Personal contact or Sunday meetings, maintaining social contacts are the major ways used to attract and retain the clients.

Proposition 5. Personal recommendations of friends/ relatives and referrals are important source of business in case of professional services of CAs.

Proposition 6. Consumer/clients look for such qualities as trustworthiness and competence the most, in seeking public accountants (selection criteria's).

Proposition 7. Over all organizational capabilities (No. of partners, office environment, equipments, prestigious locations international experience) combined with tangible evidence of the professional seller capability to provide the service are of major importance in attracting the attention of prospective users in the marketing of people intensive services.

Proposition 8. Professional accountancy services are rendered by people (professionals) and are heavily people centered, so service facility can be located at considerable distance from intended customers because. 1. The service can be sold through the use of market located sales office. 2. Customer will seek more prepurchase information. 3. Customer will travel considerable distance for the service and 4. The service capacity can be transported to the customers.

Proposition 9. Users of accountancy services evaluate the importance of source of information about accountancy services differently. Personal contacts are more important source of information for users.

Proposition 10. Prior accountancy services usage is related to perceptions of the importance of needs for accountancy services. Users are likely to have greater awareness of the usefulness of a CA, for most accounting needs, they are also in better position to place a value on accountancy services.

Proposition 11. There is direct relationship between the experience of a accountant and his income.

Proposition 12: There is difference in service quality expectations between different types of users and between professional and users.

Limitations

This is by no means an exhaustive study and it has been carried out with constraints of time and money and for which the study is limited to just professional chartered accountants. There is nonavailability of Indian literature in professional services, which has also been a main limitation. Bias of respondents is also possible.

2

Review of Literature

The services marketing literature is a phenomenon driven by a rapidly growing population of services marketing scholars and the loose-knit system of publication outlets that has emerged to publish their works. Both the scholars and the publications have been influenced by the changing nature of the economy and the needs of management, especially during the last 10 to 15 years. Not since the strong emergence of interest in consumer behavior in the 1960s has a field developed within the marketing discipline with the passion and determination of services marketing.

Academia by its nature is conservative and hidebound. New ideas and concepts gain acceptance slowly. In this context, the early services marketing scholars were true risk takers. They found relatively few publication outlets enthusiastic about their work, and they confronted a discipline debating whether services' marketing was significantly distinctive. Today services marketing scholars work in a far more receptive environment. Between 1990 and 1992, for example, 20 books and more than 150 scholarly papers and journal articles were published on the general topic of services marketing - with a number of them in the top marketing journals. This tally does not even begin to include the myriad publications in every sub field of services marketing (such as health care, financial, professional, non-profit, education, hospitality, government). And now numerous conferences and symposia are held annually not only in Europe and the United States but also in a developing country like India, allowing services researchers to present and publish their work.

In addition to the exuberance and the risk taking that have characterized the discipline's development, three other noteworthy factors influenced the evolution of the literature.

First, considerable interaction has occurred between academics and practitioners. This has resulted in a literature anchored in managerial issues.

Second, the literature has a strong interdisciplinary orientation especially involving operations and human resources management. Academics from the management field have regularly attended services marketing conferences, and their work has significantly influenced the thinking and writing of services marketing scholars.

Third, the services marketing literature has been international from the beginning, with academics in the United States, Scandinavia, the United Kingdom and France intensely involved. These factors are essential cross-fertilizing ingredients in the evolution of the services marketing literature. The focus is general services marketing literature as opposed to literature on specific services industries; further, the literature examined concentrates on the English language works of primarily American scholars. The history of the literature in an academic field can focus on key ideas, authors, or events. This history focuses primarily on the key ideas that have emerged. However, prolific authors and significant events are also chronicled. We have been fortunate to live and work during the period described in this article.

Stages of Services Marketing Literature

The evolution and legitimization of services marketing as reflected in the literature can be described in three stages: Crawling Out (pre-1980), Scurrying About (1980-85), and Walking Erect (1986-present). Scholars in the services marketing field first asserted the discipline's right to exist—the Crawling Out stage. This stage began with the first services marketing scholars struggling to publish their work and culminated with a fierce debate over whether "services marketing is different". The debate questioned the very legitimacy of services marketing as a field within the discipline; its outcome could have been the early demise of the research, and therefore the literature, had the debate been lost. In the Scurrying About stage, a thriving colony of nimble scholars contributed to the growing base of literature. This was a bustling period when enthusiastic scholars contributed to the rapid development of multiple topics and interests.

In the Walking Erect stage, scholars achieved a respected stance as services marketing became an established field within the marketing discipline. The publications on many of the primary topics matured considerably. To trace this evolution through the literature, the publishing outlets of the general services marketing literature across all three periods are classified and the major contributions summarized. The final section offers speculations about the future of services marketing.

The bibliographic data used in this are derived and from prior bibliographic work by Fisk and Tansuhaj (1985) and from an electronic database known as SERVMARK developed by Fisk et al. (1988). These bibliographies contain both general services marketing literature and industry specific services marketing literature. Four major sources of general services marketing literature are included in the bibliography: journal articles, books, conference proceedings papers, and dissertations. These four sources represent the principal outlets for disseminating knowledge in the marketing discipline. In addition, the bibliography includes original book chapters and a few early monographs from the Marketing Science Institute. Books from the popular press aimed at a broader audience than just marketing academics are included. Services marketing articles from thousands of newspapers and magazines are not included. Nor are cases and working papers a part of this review. The services marketing literature cited in the bibliography and discussed in this article is primarily from North America. There are absolutely limited information about professional services in indi and all the concepts are a true reflection of the Western content.

Scholarly services marketing literature is primarily discussed in this article, i.e. publications written primarily by academics for an academic audience. As noted earlier, the boundaries between the fields of services marketing and services management are somewhat fluid. Several services marketing topics, in other words, are not the exclusive domain of marketers. Thus, numerous publications listed were judged to be of significant interest and value to services marketing scholars, even though they were written by management professors and published in management journals. In the Crawling Out stage, 120 publications were found. During the Scurrying About stage, the literature grew rapidly to 287 publications. Growth accelerated in the Walking Erect stage to reach 720 publications. A combined total of 1,127 publications have been identified across the history of the services marketing field.

Crawling Out: Pre-1980

The Crawling Out stage was a time of discovery and risk taking. The period captures the embryonic beginnings of the services marketing literature in 1953 and continues through the goods marketing versus services marketing debate that marks the end of this stage. The entire output of the 27 years spanned by this stage is 120 publications, most of which were published in the 1970s. Many of the prominent services marketing authors today (including John Bateson, Leonard Berry, Stephen Brown, John Czepiel, Pierre Eiglier, William George, Christian Gronroos, Eugene Johnson, Eric Langeard, Christopher Lovelock and Lynn Shostack) began writing and publishing during this stage.

General Observations

The early history of the marketing discipline (Bartels, 1988) focused on selling agricultural products. Subsequently, the discipline's scope expanded to marketing physical goods. Services were given relatively little attention in this early literature as illustrated in the following quote: Still the main function of "business" is to market goods. Accounting, banking, insurance, and transportation are only aids, very important aids it is true, to the production and marketing of goods. (Converse, 1921, p. vi).

The focus on marketing physical goods was pervasive. In textbooks and other publications, the accepted wisdom that marketing meant goods marketing was rarely challenged. As the industrialized nations began the transition to service economies, the development received little notice in the marketing discipline. Although some of these nations' economies were dominated by services as early as the mid-1940s, some time elapsed before marketing scholars began to discuss and study service economies and the marketing that occurred within these settings. As noted, many of the early scholars took the significant risk of writing about the new topic of services marketing.

Many began their services research as doctoral students or as untenured professors. Yet one of the traditions of academe is the construction of new knowledge "on the shoulders of giants". When the early services scholars chose to pioneer their area, however, they put themselves in the difficult position of developing new knowledge with virtually no research model. They found themselves "seeking to be giants". The personal challenges these early scholars faced are documented by Berry and Parasuraman (1993). The majority of the literature in the Crawling Out stage is conceptual. Definitional assertions about the nature of services and their marketing were often key parts of these papers. Few publications included empirical investigations. Further, the newness of the services marketing field meant that publishing outlets for the early literature were somewhat limited.

Early Publications

Interestingly, most of the scholars studying services marketing in the 1950s and1960s did so through their dissertation research (McDowell, 1953; Parker, 1958). These academics began a pattern of innovation that was continued by 17 other budding scholars in the United States alone completing services marketing dissertations during the Crawling Out stage. Several of these scholars went on to significant prominence in the services marketing field. Johnson's dissertation (1969) was the first to ask the question, "Are goods and services different?" and launched the goods versus services debate. Regan (1963) wrote the first of three services marketing articles to appear in the *Journal of Marketing* during the 1960s. He described the United States as well advanced into a "service revolution" that would significantly change consumer behavior. Judd (1964) proposed redefining services and created a services typology.

Rathmell (1966) argued that marketing people needed to devote more attention to the service sector and offered a definition of services that is still used by many scholars today. All three of these early *Journal of Marketing* articles are descriptive, but they were important in influencing the thinking of future scholars.

Blois (1974) wrote the first services marketing article to appear in the *European Journal of Marketing*. He noted the importance of the service economy in the United Kingdom and emphasized the scarcity of services literature sources. Blois also proposed an approach to services marketing based on buyer behavior theory. Another noteworthy article from the 1970s was Donnelly's (1976) examination of distribution channels for services. He demonstrated that marketing channels for services are significantly different from those for physical goods.

At least a dozen dissertations were completed on services marketing topics during the 1970s; ten were written during the late 1970s. George studied the marketing of service industries, and his dissertation (1972) led to an early publication in the *Journal of Marketing* (George and Barksdale, 1974). George (1977) also wrote the first article in the *Journal of Retailing on retailing services*. Weinberger's dissertation (1976) tested information on services versus goods in a laboratory setting. This data became the basis for the first services marketing article in the *Journal of the Academy of Marketing Science* (Weinberger's and Brown, 1977). Gronroos' dissertation (1979) focused on the marketing function of service firms, and he continues that emphasis in his recent work (Gronroos, 1990).

The first book on services marketing was actually a research monograph by Johnson (1964). Based on personal interviews, case studies, trade association contacts and literature review, he sought to show marketing managers how to address more effectively the intangibility issues associated with services. The first full-length book was authored by Rathmell (1974). He sought to introduce the service sector to marketing and marketing to the service sector. He attempted to integrate the two areas in four sectors: sports, banking, health care and business services. Rathmell book served as a textbook at a few universities offering services marketing courses in this early period. Johnson's research monograph on the service economy (1968) was the first of many monographs published by the Marketing Science Institute (MSI). Eiglier *et al.* (1977) produced the first output of MSI's new consumer services marketing research programme. This collection of five lengthy papers served as a valuable resource to many early researchers.

The collection included: "Do We Need Service Marketing?" by John Bateson; "A New Approach to Service Marketing" by Pierre Eiglier and Eric Langeard; "A Note on the Commonality of Problems in Service Management: A Field Study" by Pierre Eiglier; "Services as Systems: Marketing Implications" by Pierre Eiglier and Eric Langeard; and "Marketing's Potential for Improving Productivity in Service Industries" by Christopher Lovelock and Robert Young. The MSI followed this monograph with Testing conceptual Framework for Consumer Service Marketing (Bate son et al., 1978). This piece built on many of the ideas Bate son described in his 1977 paper. Perhaps the major outcome of the Crawling Out stage is the literature's delineation of services characteristics. These features - intangibility, inseparability, heterogeneity, and perishability - provided the underpinnings for the case that services marketing is a field distinct from goods marketing. The advocacy for this new field, however, was met with some challenge.

Goods versus Services Marketing Debate

As the literature grew, a fundamental questioning of the legitimacy of services marketing emerged. This debate became most intense during the latter years of the Crawling Out period. The goods marketing versus services marketing debate represented a fundamental challenge to the right of the services marketing field to exist. If the marketing discipline concluded that service marketing was different, the field might gain sufficient acceptance to grow and thrive. However, if the discipline concluded that services' marketing was simply a modest extension of goods marketing, the field would be considered illogical and would die. Today, outside observers looking back at the written literature might assume that the debate was primarily one-sided. This is because virtually all services marketing authors during the 1970s felt compelled to argue that services marketing was different, at least in the introductions to their articles and papers.

Few of the critics, however, felt compelled to publish their arguments. Indeed, most advocates were reacting to verbal criticism by reviewers and conference participants. Within academic departments, this questioning continued as informal discussion and among dissertation Services committee members.

Virtually every early services scholar recognized these comments as questioning the legitimacy of their research and writing. Such challenges (even though often not in print) were career threatening, especially because many of the pioneers were young and untenured. In this context, the vigor of the response to these criticisms is not surprising. One of the few early published criticisms of services marketing appeared in the *European Journal of Marketing* by Wyckham et al. (1975). They examined the argument that services marketing are different and concluded that taxonomy of goods versus services is dysfunctional.

In the late 1970s, a landmark article altered the evolution of the services marketing field. Lynn Shostack, then a vice president at Citibank, published "Breaking Free From Product Marketing" in the *Journal of Marketing* (1977). Philip Kotler (in Gronroos, 1990, p. xii) has commented, "This article was to alter the course of our thinking about services marketing, if not general marketing itself." In her article, Shostack made the following provocative assertions (p. 73): Could marketing itself be "myopic" in having failed to create relevant paradigms for the service sector? service industries have been slow to integrate marketing into the mainstream of decision making and control because marketing offers no guidance, terminology, or practical rules that are clearly relevant to services.Shostack's criticisms stung all the more because they came from someone outside the academic community. Her article became a rallying cry that has inspired numerous services marketing scholars.

Thomas (1978), in an influential *Harvard Business Review* article, also argued that strategy differs for services businesses. More specifically, he stated that traditional strategies developed for physical goods are inappropriate for services and that services managers need to take advantage of the unique strategies available to them. The first modern AMA conference on marketing theory in 1979 served as a special forum for publicly and fervently advocating the uniqueness of services marketing. Bate son (1979) vigorously argued that services marketing required new concepts. With equal vigor and enthusiasm, Lovelock (1979) argued that marketing concepts needed to be broadened to encompass services marketing.

Berry (1980) wrote one of the most definitive assertions (entitled "Services Marketing Is Different") near the end of the goods marketing versus services marketing era. However, traces of this debate lingered in the early years of the Scurrying About stage (Enis and Roering, 1981), and challenges have even occasionally appeared in the Walking Erect stage (Williams and Mowen, 1990).

Scurrying About (1980-1985)

The Scurrying About period represents a time of high interest and enthusiasm in services marketing. For the first time, conferences on the topic brought together established and novice contributors. The first half of the 1980s also represents a bridging period for the literature. The services versus goods debate began to wane, and the foundation was laid for the flourishing "Walking Erect" stage (1986-present). During the Scurrying About period, the literature increased significantly, including four pieces in a premier journal, the *Journal of Marketing*.

General Observations

Two major developments during 1980-85 helped trigger an exponential growth in the literature that continues to this day. One development was the deregulation of service industries. The second development was the interaction among participants at a series of American Marketing Association conferences. Deregulation was ushered in at the beginning of the decade, especially in North America. Firms in air transportation, financial services, health care and telecommunications woke up to an environment of new rivals, intensified price competition and rising consumer expectations. The role of marketing within these firms was transformed from being modestly important to being a core function vital to the survival of the organization. With most of these firms recognizing the greater significance of the discipline, they were hungry to acquire and understand marketing knowledge. This need encouraged services managers and marketing academics to come together. For some academics, the first exposure to services marketing occurred almost before they fully realized what was happening. Through writing, executive education programmes, and consulting, many scholars attempted to respond to the needs of specific services industries. These educators quickly realized that services' marketing differs from goods marketing. Many also recognized the need for research that transcends specific company and industry boundaries.

At the same time, the American Marketing Association (AMA) sponsored a series of services marketing conferences. Recognizing the developments just noted, selected AMA leaders (e.g. past presidents Leonard Berry and Stephen Brown) successfully persuaded the association to make a special commitment to the rising interest in services marketing. The Services Marketing Conferences of 1981, 1982, 1983, and 1985 stimulated excitement and productive interchanges between academics and business people in Europe and the United States. In 1985, the first AMA faculty consortium featuring services was held at Texas A&M University. The Marketing Science Institute and New York University also sponsored a special conference on service encounters in New York City in 1985. Much of the literature of the 1980s and 1990s emerged from discussions at these events. An additional outgrowth of the conferences has been an ongoing sensitivity to both European and North American contributions and to managerial implications. During the Scurrying About stage, two new journals came into being: the *Services Industries Journal* (SIJ) in 1980 and the *Journal of Professional Services Marketing* (JPSM) in 1985. The "Preface" in the inaugural issue of the JPSM discussed the growing interest in services and pointed out that the journal's scope embraced generic articles for the entire service industry as well as more specific pieces for particular service sectors of the economy. The First Interstate Center for Services Marketing (FICSM) at Arizona State University was established in 1985. The center further legitimized the field by encouraging scholarly research and establishing ties with the business community. Collectively, deregulation, the practitioner-academic dialogue, and the European - United States connection had a pronounced impact on the literature of the time and on subsequently published work.

Contributions

During the 1980-85 period, the quantity of literature increased. Although the goods versus services debate was dying out in the mid-1980s, the proceedings of the AMA services conferences suggest a lingering dispute. More and more scholars, however, began to investigate substantive issues unique to the field such as service quality and service encounters. The appearance of four services articles in the *Journal of Marketing* within three years (1983-85) encouraged many services scholars and further legitimized the field among marketers. Christopher Lovelock's "Classifying Services to Gain Strategic Marketing Insights" (1983) proposed five classification schemes for services that transcend narrow industry boundaries. For each scheme, Lovelock offers insights into how the nature of the service may affect marketing strategies and tactics. The article received the journal's prestigious Alpha Kappa Psi Award and strengthened the case for the uniqueness of services marketing. Two significant *Journal of Marketing* articles by A. Parasuraman, Valerie Zeithaml and Leonard Berry were published in 1985. In the first article, the authors offered a conceptual framework summarizing the unique characteristics of services. They reported the findings from a survey of service managers concerning the strategies used to respond to marketing problems (Zeithaml et al., 1985). The authors also compared the problems and strategies cited in the literature with those reported by the managers and offered suggestions for reflection.

In addition to building a comprehensive case for services marketing, this article represents the first empirical services research published in a major journal. Two issues later, the same author team published "A Conceptual Model of Service Quality and Its Implications for Future Research" (1985). This piece launched a highly successful research programme supported by the MSI. In the article, the authors developed their Gaps Model of service quality and reported an exploratory investigation of quality in four service businesses. This landmark article and subsequent studies by Parasuraman et al. stimulated others to contribute to the area (e.g. Brown and Swartz, 1989; Cronin and Taylor, 1992). It led to service quality being a core topic for services marketing.

The third services marketing article in the 1985 *Journal of Marketing* was "A Role Theory Perspective on Dyadic Interactions: The Service Encounter" by Solomon et al. (1985). The authors presented the critical components of service encounters; they proposed that the dyadic interaction between a service provider and a customer is an important determinant of the customer's overall satisfaction with a service. This piece, plus a book edited by several of the same authors (Czepiel et al., 1985), led to further investigations and helped establish the service encounter as a viable research topic. Although the preceding works are among the most notable articles of the Scurrying About stage, other important contributions were made during this period. Papers from the AMA services conferences proceedings represent some of the most widely cited works in the literature (e.g. Berry et al., 1983; Bloch et al., 1985; Donnelly and George, 1981). Papers having a profound impact, among others, included Berry (1983) on relationship marketing, Booms and Bitner (1981) on the expanded marketing mix for services, Gronroos (1981) on internal marketing, and Zeithaml (1981) on the unique consumer evaluation process for services.

In addition to the *Journal of Marketing*, the *Harvard Business Review* (HBR) long has been an outlet for literature on services. During this period, the HBR published articles by Levitt (1981) on marketing intangibles, Takeuchi and Quelch (1983) on service quality, Canton (1984) on the service economy, and Shostack (1984) on services design. Levitt's widely cited piece, in particular, offered significant services marketing insights to both business and academic audiences. The *Journal of Retailing* also furthered the development of the field, publishing contributions by Berry (1980) on the time-buying consumer, by Kelly and George (1982) on strategic issues for retailing of services, and by Bateson (1985) on the self-service consumer. The work of management and psychology academicians, such as Richard Chase, Peter Mills and Benjamin Schneider, also had a significant impact. Their work began to enlighten marketing scholars on the human resource and operations management issues associated with services. Further, the contributions of Europeans John Bateson, Keith Blois, Christian Gronroos, Evert Gummesson, Richard Norman and others significantly influenced the services literature.

A number of noteworthy books appeared in the early to mid-1980s, each having a different orientation but pronounced influence. Lovelock (1984) published the first services marketing textbook. By bringing together cases, articles, and text material in a single text, his book provided a major resource to faculty teaching the emerging courses in the discipline. The holistic work of the "Nordic School" became particularly influential during this period as illustrated in Norman's (1984) Service Management and Gronroos' and Gummesson (1985) Services Marketing - Nordic School Perspectives. In 1985, The Marketing of Services by British academician Donald W.Cowell also was published. To assist further in services marketing teaching, Nancy Hansen of the University of New Hampshire compiled and, with the help of AMA, distributed syllabi of services marketing courses being taught in the United States. In 1985, Fisk and Tansuhaj edited the first bibliography of services marketing literature through the AMA. As noted earlier, this resource listed generic and industry-specific articles, conference papers, books and dissertations. Some of the articles, papers, and books published during the Scurrying About period continued to defend services as fundamentally different from goods. Others, however, targeted new areas of enquiry, such as service design and mapping and service encounters; they laid the groundwork for the Walking Erect period.

Walking Erect: 1986-Present

This stage in the services marketing literature can be characterized as a period of explosive growth in numbers of publications and increasing empirical and theoretical rigor in their content. There has been almost no discussion of whether services are different from goods since 1985, but rather the literature has focused on specific marketing problems of service businesses. These topics include managing quality given the heterogeneity of the service experience, designing and controlling intangible processes, and managing supply and demand in capacity constrained services, and organizational issues resulting from the overlap in marketing and operations functions. This problem focus has resulted in the field becoming increasingly cross-functional because many of the issues being researched have multiple roots and multiple solutions that span traditional functional boundaries.

General Observations

The Walking Erect period has produced an increasing number of marketing academics who have begun conducting research in services marketing. From the handful of marketing academics who provided enthusiastic moral support to each other at the first AMA Services Conference in 1981, the numbers of services researchers mushroomed most noticeably during the late 1980s and continues to the present. Established researchers (e.g. Claes Fornell, Richard Oliver, Linda Price, Roland Rust, Steven Shugan) began developing their Current research to address marketing issues in services, while every year more doctoral students have elected to pursue dissertation projects in services marketing. In addition, virtually all of those who met at the early AMA conferences (e.g. John Bate son, Leonard Berry, Mary Jo Bitner, Bernard Booms, Stephen Brown, James Donnelly, Raymond Fisk, William George, Christian Gronroos, Evert Gummesson, Eric Langeard, Christopher Lovelock, Carol Surprenant and Valerie Zeithaml) continue to contribute to the development of the field. The boom in research was encouraged by the continuation of the AMA Services Conferences annually through 1991. Research was encouraged by the first Quality in Service (QUIS 1) meeting in Karlstad, Sweden, in 1988, which was jointly sponsored by the Service Research Center at the University of Karlstad and the First Interstate Center for Services Marketing (FICSM) at Arizona State University. This meeting brought together academics and business practitioners from ten different countries. It was pivotal in moving services research ahead. QUIS 2, held in 1990 in Norwalk, Connecticut, and QUIS 3, held again in Karlstad in 1992, with 15 countries represented, encouraged the enthusiastic continuation of research in the field.

Explosive Growth

The explosion in the number of books, journal publications, conference proceedings, and dissertations dealing with services marketing issues during the Walking Erect stage is documented in Table I. Growing numbers of general services marketing publications in the top academic marketing journals characterize this period. *The Journal of Marketing* has published between one and three services marketing papers each year since 1987 (compared to a total of four between 1980 and 1985).

The Journal of Consumer Research published its first services papers in 1991 (Bolton and Drew, 1991; Hui and Bate son, 1991;Soberson-Ferrer and Dardis, 1991). The Journal of Marketing Research published two services papers early in this period, while the *Journal of Retailing* has published 11 general services marketing pieces. The *Journal of Marketing* has been the primary outlet for academic services marketing research among the field's top journals. In addition, two new journals dealing specifically with services marketing and services management were started as well: the *Journal of Services Marketing* in 1987, and the *International Journal of Service Industry Management* in 1990.

Along with the rapid growth in journal publications, the number of dissertations in services marketing doubled in the Walking Erect stage when compared to the preceding period. Because a number of years often elapse from the time a dissertation is completed until a major journal article is published.

Services Marketing Thought

The increasing number of dissertations is an early indication of more journal publications to come. A number of significant books also have been written, many by early, prominent researchers in the field of services (Bateson, 1989, 1992; Berry and Parasuraman, 1991; Bowen et al., 1990; Brown et al., 1991; Gronroos, 1990; Heskett, 1986; Heskett et al., 1990; Johnson et al., 1986; Lovelock, 1988, 1991, 1992; Sasser et al., 1991; Swartz et al., 1992; Zeithaml, et al., 1990). A new services marketing textbook was added in 1989, Managing Services Marketing written by John E.G. Bate son, with a second edition in 1992. Christopher Lovelock's 1984 Services Marketing text also was published in a second edition in 1991. Both books include short chapters followed by reprinted readings; Lovelock includes cases as well. In addition to these publications, numerous books on topics closely related to services marketing, such as customer service, relationship management, and service quality, have been published.

Focus

The cross-disciplinary and international nature of the field is becoming increasingly evident in the literature. In reviewing the citations at the conclusion of any major journal article on services, the cross-functional and international sources that support nearly all research in this area are immediately apparent. For example, a recent *Journal of Marketing* article on service environments (Bitner, 1992) cite research from management, human resources, operations and social psychology journals as well as from marketing. Similarly, a journal article on managing and coordinating service organizations in the prestigious *Academy of Management Review* (Larsson and Bowen, 1989) includes 20 marketing citations. Clearly, while the research has become more focused and rigorous, services researchers have continued to draw from related fields to solve problems and build theories for services marketing. The international focus is expanding similarly. This is apparent in article citations as well as in the addition of the International *Journal of Service Industry Management* published in the United Kingdom, the QUIS conferences, and the biannual research seminars in France. Journal publications in services marketing have become more empirically based and theory driven, as opposed to presenting conceptual discussions or debates. The differences between goods and services appear to be assumed, and researchers have begun to focus on substantive business issues and problems stemming from the implications of these basic service differences. Topics that have gained substantial attention are rooted in relatively isolated pieces of research published during the preceding periods. However, not until the Walking Erect period could a cohesive core of research be identified under these topics.

Early Revelations in Services Marketing

As a first step, we examine the validity of the current core paradigm of services marketing, namely, the assertion that four specific characteristics-intangibility, heterogeneity, inseparability, and perishability-make services uniquely different from goods. These characteristics, which for simplicity are collectively referred to as "IHIP," have been staples of service research and teaching for more than two decades. But we need to ask if they are grounded in empirical research or are merely theoretical constructs that are subject to ambiguous interpretation.

Concerns over the future of Services Marketing. In evaluating the evolution of services marketing, Schneider (2000) observed that organizations go into decline when they try to refine what makes them successful- an assertion based on the work of Miller

(1990) and Kotter and Heskett (1992)-and added rather glumly: Services marketing has been successful because it differentiated itself in the marketplace with a conceptual paradigm shift—services are different from goods. All else has followed from this conceptual leap and with increasing refinement. We have had a happy 20-year run . . . but we may need some new energy and new directions. . . . I sense a kind of malaise in services marketing. (p. 180) Berry (2000) expressed concern that the dominance of a single area of research—one in which he himself made major contributions—has effectively blocked progress in other areas.

During most of the 1990s, the field became too caught up in service quality measurement and debating the pros and cons of alternative methodologies. . . . So much research energy and journal space was devoted to this subject matter that the field seemed to lose its bearings. (p. 10) Perhaps reinforcing the drift to which Schneider (2000) and Berry (2000) referred was the emergence during the late 1990s of the Internet as an important business tool and the resulting explosion of interest in e-commerce. Internet technology offers the potential for creating new business models, radical new approaches to delivering information- based services, and new ways of relating to customers (Peterson, Balasubramanian, and Bronnenberg 1997; Reichheld and Schefter 2000; Rust and Kannan 2002). Some scholars have expressed concern that existing service concepts are not readily applicable to Internet services. Brown (2000) argued that "the ability to obtain and consume services without interacting with a human provider challenges much of our existing knowledge" (p. 62). Reinforcing this viewpoint, D. E. Bowen (2000) concluded, "It now seems that most of what we know about services marketing and management has been derived from the study of face-to-face service encounters or at least over the telephone" (p. 46). In a subsequent review and commentary, Grove, Fisk, and John (2003) observed, Services marketing now faces a challenge that confronts many maturing fields of study. Specifically, as the domain of services has expanded, the boundaries that define it have become more obscure. Further, like so many other evolving disciplines, the direction in which services marketing is headed is unclear. Issues regarding the scope and the future of services persist. In short, as the field has grown, it has become more diffuse. A basic question now facing the services marketing sub-discipline is "where do we go from here? (p. 106)

The Power of Paradigms

As clarified by Kuhn (1970), progress in any scientific field requires a paradigm, which he conceives as a fundamental set of assumptions that is shared by members of a particular scientific community. A paradigm shapes the formulation of theoretical generalizations, focuses data gathering, and influences the selection of research procedures and projects. Although paradigms can facilitate research and generate axioms that are useful for both teaching and practice, they are only temporary postulates, and the validity of the underlying assumptions must always be open to challenge. We should be mindful of Schumpeter's (1950) famous treatise on entrepreneurship and the drivers of development demanding "creative destruction through innovation." Such a perspective seems applicable to theory development as well. For this reason, we argue that it is desirable to open a dialogue on paradigmatic issues.

How does the Marketing Discipline as a Whole View Services ?

A case can be made that the received wisdom of marketing is perhaps best captured in mainstream textbooks employed for required courses in the field. As scholars, we should be concerned about how mainstream texts present our field, because this content will be as much as most people ever learn about it. With few exceptions, courses in services marketing are taught as electives at both undergraduate and graduate levels. However, most business schools require all students to take an introductory course in marketing, in which treatment of services marketing is necessarily limited—if, indeed, it is covered at all. Hence, we can infer that only a fraction of all students are actually exposed to in-depth coverage of services marketing. Although services dominate developed economies, "textbook theory" treats services marketing as a sub discipline of manufacturing—based marketing management. Gummesson (2002a, pp. 325-26) noted that marketing textbooks offer a smorgasbord of dishes but laments that the smorgasbord text often offers minuscule context.

New theories and concepts tend to be presented as a special case and an add-on. Developing general marketing theory requires either integration of new lessons at a higher conceptual level than the theory already in existence or, more radically, a change in its very foundations. As argued by Schneider (2000), the underlying paradigm in services marketing since the 1980s has been that services are different from goods, a claim supported by an in-depth literature review by Fisk, Brown, and Bitner (1993), who concluded that "[four] features—intangibility, inseparability, heterogeneity, and perishability—provided the underpinnings for the case that services marketing is a field distinct from goods marketing" (p. 68). In reviewing introductory marketing management texts recently published in the United States, we identified four established textbooks—defined as being in their third or later edition—that contained an entire chapter devoted to services (Kerin et al. 2003; Kotler 2003; Pride and Ferrell 2003; Solomon and Stuart 2003).

In each instance, the authors attribute specific characteristics to services that implicitly or explicitly differentiate them from physical goods (see Table 1). Despite differences in both sequencing and terminology (notably Kerin et al's alliterative effort to create the Four I's of services and Kotler's and Solomon and Stuart's use of the term variability instead of heterogeneity), each text essentially discusses the four IHIP characteristics. Pride and Ferrell claim two more: client-based relationships and customer contact. As evidenced by the content of these widely used textbooks, we conclude that the paradigm that services differ from goods, reflecting the "basic"/"major"/"unique" IHIP characteristics, constitutes today's received wisdom in the broader academic marketing community. However, without empirical evidence, we cannot conclude that practicing managers either accept or act upon this paradigm. Texts in services marketing are, of course, directed at a much smaller and more focused market than introductory marketing texts. Although services marketing texts agree that services differ from goods, they display less unanimity in their depiction of specific distinguishing characteristics. Among texts published between 1998 and 2004, five(Fisk, Grove, and John 2004; Kasper, van Helsdingen, and de Vries 1999; Kurtz and Clow 1998; Hoffman and Bateson 2001; Zeithaml and Bitner 2003) build their discussion of differences around the IHIP characteristics. However, five other texts (Bateson and Hoffman 1999; Gronroos 2000; Gonçalves 1998; Lovelock and Wirtz 2004; Lovelock and Wright 2002) enumerate significantly longer lists of differences between goods and services. Books in the latter group do not always include all four IHIP characteristics. This situation supports Grove, Fisk, and John's (2003) contention that the field has become more diffuse.

Development of the Goods Versus Services Paradigm

During the 1970s and early 1980s, service researchers (primarily marketers but also specialists in operations and human resources) put forward a broadly similar message. Services, they argued, raised distinctive management challenges that were not being addressed by existing research and teaching grounded in manufacturing and agricultural production, whose physical output was collectively referred as goods

-How Introductory Marketing Management Texts Portray Service Characteristics Statement of Service

Authors Characteristics (direct quotes)

Kerin et al. (2003, p. 323)

There are four unique elements to services: intangibility, inconsistency, inseparability, and inventory.

Kotler (2003, p. 446) Services have four major characteristics that greatly affect the design of marketing programs: Intangibility, inseparability, variability, and perishability.

Pride and Ferrell (2003, p. 325)

Services have six basic characteristics: intangibility, inseparability of production and consumption,perishability, heterogeneity, client based relationships, and customer contact

Solomon and Stuart (2003)

Regardless of whether they affect our bodies or our possessions, all services share four characteristics: intangibility, perishability, inseparability, and variability

During that era, the prevailing marketing theory, which claimed to be generalizable, rested mainly on a business to-consumer (B2C) depiction of market transactions in physical goods, with business-to-business (B2B) marketing presented as a special case (Bartels 1976). Services were rarely discussed, except in relation to transportation of goods through physical channels, repair and maintenance of products, and provision of customer service as part of the augmented product (LaLonde and Zinszer1976; Rakowski 1982). Academics who were interested in how services were created, designed, delivered, and marketed found that published insights and practical examples were in short supply.

In these circumstances, it is not surprising that many marketing scholars fell back on their own experiences as customers of airlines, banks, hotels, restaurants, and retail stores. Fisk, Brown, and Bitner (1993) noted that little empirical research on services was published during the 1970s; instead, scholarly efforts focused on conceptualization. Apart from early discussion of professional services (Gummesson 1981;Wilson 1972) and a few cases on high profile firms like Federal Express, relatively little attention was paid to B2B services. This experience-based approach to services made early conceptualization unusually consumer centric, emphasizing individual needs, customer satisfaction, and involvement in service encounters (Czepiel, Solomon, and Surprenant 1985). Advocacy for the new field did not go unchallenged (Enis and Roering 1981; Wyckham, Fitzroy, and Mandrey 1975). However, most of the opposing arguments took the form of internal debates within academic institutions where service pioneers often encountered resistance from established colleagues committed to the status quo (Berry and Parasuraman 1993; Fisk, Brown, and Bitner 1993). Nevertheless, a consensus emerged that (a) services- broadly defined as acts, deeds, performances, or efforts- had different characteristics from goods-defined as articles, devices, materials, objects, or things (Berry 1980; Rathmell 1966); (b) these characteristics posed vexing marketing problems not faced by goods marketers; and (c) developing marketing strategies to address these problems based on knowledge accumulated from goods marketing was often insufficient and even inappropriate (Zeithaml, Parasuraman, and Berry 1985).

Evaluating the Four "Unique" Characteristics of Services

Scholars conceptualized a variety of characteristics that were believed to distinguish services from goods. In a review of 46 publications by 33 authors during the period 1963-83, Zeithaml, Parasuraman, and Berry (1985) determined that the most frequently cited characteristics were intangibility (mentioned by all), inseparability of production and consumption or simultaneity (cited by the great majority), heterogeneity or nonstandardization (noted by about 70%), and perishability or inability to inventory (cited by just more than half of the authors). The earliest author cited in this review was Regan (1963), who identified intangibility, inseparability, perishability, and ubiquity but, rather surprisingly, neither defined nor explained them.

However, in a still earlier work, Parker (1960, p. 33) declared the two most important characteristics were intangibility and perishability. The first authors to cite all four characteristics (and only these four) were Sasser, Olson, and Wyckoff (1978), who presented them in a pioneering service operations textbook; they used the term simultaneity rather than inseparability. Although many subsequent authors citing IHIP have referenced Zeithaml, Parasuraman, and Berry (1985) as the source, it is important to emphasize that this distinguished trio of researchers did not invent IHIP but simply ratified it on the basis of an extensive literature review, conducted as a preliminary input to an empirical study (which we discuss below). An even more detailed review by Edgett and Parkinson (1993), covering 106 publications during the period 1963-1990, yielded similar results. These reviews effectively enshrined the "four unique characteristics of services" as received wisdom. However, in the process, other, less frequently cited characteristics were largely overlooked, most notably the absence of ownership in service purchases (Judd 1964; Rathmell 1966, 1974).

The extensive set of publications referenced in these reviews confirms that individual components of the IHIP framework were widely used by scholars as organizing concepts for the young field. Two important root sources that were frequently referenced in subsequent literature were Rathmell (1974) and Shostack (1977).

But in neither instance do their conclusions about service characteristics appear to be based on empirical research or to build on past foundations in the marketing literature, although one may infer that both authors were well exposed to business practice.

In fact, Shostack was a bank executive, not an academic. Her much-cited article, "Breaking Free From Product Marketing," was extremely influential in accelerating the early development of services marketing but is noteworthy for containing only six references. A similar phenomenon can be observed in an influential article by Kotler and Levy (1969) that argued for broadening the concept of marketing to include the activities of non-business organizations; this article contained only four references. Both articles built on syntheses derived from the authors' interpretations of received theory and inductive observation. By definition, a new paradigm is based on new fundamentals instead of using a stream of existing theory and research as its primary foundation. In discussing scientific method, S. D. Hunt (1976, pp. 16-20) drew a distinction between discovery and justification. Discovery can originate through observation (a variant of the inductivist route) and speculation (a generalized deductivist route), as well as through serendipity in the form of dreams and Eureka!-like events. At some point, however, the generalizations that emerge need to be tested through empirical research in the context of justification. New theory can also develop from new interpretations and innovative combinations of extant theory (Gummesson forthcoming). Hence, discovery and testing need not constitute two distinct stages but can be a continuous, iterative trial-and-error process in which we keep interpreting and combining both old and new data with the purpose of improving validity. Knowledge management is centered on the release of tacit knowledge, knowledge sharing, and ongoing dialogues (Nonaka and Takeuchi 1995). However, we have found no evidence that the IHIP characteristics have been validated by research as being either generalizable to more than limited service situations or having collective relevance for understanding how companies design and implement their marketing strategies or how customers make choices. In the study noted earlier, Zeithaml, Parasuraman, and Berry (1985) identified eight specific marketing problems associated with each of the IHIP characteristics and then conducted a mail survey of 1,000 managers across a wide array of service industries to determine their views on these specific problems.

Although 47% of the 323 respondents viewed demand fluctuation as a problem (one that is exacerbated by perishability), the proportion agreeing that each of the remaining seven items presented difficulties for their firms ranged from a modest 23% to a mere 9%. Seeking to explain these findings, Zeithaml et al. could only hypothesize that the responding firms might have already internalized the stated problems and were successfully dealing with them. Perhaps these authors' most significant conclusion was that "important differences exist among service firms, not just between service firms and goods firms" (p. 43). In particular, they noted a wide dispersion among responding firms in the need for customers to be present during service production. Although the authors did not say so specifically, this latter finding implicitly challenges the notion of inseparability of production and consumption.

Tracing The IHIP Characteristics to their Conceptual Roots

Where did the IHIP characteristics come from? Analysis of numerous publications by service marketing and operations scholars during the 1970s and early 1980s reveals very few citations of references predating the 1960s. Nevertheless, the concepts of intangibility, inseparability, heterogeneity, and perishability actually originated in classical and neoclassical economics.

Origins of the Intangibility, Inseparability, and Perishability Concepts

Neither marketers nor operations specialists created the distinction between tangible goods and intangible services. As we will show, the notions of intangibility (or immateriality), inseparability (or simultaneity of production and consumption), and perishability (with its implications of inability to inventory service output) were all derived from early economic thought. More important, all three were closely interwoven from the outset. The discussion that follows is closely based on the literature reviews of Delaunay and Gadrey (1992), T. P. Hill (1977), and P. Hill (1999).

History of Services Marketing

Debate on the distinction between goods and services originated with Adam Smith. Classical economists posited that goods (initially referred to as "commodities") must be entities over which ownership rights could be established and exchanged. In his *Wealth of Nations*, Smith (1776/1969) distinguished between the output of productive labor, which can be stored in inventories of vendible goods that can subsequently be exchanged for other items of value, and "unproductive" labor that however "honorable,. . . useful, or . . . necessary . . . produces nothing for which an equal quantity of service can afterwards be procured.... [This type of] work . . . perishes in the very instant of its production." Early discussion of services took place in a philosophical context that emphasized the importance of capital(which translated into wealth) and capital formation. Ownership of goods represented wealth. Describing service providers as "unproductive" was provocative, but Smith was not implying that the perishable output of government officials, the armed forces, clergy, lawyers, physicians," men of letters," musicians, entertainers, or "menial servants" actually failed to create valued benefits.

Writing in French, Say (1803/1964) was the first to employ the term immaterial (immaterial or intangible) and to introduce the concept of simultaneity. He used the example of a physician who visits a patient, prescribes a remedy, and then leaves without depositing any product: "'The physician's advice has been exchanged for his fee. . . . The act of giving was its production, of hearing [by the invalid] its consumption, and the production and consumption were simultaneous. This is what I call an immaterial product"(cited in P. Hill 1999, p. 430). Peter Hill (1999) characterizes Say's choice of the term immaterial as "unfortunate" and draws attention to a foot-note in which the French economist admits that his first intention was to use the term perishable product, but that he discarded this on the grounds that certain physical commodities were also perishable. Other adjectives that he considered and rejected were in transferable, transient, and momentary.

We might also argue that it was unfortunate that Say should have restricted his definition of consumption to the act of hearing the physician's advice and thus implicitly excluded the patient's subsequent actions in following that advice. The challenge of selecting an appropriate label for a new concept is one that faces scholars in all disciplines. Unfortunately, an infelicitous or inappropriate choice of terminology may cause problems for future generalizations of researchers when it results in alternative interpretations and meanings.

During the nineteenth century, the terms material products and immaterial products became well entrenched. Marshall (1890/ 1962) introduced the term goods into general economic usage, replacing the older term, commodities. Karl Marx treated activities such as transportation of merchandise and repair and maintenance operations not as services but as part of merchandise production (Delaunayand Gadrey 1992, pp. 49-51). In time, other economists began representing services such as freight transportation and the distributive trades as extensions or continuations of the process of producing material goods, because they added to the value in exchange of the final product.

By the mid-20th century, most economists-with the exception of some in socialist countries-tended to dismiss the distinction between productive and unproductive labor as irrelevant and obsolete. In particular, they came to see the ultimate end of economic activity as consumption rather than capital formation, thereby validating the economic contribution of services that could be sold at a price because they offered consumers value in use. Yet few perceived the distinction between material goods and immaterial services as having any great economic significance. Peter Hill (1999), himself an economist, cautions that the economics literature is full of statements to the effect that goods are material, or tangible, whereas services are immaterial, or intangible. Such statements are casual or conventional, rather than scientific, as the nature of an immaterial product is not explained. (p. 426)

Origins of Heterogeneity: Unlike the other three IHIP characteristics, the concept of product heterogeneity (also referred to as variability, inconsistency, or nonstandardization) is of 20th-century origin. It was introduced by Robinson (1933, 1969) in her discussion of the distinction between "perfect" and "imperfect" competition, and elaborated by Chamberlin(1933/1962) in the context of both natural and planned differentiation of commodities. Early service scholars focused on the need for standardization of work procedures, service technologies, and self-service in order to "routinize" service operations and make service faster, cheaper, and more convenient (Judd1968; Rathmell 1966). In some of the subsequent services literature, the term heterogeneity was also used to describe an entirely separate phenomenon, the extreme diversity of service establishments and their operations (Rathmell 1974, pp. 8-9; Riddle 1986, p. 8; Shelp 1981, pp. 2-3).

In hindsight, it would have been better if service scholars had settled on the term variability, which operations specialists often see as a key difference between manufacturing and service operations (Morris and Johnson 1987).

Are the IHIP Characteristics Truly Generalizable?

Despite an undercurrent of skepticism about the component elements (Gronroos 2000; Lovelock 1983, 2000) and a highly critical stance by Gummesson (2002b, pp. 288-89), the IHIP framework remains a unifying theme for services marketing. It continues to be presented as received wisdom in chapters on services marketing in introductory marketing texts and with varying degrees of certitude in several, but not all, specialized services marketing texts. However, as we will demonstrate, the framework has serious weaknesses as a generalizable underpinning for the paradigm that services are different from goods. We examine each characteristic in turn.

Characteristics of Services

1. Intangibility: Intangibility is not only the most widely cited difference between goods and services but has also been described by Bateson (1979) as the critical distinction from which all other differences emerge. Bateson drew a distinction between physical intangibility, that which is impalpable or cannot be touched, and mental intangibility, that which cannot be grasped mentally, and concluded," The crucial point about services is that they are doubly intangible"(p. 139). Later, McDougall and Snetsinger (1990) sought to operationalize mental intangibility as" the degree to which a product can be visualized and provide a clear and concrete image before purchase. "Laroche, Bergeron, and Goutaland (2001) argued that intangibility includes a third dimension, generality (which encompasses the notions of accessibility versus inaccessibility to the senses, abstractness versus concreteness, and generality versus specificity) and developed a scale for measuring all three dimensions.

However, on the basis of two subsequent empirical studies, Bielen and Sempels (2003, p. 12) confirmed Bateson's original conceptualization and concluded that intangibility is a bidimensional concept comprising (a) a physical dimension specific to the degree of materiality of the product or service studied and (b) a mental dimension tied to the degree of difficulty involved in defining, formulating, or understanding in clear and precise fashion the product or service in question. Nevertheless, the received wisdom presented today in introductory marketing textbooks fails to make an explicit distinction between physical and mental intangibility. Pride and Ferrell (2003) stated simply that "intangibility means that a service is not physical and therefore cannot be touched . . . or physically possessed." (p. 324).

The other three texts present physical intangibility as a prepurchase phenomenon that results in uncertainty and difficulty of evaluation. Kotler (2003) stated that "unlike physical goods, services cannot be seen, tasted, heard, felt, or smelled before purchase" and then linked this point to the need to reduce prepurchase uncertainty (p. 446). Kerin et al. (2003) stated that services "can't be held, touched, or seen before the purchase decision" and are thus more difficult to evaluate (p. 323).

Solomon and Stuart (2003) made the same point. Of course, we can argue that the same prepurchase phenomenon happens to be true of numerous manufactured products, including foodstuffs, cosmetics, medicines, and audio or video recordings, whose sensory stimuli are often hidden within protective packaging, making it possible for only the most seasoned buyers to fully evaluate them in advance of actual use. The growth of telephone ordering, ecommerce,and build-to-order products further insulates buyers from merchandise in advance of delivery. Yet many services involving delivery of tangible elements can be evaluated before use. For instance, the core product in hotel or motel is the room. Travelers can check out hotel or motel rooms before registering and may even decide to try another facility if they do not like the look of the facilities, the appearance and attitude of the staff, or even the feel of the bed.

Laroche, Bergeron, and Goutaland (2001) provided empirical support for Shostack notion of a tangibility-intangibility spectrum. They asked respondents to rate six product categories, composed of three goods (jeans, a computer, and a compact disk) and three services (a pizzeria dinner, a haircut, and a checking account) on a set of 9-point Likert-typescales measuring physical intangibility, mental intangibility, and third construct they called generality. The findings showed a different sequencing of the ratings for the six products on physical and mental intangibility, clearly indicating that consumers do not necessarily view all goods ashore physically and mentally tangible than all services and vice versa. In particular, the results showed that although a haircut was viewed as combining a roughly equal mix of physical tangibility and intangibility, it was clearly positioned in consumers' minds as mentally tangible.

2. Heterogeneity: The problem of variability has attracted attention from service researchers in both marketing and operations, primarily in relation to the difficulty of achieving uniform output, especially in labor-intensive services. Sasser, Olsen, and Wyckoff (1978) described the challenge of establishing standards when behavior and performance vary not only among service workers but even between the same employee's interactions from one customer to another and from one day to another. But Rathmell (1974) explicitly recognized that performance variability was much less problematic in machine-intensive service industries and that performance standards would become easier to attain as more services converted from human-intensive to machine-intensive operations. Levitt (1972) argued for "industrialization" of service operations, highlighting the use of equipment, procedures, and technology to remove human discretion and eliminate physical factors that caused variations in delivery.

Eiglier and Langeard (1975, 1977) noted the difficulty of controlling service quality when customers are actively involved in the production process. Morris and Johnston (1987) contrasted materials processing (manufacturing) and customer processing (service) operations, pointing to the variability in services of both the transforming resources and the transformed input (customers). Although the case for heterogeneity in services is based primarily on variations in worker performance, Zeithaml and Bitner (2003) noted that no two customers are precisely alike and thus will have unique demands or experience the service in a unique way. As additional factors creating variability in service performance, Desmet, VanLooy, and Van Dierdonck (1998) cited the presence and behavior of other customers during service delivery and variations in external conditions—weather, crowding, and differences between service locations.

However, we need to distinguish between variations in the consistency of service delivery that result from customer interactions with the service operation (a phenomenon derived from the characteristic of inseparability) and variations in customer perceptions of service experiences. The latter is not unique to services, because customers' expectations of, and experiences with, physical goods can also vary widely. Similarly, the notion of variability between customers is not unique to services and is embodied in relationship marketing, customer relationship management (CRM), and one-to-one marketing (Copulsky and Wolf 1990; Gronroos 2000; Gummesson 2002b; Peppers and Rogers 1999). Such customization strategies are as relevant to manufactured products as to services in both B2B and B2C contexts. Just as in consumer goods marketing there may be opportunities for product differentiation through mass customization (Pine 1993), research suggests a trend toward customization of services (Sundbo 2002). What is the received wisdom on heterogeneity? Among marketing management text authors, only Pride and Ferrell (2003) employed the term heterogeneity.

Kotler (2003) and Solomon and Stuart (2003) both used the more appropriate term, variability, whereas Kerin et al. (2003) employed inconsistency. All four texts link variability to human involvement in service delivery and resulting quality problems. Pride and Ferrell emphasize that "heterogeneity usually increases as the degree of labor intensiveness increases. Equipment-based services, in contrast, suffer from this problem to a lesser degree"

(p. 326). But it may not be a negative. Solomon and Stuart no tee that standardization is not even desirable for many services and that individuals often appreciate customization to meet their specific needs. The service literature makes frequent use of the standardization/ nonstandardization dichotomy. Yet this represents an incomplete depiction of the issue.

A better conceptualization, derived from manufacturing, is standardization, modularization, and customization. Many so-called standardized services, from banking to transportation, actually represent a strategy of mass customization (Pine 1993), in which customers make selections from a variety of modules (standardized in themselves) to create the service package that best suits their needs. For example, scheduled airline service is highly standardized in design but offers modules for customizing specific elements, such as alternative schedules; service to or from different airports in the same metropolitan area; different classes and prices; seat location; and a selection of drinks, food, and other amenities. Actual execution, of course, is variable.

3. *Inseparability:* Inseparability of production and consumption is linked to the concepts of interaction and the service encounter (Czepiel, Solomon, and Surprenant 1985). The latter concept was dramatically illustrated by the "50 million moments of truth per year" that Scandinavian Airlines (SAS) stressed in their pioneering and service-focused turnaround in the early 1980s (Carlzon 1987). A simultaneous production and consumption process involving such factors as the presence of the customer, the customer's role as co producer, customer-to-employee, and customer-to customer interactions is readily observable in many service environments and can form a critical distinguishing property between goods and many types of services. Although, as Prahalad (2004) recognized, there are multiple approaches to customer engagement, we use the term co-producer here in the narrow sense of a transfer of work from the provider to the customer. The literature on co production (Benapudi and Leone 2003; Bitner et al. 1997; Edvardsson et al. 2000; Firat, Dholakia, and Venkatesh 1995; Namisvayam 2003) highlights the productivity benefits as well as the managerial challenges that arise when customers become "partial employees."

In its purest form, co-production means that customers engage in self-service, using systems, facilities, or equipment supplied by the service provider. Bateson (1985), Lovelock and Young (1979), and Meuter et al. 2000) offer compelling evidence of the value of this approach to service delivery, the differing forms it can take, and the role of technology.

Separable services. Despite the inseparability claim for services, there is a large group of separable services that do not involve the customer directly, with the result that production and consumption need not be simultaneous. Simple observation will show that numerous widely used business and consumer services delivered to customers' physical possessions—such as transporting freight, laundering clothes, and undertaking routine cleaning and maintenance on a wide array of equipment and facilities- are most commonly performed in the customer's absence. The same is true of many government services such as defense and maintenance of infrastructure.

Consumers purchase such services as laundry and dry cleaning, oil changes for their cars, lawn care, and parcel delivery precisely to avoid having to involve themselves in these tasks. They are willing to pay money to save time and effort and to allow a professional to do the job-often perceived as an unpleasant one-better than they could themselves. Dropping off an item at a retail repair site or giving instructions to a provider of lawn care services does not constitute involvement in actual production of the core service activity. Similarly, corporate customers outsource such repetitive tasks as freight transportation, payroll administration, landscaping, and office cleaning precisely in order to disengage from performance of these activities. In some cases, the tasks are performed at a different physical location; in others (such as office cleaning or building repairs), they may be deliberately scheduled at night or weekends when hardly anyone is around. Although there may be some initial collaboration between the customer and the service provider, once the outsourced operation is running smoothly, there is usually little reason for the customer to remain engaged in the production process. In many separable services, there is an inevitable decoupling of production and consumption. Consider cleaning, repair, and maintenance services, where consumption of the benefits can only take place after the customer reclaims the item, typically some time after production has been completed. In a few instances, consumption of benefits actually precedes production, as in banking when a customer pays a bill by writing a check that may not be processed until several days later.

4. Perishability: There are multiple perspectives on the meaning and implications of perishability, and consequently, the literature on this topic embraces several strands. What, then, is the received wisdom? A common claim is that services cannot be saved, stored for reuse at a later date, resold, or returned (Edgett and Parkinson 1993; Zeithaml and Bitner 2003). Kotler (2003, p. 449) stated simply that services cannot be stored, and Solomon and Stewart (2003) concurred. Pride and Ferrell (2003) declared that "the unused service capacity of one time period cannot be stored for future use" (p. 325), and Fitzsimmons and Fitzsimmons (1998) specifically stressed the time dependency. If demand is low, unused capacity is wasted. If demand exceeds capacity, it goes unfulfilled and business may be lost.

Bringing demand and supply into balance requires management of both demand and available capacity (Lovelock 1984; Sasser 1976). Kerin et al. (2003) took a slightly different perspective. Using the heading "Inventory" rather than "Perishability," they argued that inventory of services is different from that of goods: "Inventory problems exist with goods because many items are perishable and because there are costs associated with handling inventory. With services, inventory carrying costs are related to idle production capacity" (p. 325). In one sense, perishability and inventory present a more challenging issue for manufacturers than for service organizations. When producing for inventory, manufacturing firms incur both maintenance costs (such as storage, security, and insurance) and financial carrying costs. With an expanded role for the finance function, demands for earlier and higher return on capital and minimizing inventory and its associated costs have become overriding concerns for many companies. Service firms do not have inventory costs of this nature. But the problem of achieving efficient capacity italicization is universal: Perisha bility of productive capacity is as relevant to the manager of a factory producing beds as is it is to a hotel manager worried about unrented rooms. Perishability of capacity from the producer's standpoint is not the same as a perishable experience for a customer, although both are rooted in the passage of time. And perishable capacity is not the same as perishable output, for without customers who require service at a specific time, either to themselves or their possessions, there can be no output at most service organizations. Consumers may view output differently from producers.

Most service performances are transient experiences, but this does not mean that the output itself is also perishable, since some services create durable results, thus raising the question of how best to define output. For instance, from a hospital's perspective, a surgical procedure represents output; from the patient's perspective, it is the outcome of that surgery that is relevant. However, there is an exception to the rule that, unlike manufacturers, service firms cannot produce for inventory and sell their products later. Certain types of live performances—such as education, entertainment, music, religious services, and news—can be recorded for subsequent use through broadcasting or transformed into a reusable physical good in the form of DVDs, tapes, or other storage media. We propose an expanded concept of inventory that better represents the challenges facing both manufacturers and service providers.

Classic use of the term refers to a store of physical goods (including foodstuffs and raw materials) following completion of manufacturing, agricultural, or extractive production. But in a context of build-to order and just-in-time delivery, where even manufactured products are often ordered or reserved in advance, it is relevant and important to examine the characteristic of preproduction inventory. Today, many service industries explicitly calculate their future productive capacity for specific dates and even times of day, relating it to such variables as hours of service and number of employees available. Planned variations in this capacity can be reduced if customers are willing to queue. Growing attention is now being paid to maximizing yield per unit of available capacity, by varying prices between time periods and charging different rates to different types of customers (Kimes and Chase 1998). This capacity is then defined in terms of specific units of service production, which may be further categorized by nature of output. Thus, hotels categorize room nights by type of accommodation; airlines categorize seats by service class, route, and schedule; consulting firms may allocate billable hours among staff with different levels and types of skills; and maintenance services may allocate labor and machine time among different applications under both routine and emergency conditions. This notion of preproduction inventory is central to development of revenue (yield) management programs (Kimes 2003).

Noting the extent to which manufacturing organizations have reoriented themselves around services, Schneider (2000) observed that "the field has been so successful that it is now just another facet of marketing" (p. 180). Why, then, is services marketing more often presented as a special chapter in marketing management textbooks than integrated into general marketing theory? In Kuhn's spirit, the major reason is that the marketing literature has been unwilling to abandon mainstream marketing management concepts and categories and to acknowledge services as an integral part of every industry and product—a position championed by Gronroos (2000) and Vargo and Lusch (2004a, 2004b). Such an outcome would be a final vindication of Levitt's (1972) prescient claim that "everybody is in service." Even earlier, Norris (1941) concluded that "goods are wanted because they are capable of performing services" (p. 137).

Much of the marketing-oriented research reported in some of the service journals is not service-specific in its application. For instance, the study of customer satisfaction and dissatisfaction, a key topic in developing satisfaction related measures of service quality, originated with research on goods (Anderson 1973; Cardozo 1965; H. K. Hunt 1977). Relationship marketing has benefited from service-specific research (Berry 1983; Crosby, Evans, and Cowles 1990; Gummesson 1994, 2002b) but also applies to consumer durables (especially those of high value) and industrial goods. The emerging field of customer equity management has its roots in several overlapping research streams including direct marketing, service quality, and relationship marketing, and brand equity (Hogan, Lemon, and Rust 2002). To the extent that such studies yield managerially useful results, these are healthy developments. Perhaps a case can now be made by service marketers for declaring victory and claiming dominion over all marketing, on the grounds that service thinking has thoroughly infiltrated most aspects of goods marketing (Rust 1998). But this beguiling perspective conceals an intellectual and managerial trap. Lovelock and Wirtz (2004) emphasized that there is an important distinction "between marketing of services-where a service is the core product -and marketing goods through service" (p. 23). In the latter case, a manufacturing or natural resource firm bases its marketing strategy on a philosophy of serving customers well by adding supplementary services that enhance the value of the core product. However, that core product still remains a physical good.

Nonownership: One Potential basis for a New Paradigm

Early researchers emphasized that there was no transfer of ownership in services (Judd 1964; Rathmell 1974). Yet subsequent theorizing has largely ignored this striking characteristic. In pursuit of an ideal paradigm, we propose creation of a new one around the notion that marketing transactions that do not involve a transfer of ownership are distinctively different from those that do. We believe that at this stage in the evolution of services marketing theory, this perspective offers the potential to uncover new and different dimensions of service reality.

Exploring the Characteristic of Nonownership

In dusting off the characteristic of nonownership, we do not claim that it offers a panacea with necessarily general properties. Rather, we propose it as a lens to present aspects not clearly visible in current theory. If customers do not receive ownership when they purchase a service, then what are they buying? We contend that services involve a form of rental or access in which customers obtain benefits by gaining the right to use a physical object, to hire the labor and expertise of personnel, or to obtain access to facilities and networks. Although we use the terms rental and access, we remain open to the use of other terminology and acknowledge the subtle distinctions between words such as rent, hire, and lease. Several broad categories can be identified within the nonownership framework.

Rented goods services (Judd 1964). Customers obtain the temporary right to exclusive use of a physical good that they do not wish to own or cannot afford to purchase outright. Examples include vehicles, power tools, furniture, construction equipment, and formal clothing.

Place and space rentals. Customers obtain exclusive use of a defined portion of a larger space in building, vehicle, or other area. Examples include hotel room, a seat in an aircraft, or a suite in an office building. The space is sometimes designated by location, but in other instances, as in so-called open seating, customers may be free to select one space per ticket.

Labor and expertise rentals. Customers hire other people to do work that they either choose not to do for themselves (e.g., cleaning a house) or are unable to do because they lack the necessary strength, tools,or skills. In many instances, customers may effectively rent an entire team as in car repair, surgery, and management consultancy.

Physical facility access and usage. Customers rent admission to a facility such as a museum, theme park, spa, or conference site and can then take advantage of it during the period of validity.

Network access and usage. Customers rent the right to participate in a specified network such as telecommunications, utilities, banking, insurance, or specialized information services. Differing terms ofaccess may be developed to meet varying customer needs and abilities to pay. In many instances, a service may combine elements from several of the above categories, plus direct transfer of one or more physical items. One way of representing such a package is through the molecular modeling of market entities proposed by Shostack (1977).

Implications of the Rental/Access Paradigm

The division of marketing exchanges into two broad categories-those that involve a transfer of ownership and those that do not-offers scholars and practitioners a new lens through which to observe marketplace activity and examine data. In the process, there may be opportunities to see things that were previously missed. Butterfield (1949) described such a reorientation as "picking up the other end of the stick." Let us consider what issues immediately jump into focus and demand our attention. Manufactured goods can form the basis for services. Both household and business customers often find that solutions to temporary needs are better met by renting a durable good than owning it. Advertisements can be found in most Yellow Pages for rentals of a wide array of products, including vehicles, construction and excavation equipment, generators, tents, party supplies, power tools, furniture, formal wear, and sporting goods. Users purchase temporary possession utility and return the items when no longer needed. Marketing goods through rentals raises distinctive challenges.

Consider car rental, where customers obtain the right to use the car for a defined period within the terms of the rental agreement. Although the core product remains a physical good, customers' brand preferences shift from the characteristics of the vehicle to those of the rental firm, being shaped not only by price but also by ease of reservation, convenience of rental office locations for pickup and drop-off, performance of rental agents, and benefits of loyalty programs. Service often involves selling slices of larger physical entities. In the category "place and space rentals," the physical entity becomes a "sausage" from which customers buy slices. Customers gain the right to exclusive but temporary use of a portion that they can legitimately describe as "my seat," "my room," "our offices." The fact that the items rented represent subdivisions of a larger entity enables customers to participate in the economies of scale derived from sharing a larger space with many users, while enjoying varying degrees of separation and even privacy. In some instances, the proximity of other customers and interaction between them is regarded as a positive experience; in others, it may be seen as a trade-off against more expensive alternatives.

The object is often desired less for its intrinsic qualities than as a means to a broader end. A restaurant table provides a surface for meals; a theater seat offers a resting place from which to view performance. In both instances, some locations may be perceived as more desirable than others. In the category "physical facility access," customers are not assigned a specific physical slice but instead have a certain freedom during the period of validity to select and experience different elements of a facility.

Labor and expertise are renewable resources in services. Abraham Lincoln's remark that "a lawyer's time and expertise are his stock in trade" can be applied to all skilled service jobs. Sometimes the desired task requires physical stamina, but increasingly it is intellectual skills that customers seek. Assuming adequate rest and good health, the service provider's expertise is a renewable resource, but time itself is perishable.

Time plays a central role in most services. The rental paradigm explicitly focuses our interest on time as a key construct for both suppliers and customers. Ownership is for as long as the object lasts or until the owner chooses to dispose of it. Rental nearly always relates to a specified time period. We live in the most time-conscious era in human history. McKenna (1997) highlights changing expectations of speedy delivery and the evolving technologies and procedures that make this possible. Berry, Seiders, and Grewal (2002) cite the importance for firms of understanding consumers' perceived expenditures of time in order to create transaction convenience. But despite Scientific American's contention that "time has become to the 21st century what fossil fuels and precious metals were to previous epochs" (Stix 2002), the study of time in a service management context has not received the attention that it merits.

In contrast to the sustained effort to study such constructs as service quality and customer satisfaction, only spasmodic attention has been paid to improve our understanding of how customers perceive, budget, consume, and value time (Graham 1981; Herlow 1981; Le Clerc,Schmitt, and Dubé 1995; Soman 2001). The most commonly discussed applications relate to management of waiting lines (Durrande-Moreau and Usinier 1999; Jones and Peppiatt 1996; Kostecki 1996; Rossiter 2003) and shaping customers' decisions on when to use a service (Lovelock 1984; Kimes and Wirtz 2003). Examining services from a rental perspective should stimulate research interest in this important area and enable us to build on existing prescriptions for minimizing the perceived burden for customers of waiting time (Maister 1985; Jones and Peppiatt 1996; Katz, Larson, and Larson 1991).

Service pricing

New thinking is needed on service pricing. The distinction between ownership and rental offers a different perspective for pricing analysis and strategy, beyond the obvious ones of relating price to quality and value. A logical approach in rental and access situations is to relate pricing to units of time-how long customers rent, how long they are entitled to share a defined space or access a physical facility or network, and how much time they receive from a service provider. This approach is straightforward and can work well for suppliers if they can document their time and have a good understanding of the costs associated with delivering a specific unit of service. Although activity-based costing is widely applied in manufacturing firms (Cooper and Kaplan 1991), little has been published on its application to different types of services (Lovelock and Wirtz 2004, pp. 154-56). Circumstances may require modification of time-based pricing, including incorporation of the cost of physical goods supplied as part of service delivery (such as food, medical drugs, or spare parts).

Revenue management strategies (also known as yield management) recognize that many customers explicitly place more value on some time periods than others and that different segments vary widely in their price sensitivity (Kimes and Chase 1998; Kimes and Wirtz 2003; Shugan and Xie 2000). Historically, revenue management has been practiced primarily by airlines, hotels, and rental car companies, but there may be opportunities to employ this strategy among many other capacity-constrained service suppliers that face significant but predictable swings in demand over time, ranging from golf courses to restaurants and professional firms (Kimes 2003). Customers who are time sensitive may also be willing to pay extra for speed. Services offer opportunities for resource sharing.

Renting is a way for customers to enjoy use of physical goods and facilities that they cannot afford to buy, cannot justify purchasing, or prefer not to retain after use. In addition, renting-in the form of access fees-offers a means to participate in network systems that individuals and most organizations could not possibly afford to own and operate for themselves. This insight has two important implications for today'sworld. First, in developing economies, prospects for improved quality of life may revolve around finding creative ways of sharing access to goods, physical facilities, systems, and expertise, in ways that bring the price down to affordable levels. Second, in a world where many resources are believed to be finite, replacing ownership by rental may be the best way in both merging and developed economies to allocate use of the products that incorporate these scarce resources.

The foundations of services marketing were laid down more than a quarter-century ago. The pre-1980 era that Fisk, Brown, and Bitner (1993) referred to as the "Crawling Out" phase of services marketing was one in which scholars were debating what made services different from goods as they sought to legitimate the need for a new field. In that era, there were no personal computers, no Internet, and little opportunity for consumers to make toll-free long-distance calls to service suppliers. International trade in services was restricted, most firms still preferred to perform service activities in-house rather than to outsource, and there was no body of knowledge on how to improve service quality. Although vending machines had a long history, applications of technology-based self-service were only just getting off the ground-primarily in banking and gasoline retailing.

Today, the environment of services marketing is radically different. The "goods versus services" debate of the 1970s and early 1980s was useful and fruitful in highlighting the crucial but neglected role of services in management and marketing, yet the very nature of that debate obscured the necessary synergies between manufacturing and service businesses, and much work remains to be done to develop an understanding of the mutual interaction and interdependence between goods and services.

Early theorizing created a paradigm that services possessed four unique characteristics (IHIP) that made them different from goods. This paradigm was enshrined in landmark articles, service textbooks, and many professors' lecture notes, ultimately becoming part of the received wisdom of marketing through repetition in successive issues of mainstream marketing texts. Although it served a useful purpose in facilitating evolution of the field of services marketing, we contend on the basis of our review that the underlying premises of this paradigm no longer bear up under examination. Vargo and Lusch (2004b) have independently reached a similar conclusion, dismissing many of the arguments for IHIP as myths. In Kuhn's (1970) terminology, the core paradigm of services marketing has long been in "crisis."

To continue pretending that the IHIP-based paradigm is an appropriate lens through which to view the entire service sector risks transforming what was once a building block into a stumbling block. But Kuhn also warns us that "to reject one paradigm without simultaneously substituting another is to reject science itself" (p. 79). We are not alone with Schneider (2000) in explicitly calling for new directions. In their own review of the future of services marketing, Grove, Fisk, and John (2003) declared, "In our information age economy, where new business models are constantly emerging and disappearing, the struggle to discover successful new frameworks raises questions regarding existing paradigms. Newer paradigms must evolve." (p. 119). Changes in such factors as corporate and consumer attitudes, marketplace behavior, and political agendas are also shaped and reinforced by technological change. Technological development presents marketers with new tools and opportunities (Rust 2004).

At the same time, it also has the potential to undermine the foundations of existing marketing thought. Deighton (1997) argued that with the advent of the Internet, "the rate of intellectual capital depreciation in marketing today exceeds that at any time in this [20th] century" (p. 347). Accepting the need for new directions in services marketing is potentially threatening. As the 16th-century English theologian Richard Hooker once observed, "Change is not made without inconvenience, even from worse to better." Shugan (2004) warns that "generality is a traditional holy grail of academic research. The developers and stewards of traditional methods and theories will enthusiastically proclaim that new methods are unnecessary" (p. 25). Yet the evidence is compelling that the field must adopt new directions if it is to remain relevant. Earlier, we laid out several alternative routes for services marketing.

One option is to argue that services marketing and goods marketing should be reunited under a service banner. This would be consistent with Vargo and Lusch's 2004a, 2004b) belief that a new dominant logic is emerging in marketing in which service provision, rather than goods, is fundamental to economic exchange. Another option would be to acknowledge that there continue to be important differences between the ways in which the core products of manufacturing and service enterprises are created, marketed, distributed, and consumed, but that the differences among services are equally significant and must be acknowledged by developing separate paradigms for different categories of services. For instance, we could have one paradigm for tangible services to the person of the customer, one for e-services, one for separable services, one for what Peter Hill (1999) termed "intangible goods," and lastly, consider retaining or modifying the IHIP-based paradigm for services that still meet the criteria posed by those characteristics. The third option we put forward was to look for a new paradigm that would cut across the traditional goods and services dichotomy. Therefore, we proposed an alternative set of assumptions tentatively labeled the rental/access paradigm. In this paradigm, based on the premise that those marketing exchanges that do not result in a transfer of ownership from seller to buyer are fundamentally different from those that do, services are presented as offering benefits through access or temporary possession, rather than ownership, with payments taking the form of rentals or access fees.

We make no claim that the proposed new paradigm offers a panacea with necessarily general properties. Rather, we present it as a lens to explore aspects of services marketing and consumption not clearly visible in current theory. It holds the potential to stimulate new approaches to both research and practice, and it provides a bridge to manufacturing by explicitly recognizing the role of service-based rentals as an alternative to direct sale of durable products. Because it does not undermine the existing services marketing field, it is consistent with Kuhn's (1970) belief that new paradigms "usually preserve a great deal of the most concrete parts of past achievement and they always permitadditionalconcreteproblem-solutions besides" (p. 169). At this point, the proposed "rental/access paradigm" is a set of assumptions.

It cannot be described as a paradigm shift in the Kuhnian sense until it is shared among other scholars and starts to shape the formulation of theoretical generalizations, to focus data gathering, and to influence research procedures and projects. In particular, we believe there is a need for systematic field research in services, employing both qualitative and quantitative methods that go beyond consumer satisfaction studies to include in-depth case studies of business practice and customer behavior. Early development of the field of services was stimulated by a combination of inductive and deductive research involving both scholars and practitioners from several continents. Future advances in theory and practice will profit from similar collaboration around the world.

Specific Topics

Service Quality

The single most researched area in services marketing to date is service quality. The interest in service quality parallels the focus on quality, total quality management, and customer satisfaction in business during the last decade. The roots of the service quality research reside in early conceptual work from Europe (e.g. Gronroos, 1983; Lehtinen and Lehtinen, 1982), and customer satisfaction theory (e.g. Oliver, 1980). Most of the recent work on service quality in marketing can be credited to the pioneering and continuing contributions of A. Parasuraman, Leonard Berry and Valerie Zeithaml. Their ongoing research, supported by the Marketing Science Institute, has produced a well-received conceptual framework (the Gaps Model) and a measurement instrument, SERVQUAL, for assessing service quality. While there is healthy - and for the most part productive - debate regarding the dimensionality of SERVQUAL across industries, and the precise wording of the SERVQUAL items, researchers generally agree that the scale items are good predictors of overall service quality (Babakus and Boller, 1992; Bolton and Drew, 1991a,b; Brown and Swartz, 1989; Carman, 1990; Cronin and Taylor, 1992; Parasuraman et al., 1991).

The debate underscores the importance of the topic and the significance of the contributions to date. Such interchange will help refine the meaning of service quality. Other researchers have contributed empirical studies on service satisfaction, a closely related topic that is sometimes difficult to distinguish from service quality (Bitner, 1990; Bitner et al., 1990; Crosby et al., 1990; Oliva et al., 1992). While service satisfaction and service quality are clearly related, researchers do not share common definitions of the terms, nor is there clear understanding expressed in the literature of how the two relate. Exploration and discussion of these issues will certainly continue in the near future (see Rust and Oliver, 1993).

The emergence of service quality and its assessment has attracted the attention of numerous researchers in the past two decades or so. In this sense, there are two main lines of thoughts on measuring service quality (Kang and James, 2004): an American and a European perspective. Brady and Cronin (2001) suggest that the researchers generally adopt one of the two conceptualizations in their work. The focus on functional quality attributes is referred to as the American perspective of service quality while the European perspective suggests that service quality considers two more components. The European perspective considers additional aspects other than the process of service delivery. Grönroos (1984), for instance, noted that the quality of a service as perceived by customers consists of three dimensions: functional (the process of service delivery to customers), technical (the outcomes generated by the service to the customers), and image (how the customers view the company).

Considering those dimensions, the quality of the service is dependent upon two variables: the expected service and the perceived service. More details of the previous argument are provided by Grönroos (1984). Functional quality of a service is often assessed by measures of customers' attitudes, as in customer satisfaction questionnaires. As described by Hayes (1997), the process of identifying customers' attitudes begins with determining customers' requirements or quality dimensions. Parasuraman et al. (1985) identified in a first study 10 quality dimensions based on a series of focus group sessions. From this study, the authors concluded that customers use the same criteria to assess service quality independently of the type of service For Hayes (1997), however, some quality dimensions are generalised across many services, but some will apply only to specific types of services, and it is necessary to understand quality dimensions to be able to develop measures to assess them. The author explains then two ways of identifying important quality dimensions of services:

quality dimension development approach and critical incident approach. The first one uses different sources of information, such as opinions of providers and literature. The other one is a process to obtain information from customers.

The 10 determinants of service quality established by Parasuraman et al. (1985) provide a list that can guide investigation on the first approach. The authors subsequently developed SERVQUAL (Parasuraman et al., 1988), a two-part instrument for measuring service quality that was refined later (Parasuraman et al., 1991). Much of the research to date has focused on measuring service quality using this approach and its use has become quite widespread (Brown et al., 1993; Kang and James, 2004). SERVQUAL instrument consists of a 22- item instrument for assessing service quality based on customer's perceptions, which is, by his turn, the difference between the customer's perceived quality and his/her expectation. The perceived quality is assessed based on service quality dimensions that correspond to the criteria used by consumers when assessing service quality.

There are 10 potentially overlapping dimensions: tangibles, reliability, responsiveness, communication, credibility, assurance, competence, courtesy, understanding/knowing the customer, and access. A more detailed description of those dimensions can be found in Zeithan et al. (1990). Afterwards, these dimensions were reduced to five, namely: tangibles, reliability, responsiveness, assurance, empathy. Using those 10 or 5 dimensions as the evaluation criteria the specification of service quality becomes the gap between customers' expectations and their perceptions (Parasuraman et al, 1985). This performance-expectation model was also adopted by other authors (e.g. Brown and Swartz, 1989). However, there has been an extensive debate whether the perception-minus-expectations specification would be appropriate or assessing perception alone would be sufficient.

Some concerns about the SERVQUAL instrument were raised by Cronin and Taylor (1992; 1994) and Teas (1993; 1994). The authors argue that there are serious conceptual and operational drawbacks associated with the SERVQUAL model, inducing Cronin and Taylor (1992) to propose a perceived quality model called SERVPERF. The perceived quality model postulates that an individual's perception of the quality is only a function of its performance. Considering that the 22 performance items adequately define the domain of service quality, Cronin and Taylor (1992) proposed the SERVPERF instrument, which is a more concise performance-based scale; an alternative to the SERVQUAL model. In addition, they compared the SERVPERF model with SERVQUAL and two other alternatives: the weighted SERVQUAL and the weighted SERVFERF models. Those weighted versions consider the importance of a quality attribute as a determinant of

Table: 2.1 Proposed models for measuring service quality (Adapted from Cauchick Miguel and Salomi, 2004)

Autor	*Model*	*Main Characteristics*	*Application*
Gronroos (1984)	Thiere is no mathematical representation	Quality is a function of expectations, outcome and image	Different types of services
Parasuraman et al. (1985, 1988)	SERVQUAL $Q1 = P_1 - E_1$	22-item scale using 5 quality dimensions	Different types of services
Brown and Swartz (1989)	$Q_1 = E_1 - D_1$	Use 10 quality dimensions defined by Parasuraman et al. (1985)	Medical surgery
Botton and Drew (1991)	Assessment model of service and value. There are many equations representing the model	Use four developed by developed by Parasuraman et al (1988) and introduce the concept of value for quality assessment	Telephone services
Cronin and Taylor (1992)	SERVPERF $Q_1 = P_1$	Use 5 quality dimensions defined by Parasuraman et al. (1988)	Different types of services

perceived quality. In response to the criticisms, Parasuraman et al. (1994) claimed that many of those concerns are questionable and offered a set of research directions for addressing unresolved issues.

SERVQUAL was adopted as the instrument for this research work to assess service quality according to the literature (Parasuraman et al., 1985; 1988). Although there is no consensus in the literature of which instrument is most effective, SERVQUAL was chosen because it was tested in a similar work conducted by Zeithaml et al. (1990) and it is useful to provide evidence of service quality for further service operation improvement (Page Jr. and Spreng, 2002).

Service Encounters/Experiences

Another prominent stream of research relates to service encounters/experiences or "moments of truth" (Carlson, 1987). The underlying assumption is that customer perceptions of service encounters are important elements of customer satisfaction, perceptions of quality, and long-term loyalty. Service encounter research focuses on the interactions between customers and employees in service firms. Research published recently can be traced to the book entitled *The Service Encounter* (Czepiel et al., 1985) that emanated from a symposium by that name, the first Journal of Marketing Publication on service encounters (Solomon et al., 1985), and numerous conference proceedings papers published in the early 1980s. Currently the research on service encounters can be divided into three primary types. First, considerable attention is being paid to the management of customer and employee interactions in service encounters and to understanding how customers evaluate individual service encounters (e.g. Bitner, 1990; Bitner et al., 1990; Czepiel et al., 1990; Lewis and Entwistle, 1990; Mills, 1990; Surprenant and Solomon, 1987). A second research focus is on customer involvement in service encounters and the customer's role in service production and delivery (e.g. Goodwin, 1990; Kelley et al., 1990; Larsson and Bowen, 1989). The roots of this research are in Bate son's early work on self-service customers (Bate son, 1983). The third research focus on service encounters examines the Services Marketing Thought Role of tangibles and physical environment in the customer's evaluation of encounters (e.g. Berry and Parasuraman, 1991; Bitner, 1992; Hui and Bate son, 1991). Service design. Because services are processes, the actual steps involved in delivering and receiving the service (traditionally called the service "operation"), assume tremendous marketing importance. The growth of total quality management (TQM) has provided another catalyst for research on service processes because TQM is process oriented.

However, service industries typically do not apply rigorous process design standards prior to introducing new services, and service processes are typically less controllable because of the human element. Although this topic is likely to receive greater attention in the near future, most contributions to date have been in service blueprinting and service mapping, an area pioneered by Lynn Shostack (1984; 1987; 1992) and Jane Kingman-Brundage (1989; 1991). A primary difference between service blueprinting and typical operations flowcharts is that a blueprint incorporates the customer and the customer's actions on the same flow diagram as the rest of the operation. Thus, the entire design of the service operation can be seen as if through the customer's eyes. Others have contributed to an increased understanding of the marketing impact and role of service operations and process design (e.g. Baum, 1990;George and Gibson, 1991; Johnston, 1987; Scheuing and Johnson, 1989).

The role of technology in service process design and its impact on service quality are related topics that have received attention outside of marketing; these topics are sure to influence services design research (e.g. Quinn et al., 1990; Quinn and Paquette, 1990).

Customer Retention and Relationship Marketing

Services researchers since the early 1980s have drawn attention to the need to retain, as well as attract, customers (Berry, 1983). Relationship marketing recognizes the value of current customers and the need to provide continuing services to existing customers so that they will remain loyal. For marketers, this is a definite shift away from more traditional marketing approaches. Since the late 1980s, even more research has been directed at customer retention issues (e.g. Gronroos, 1990).

The research on relationship marketing and customer retention has taken various forms. For example, some research focuses on constructs, such as trust and relationship commitment and how these constructs relate to customer satisfaction and loyalty (e.g. Crosby and Stephens, 1987; Crosby et al., 1990). Other researchers have focused on specific breakthrough strategies for retaining customers, such as building an effective recovery strategy for service failure situations (e.g. Berry and Parasuraman, 1991; Hart et al., 1990) or offering service guarantees to reduce risk and build loyalty (e.g. Hart, 1988). Understanding and calculating both the long-term value of a customer and the lost revenue-profits for defecting customers (e.g. Reich held and Sasser, 1990) are two other research topics that fall within the relationship marketing focus. These latter topics (recovery, guarantees, and the cost of defecting customers) have been embraced quickly by business practitioners and would benefit from additional academic research.

Internal Marketing

Two basic ideas underlie the concept of internal marketing, and kernels of both ideas emerged in the early services literature. First, "everyone in the organization has a customer" (Gronroos, 1981). It is not just contact personnel who need to be concerned with satisfying their customers. Everyone in the organization has someone whom he or she must serve. The second basic idea is that internal customers must be sold on the service and happy in their jobs before they can serve the final customer effectively. This idea suggests that marketing tools and concepts (e.g. segmentation, marketing research) can be used internally with employees (Berry, 1981).

The basic premise of internal marketing is that satisfied employees (or well served internal customers) will lead to satisfied customers (or well-served external customers). George (1990) provides an excellent review of internal marketing. The terminology and concept of internal marketing has quickly pervaded the business community. A few years ago, no one used the term, but now it is commonly discussed and written about in the business press. A number of recent contributions on internal marketing have appeared in both the marketing and management literature

(Berry and Parasuraman, 1991; Gronroos, 1990; Gummesson, 1987; Schlesinger and Heskett, 1991a,b; Tansuhaj et al., 1988). Empowerment is highly relevant to internal marketing, and this topic has received solid and thought-provoking coverage in a recent services management publication by Bowen and Lawler (1992).

Service Design and Delivery

Service blue printing and mapping have received some attention both in the literature and in practice. Yet, compared to the engineering and production emphasis associated with the development and manufacturing of goods, research on the parallel activities for services is meager. In the workplace, TQM is encouraging organizations to develop and use process design techniques that incorporate customers' and employees' needs with all elements of the design focused on service quality throughout the process. We believe that service engineering, design and execution should and will be key areas for scholarly and managerial inquiry. Services marketing scholars have special opportunities to incorporate the customer's needs into design and delivery of services.

Service Encounters and Service Experiences

As noted earlier, literature on contact employee and customer relationships has emerged recently. This research documents the importance of service encounters, or what Kotler calls "interactive marketing". As customer expectations increase, we envision front-line service employees assuming the role of consultant and salesperson more frequently. In other words, organizations will rely on these representatives not only to provide the service but also to solve customers' problems, gather information on customer needs and preferences, and cross-sell additional services. We foresee research on longer-term service experiences beyond one-time, brief transactions. We also expect greater focus on the relationships among service encounter issues and other organizational concerns such as quality and profitability.

Service Quality and Customer Satisfaction

Certainly the dominant theme in recent services research has been quality. We foresee this interest continuing and assuming broader, deeper dimensions. We expect more research on internal as well as external quality and the interrelationships between the two areas. The dynamics of quality are also likely to be investigated by researchers via studies of multiple exchanges over time and through a hierarchy of quality measurements ranging from individual service encounters to overall firm or even industry assessments. Finally, we see a coming together (if not a merging) of the heretofore-independent research streams of customer satisfaction and service quality. How to establish clear linkages between customer satisfaction and quality on the one hand and internal measures of efficiency and employee compensation on the other are important future directions for research.

Other New issues in Services

Although the observations on the preceding three areas are reasonable predictions given the past, we also envision a future that could - and undoubtedly should - include research on some of the following topics:

Service Recovery

Despite TQM's call for "zero defects" and "doing it right the first time", service providers typically cannot meet these high expectations. Unlike tangible goods, 100 per cent quality cannot be engineered into a service, especially when even the definition of the service is in the eyes of the beholder. This recognition indicates special needs and opportunities for research on topics such as consumer complaining behaviors, managerial responses to these behaviors, and employee-customer complaint interactions and resolution.

Reverse Marketing

This topic focuses on the service provider improving relationships with suppliers and vendors to provide the final customer with higher service quality. Some organizations, for example, are asking their suppliers to meet or exceed the same customer satisfaction standards they set for themselves. To date, services researchers have virtually ignored the value-added chain and instead have chosen to focus on the final consumer. We see a need to broaden the scope of services research to embrace topics like reverse marketing and other forms of organizational alliances.

Internal Marketing and Support Services

The view of employees as customers and their exchanges and relationships have been discussed in the literature but not subjected to extensive research. Further, the considerations associated with providing a service internally or looking to the external market (outsourcing) is an additional area of needed research. For example, can we transfer our understanding of external customer satisfaction and external service encounters to the provision of internal services? And what about internal service guarantees - can they work and what should be guaranteed?

Modeling and Measurement

The existing literature is replete with unsubstantiated principles about service excellence, service quality and related topics. Yet too little evidence exists to substantiate whether these principles result in outcomes such as long-term customer satisfaction and profitability. Understanding the linkages between customer satisfaction and employee satisfaction also demands further research. Furthermore, alternative measures and methods for understanding these principles and related factors still need to be developed and refined. For example, while SERVQUAL is a popular measure for service quality, refinements and alternative approaches are needed in measuring this important construct.

Technology Infusion

The current services literature is implicitly mired in the paradigm of "low tech and high touch". The typical need for high levels of human interaction has even led some writers to downplay explicitly the potential contributions of technology to services marketing. In the workplace, however, new technology is helping empower service employees by giving them more information more quickly for use in deciding how best to serve customers. Technology can also help organizations design and engineer services processes. Researchers have opportunities to break out of the prevailing low-tech paradigm and study customers' relative preferences for high-tech service in and of itself and in conjunction with high-touch experiences. The impact of technology on the entire service industry and organizational structures and business methods demands further research as well (see Quinn, 1992).

This discussion of future research needs is far from exhaustive. Topics such as Customer retention and customer value, managing supply and demand for a perishable inventory or capacity, and service quality and productivity in the public sector could easily be added to this list.

Continuing Evolution: Envisioning the Future Literature

The explosion of articles, papers, books and dissertations has been remarkable, leading us naturally to ask: What will the literature of the future be like? What will the next stage of the evolution generate? Based on documentation of the past and our positions as active Researchers and participants in the field, we will attempt to look ahead. Recognizing that the past often predicts the future, we are fairly comfortable in projecting from the present trends. However, it also gives an opportunity to speculate, dream, and envision the next era. Based on the previous 40 years, but particularly the last 15, one would expect a continued broadening, deepening, and sharpening of the research. By increasing breadth, it means that a continuation of the trend to incorporate theories and ideas from disciplines outside marketing, particularly management, operations, and human resources.

This trend is consistent with the desire of businesses to break down functional barriers in their organizations to improve effectiveness; this removal of barriers is often particularly essential for service businesses. By increasing depth, it means extended development of current research topics such as service quality, service satisfaction, service encounters and service design through the enhancement of current thinking on these topics. One can also expect to see the literature continue to sharpen in theoretical and methodological rigor, making ever-greater contributions in all of these areas with the recent entry of researchers into the field whose expertise is in measurement, statistics and decision support modeling, one also would expect more quantitative contributions. The practical focus and managerial relevance of services research is likely to develop even further as a result of the continuing involvement of practitioners in helping formulate research issues and supporting the research efforts of scholars.

The involvement of a global community of scholars will continue as well. We envision even closer working relationships and co-authoring among scholars from different countries as opportunities to interact become more frequent, and service business problems become increasingly global. One can also expect the growing interest in services marketing to continue among many academic researchers. Given the dramatic increase in dissertations on services topics each year, one can expect journal contributions from new scholars.

In addition, one can observe a rising number of established, well respected academics turning their research interest at least partially to services issues. The field is attractive to both new and established academics because the research issues are practical and plentiful, the community of researchers and practitioners is receptive and open, and a growing number of outlets for services publications exist.

Further, more and more opportunities occur for these researchers to interact as well, both in Europe and in North America through university, association, and business events. One can also speculate about the topics that will continue to draw research interest, as well as those that may be new, potential areas for contributions.

Subject of the Study

The professional service organizations need to be market oriented and marketing becomes extremely important to them, to cope with such changes as changing expectations of clients; an over supply of professionals resulting in increased competition; changes in legal environment, as tax laws have changed; increase in literacy and information explosion etc. So a study of exploratory nature, entitled "Marketing Professional Services—a case study of CAs of Visakhapatnam is undertaken by the researcher, to bring about important marketing insights in the field of professional services of CA's.

The study has been confined in professionals to CA's only on several counts discussed in the limitations of the study. Although has study is comprehensive one, but still a lot more work, however needs to be done in this direction on all-India basis, to bring out more realistic results (future area of research).

The development of human resources over the remaining twelve years of the century will result in the establishment of a modern self-reliant economy and substantial improvement in the levels of living of the people. It is the service sector, which will substantially contribute to social development and improvement in the quality of life. Further, it is being realized that growth in employment over the seventh plan period will come from the growth in services. Banking and the spread of credit institutions will provide opportunities for self-employment. The increasing importance of this sector of the economy is apparent.

It is also being realized that marketing concept is needed by this sector to give expected satisfaction. The Marketing Concept holds that the key to meeting an organization goal is the customer needs and wants orientation backed by integrated marketing efforts aimed at generating and delivering customer satisfaction more effectively and efficiently than competitors.

The nature of the industry in which a firm operates does much to shape the possible and appropriate form of marketing. Service industries generally have the following characteristics.

There is a direct contact between the producer of goods and services and the consumer. This highlights the importance of interaction between manager/staff and the customers.

Services are highly personalized and there is a simultaneous production and consumption of the services. So from marketing stand point, distribution channels are direct. some service industries are subject to fluctuations in demand where peaks and stacks occur during the day as well, as over season, and thus add to the degree of market orientation required by the business.

"lets wait and watch what new service revolutions are going to take on in the future. There is a mad need for the service literature to generate new ideas to keep the concept of services marketing alive."

3

Research Methodology

Methodology

The purpose of this chapter is to describe the procedures used to answer the research questions proposed in Chapter 1.

Overview of Research Methodology

Types of Research

Qualitative. The two types of research design include qualitative and quantitative. Qualitative research is defined as a "variety of research approaches that study phenomena in their natural settings, without a predetermined hypothesis" (Ary, Jacobs, & Razavieh, 2002, p. 565). This method avoids numeric data and gathers information through detail obtained via interviews and observation. The techniques include ethnography (field research), case studies (examination of one unit), content analysis, naturalistic observation, focused interviews, phenomenological studies (meanings vary by subject), grounded theory, and historical research (Ary et al., 2002).

Quantitative. Quantitative research is defined as an, "objective measurement and statistical analysis of numeric data to understand and explain phenomena" (Ary, et al., 2002, p. 22). The purpose of this method is to examine either relationships or cause and effect. It requires large samples examined through instruments that test a theory created prior to the study. Quantitative studies consist of experimental and non-experimental research (Ary et al., 2002).

Within qualitative or quantitative research, there are numerous types of studies.

They are (a) descriptive, (b) associational, and (c) intervention-type. A descriptive study helps describe events or things as carefully as possible. Associational research investigates relationships, and intervention studies observe how a method or treatment influences outcomes (Fraenkel & Wallen, 2000).

Survey research. Within descriptive studies, the most common method to answer the research question is a survey. Surveys attempt to answer the question "What exists?"

The advantages of survey research include: (a) the possibility to collect a wide scope of information from a large population, (b) the opportunity to deal with real situations, and (c) the development of research beyond description only (Fraenkel & Wallen, 2000). Surveys are sent to individuals who are known as respondents. The answers of the respondents allow researchers to summarize the characteristics of individuals, groups, or physical environments to the targeted population (Fraenkel &Wallen, 2000). The population refers to the individuals that the findings of the survey represent. Surveys may be accomplished in census form, where the entire population is surveyed or a sample survey where only part of the population is studied (Ary et al., 2002). Surveys are limited to studying tangibles and intangibles. Tangibles are items that can easily be measured such as frequency of physical activity at a recreational center. Intangibles are limited to psychological and sociological constructs such as attitude and opinions (Ary et al., 2002).

In addition, surveys are classified into two categories according to the time the data was collected. The first is longitudinal which looks at information gathered at points in time; this helps to observe changes over the time frame. A longitudinal study may be accomplished by three methods: (1) a panel, where the same group is studied over time, (2) a trend, where a different people from the same population are studied, or (3) by a cohort study, where the same groups of people are followed over time. The second category, cross-sectional studies, examines a sample of the population at a specific time (Ary et al., 2002).

Marketing Professional Services

The professional service organizations need to be market

oriented and marketing becomes extremely important to them, to cope with such as changes in the expectations of clients; an over supply of professionals resulting in increased competition; changes in legal environment, as tax laws have changed; increase in literacy and information explosion etc. So a study of exploratory nature, entitled "Marketing Professional Services—a case study of CAs of Visakhapatnam is undertaken by the researcher, to bring about important marketing insights in the field of professional services of CA's.

The study has been confined to professional CA's only on several counts discussed in the limitations of the study. Although has study is comprehensive one, but still a lot more work, however needs to be done in this direction on all-India basis, to bring out more realistic results (future area of research).

Research on marketing has focused primarily on qualitative as well as quantitative methods. Therefore, a quantitative, descriptive, cross-sectional survey study design was used to answer the research questions asked in Chapter 1. The aforementioned research studies were explained in Chapter 2 but each utilized a different instrument and approach to examine marketing professional Services.

Of these studies, many researchers utilized survey instruments for their study like Ahmed et al., 2002; Foreman & Money, 1995; Fram & McCarthy, 2003; Lings & Brooks, 1998; Naude et al., 2003. Four out the five mentioned above were created through a review of literature (Ahmed et al., 2002; Foreman & Money, 1995; Fram & McCarthy, 2003; Naude et al., 2003).

The researchers modified the items to examine the perceptions of both professionals and their clients.

The specific instrument utilized in the current study is described in greater detail.

Subject Selections Setting

The setting of this study, in order to examine marketing of professional services, is a study of Chartered Accountants in Visakhapatnam, Andhra Pradesh, India. The examination of marketing professional services is best accomplished in a single setting due to the differences that exist within each organization (i.e., Peccei & Rosenthal, 2000; Stuart, 1998). Ary, Jacobs, and Razavieh (2002) described case studies as "an attempt to describe the subject's entire range of behaviors and the relationship of these behaviors" (p. 440). It allows for depth and understanding into the present status of an entire institution and allows for the development of future hypotheses, which is ideal for the study.

Sampling Method

"A sample consists of all units of the population that are drawn for questionnaires" (Dillman, 2000, p. 126) and the population refers to the people in the organization for whom you may generalize the results. Two major types of sampling exist: probability and nonprobability. Probability sampling generates a sample through chance, while nonprobability sampling is not created through chance (Ary et al., 2002).

This study used probability sampling and the four most common types include:

(1) Simple random sampling, (2) stratified sampling, (3) cluster sampling, and (4) systematic sampling (Ary et al., 2002). Simple random sampling allows everyone in a population the equal chance to be selected. This is often accomplished through the assignment of identification numbers to each member of a population and the use of a Table of random numbers to select the subjects. Stratified sampling is used when various subgroups exist and it is believed that various groups will provide different responses.

The division of groups may be accomplished through any characteristics and randomly selected independent samples develop from each stratum. Cluster sampling allows a researcher to examine a group not simply individuals. People are placed into groups based upon similar characteristics and the clusters are randomly selected, then all members of the cluster are examined. Systematic sampling allows a researcher to examine every Kth case from a population where the first number is selected randomly (Ary et al., 2002)

Simple and Stratified random sampling: The present study utilized a simple and also a stratified sampling approach based upon involvement within the Profession (Chartered Accountants and Clients). This sampling approach allows the researcher to examine various subgroups, the use of this method recommends equal sample sizes but, "when the population to be sampled is not homogenous but consists of several subgroups, stratified simple random sampling may give a more representative sample than simple random sampling" (Ary et al., 2002, p. 167). A random sample of 150 practicing chartered Accountants enrolled for their practice in Visakhapatnam was selected. A list of members of Chartered Accountants updated till 1/4/2006 was made available and from that list, a list of chartered accountants in practice was prepared, and then from that list of 438 practicing CA's enrolled in visakhapatnam, a random sample of 150 CAs was selected covering the entire visakhapatnam area, located in Andhrapradesh, India.

Another sample of 400 clients, which included both individual clients and organizations and professionals, was selected based on judgment and convenience from Visakhapatnam area only. Attempt was made to cover entire city. Two type of samples were chosen because the nature of the study was such as divided in to two parts (1) covering the marketing of professional accounting services (2) Second part, the client survey to uncover various aspects of selection criteria, need for professional accountants, etc.

The number of respondents in the later case was kept high to 400 so as to make this segment of people/organizations/ professionals more representative of the over all universe.

The sample distribution is like: -

1.	Chartered Accountants	=	150
2.	Users of CA's firm	=	200
3.	Non-Users (Non-Clients)	=	200
But potential clients total		=	550 Respondents.

The reasoning for the three strata in client groups (Individual clients, institutional clients, and other professionals) developed from the review of literature. The implementation of internal marketing requires the support of management (Crosby & Johnson, 2003) and for knowledge exchange patterns to exist this process must begin at the top of the organization (Ballantyne, 2003).

Professional Chartered Accountants

They are the certified professionals by ICAI, Institute of chartered Accountants of India who consists of full-time members and part-time practicing professionals. The sample size is 150 Professionals out of 438 Practicing professionals in Visakhapatnam Area.

Clients

The clients consist of Individual, Institutional and other professionals like Doctors, Engineers etc. There are currently 200 users of professionals services and 200 non-users of professional services who make the sample size of the study. The sample size is determined through convenience sampling for both professionals and clients.

A random sample of the professionals and clients was conducted by placing each separate group in alphabetical order where each member of the population was assigned a number. Then with the assistance of Research Randomizer (www. randomizer.org), sets of numbers were randomly generated by the computer to identify test subjects. The people randomly selected created the sample.

Marketing develops through communication to remove barriers (Lings, 1999) and develops internal relationships (Ahmed & Rafiq, 2003).

Experience. The independent variable in research question one given for chartered accountants is years of experience (below 5, 05-10,10-15,15-20,20-25 and 25 and above).

Dependent Variables

Cases handled by Professionals. In research question two given for chartered accountants. Major area of specialisation acts as the dependent variable. It is a process of selecting the type of services to be provided by a Chartered Accountant.

Service Quality. The dependent variable in research questions four given to clients is service quality. In question four, service quality is examined based upon level of involvement. Gronroos (1994, p. 14) stated, "without active and continuous internal marketing efforts, the interactive marketing impact on customers will deteriorate, service quality will suffer, and customers will defect" and encourages the examination of differences in perceptions.

In question four-service quality is examined versus the 22 items. One outcome identified through the literature review is a belief that as service quality perceptions improve within professionals, they become satisfied and improve their treatment of external customers (Ahmed & Rafiq, 2003). If the Chartered Accountant provides better service, then the perceived service quality of external customers is expected to improve. Therefore, the Perceptions of service quality internally impact the perceptions externally and are a result of internal marketing. The current study attempts to examine the gaps in service quality through finding the difference between perceived and expected quality, a partial replication of the Ko (2000) instrument.

Scale Instruments

The instrumentation for this study involves both previously tested questions and items developed through a review of literature. The use of a previously developed instrument was recommended by Fraenkel and Wallen (2000, p. 130) who stated, "selection of an already developed instrument when appropriate ... is preferred."

Two survey instruments. Two survey instruments were created for this study: one for Chartered Accountants (Appendix A) and one for Clients (Appendix B).

The Chartered Accountants instrument consists of questions on experience, major areas of practice, cases handled, defining client groups, identifying specific client groups, attributes that grant success in accountancy profession, sources of clientele, sources of referrals, perceived selection criteria used by clients, service quality and marketing orientation. The clients instrument consisted of questions on income, nature of services hired, professional tactics as perceived by clients as important, service quality, selection criteria to hire services, sources of referrals. Most of the items in the service quality, and feedback sections utilize 6-point likert type scales that range from extremely Important to unimportant, and three point scales from strongly agree to disagree.

Scale Development

The instrument for the study involves both items previously examined and new items developed from a review of literature, therefore validity and reliability must be examined. The ability to address these issues reduces alternative explanations, generalizability, and consistency in measurement.

Field Test

A field-test was administered to further strengthen face and content validity and to identify any further misunderstandings that were missed by the researcher. This was accomplished by administering the questions to a 30 professional Accountants and 50 clients the respondents were not asked to fill-out the questionnaire, but to provide comments and suggestions regarding content, wording, format, clarity, focus, ease of use, and appropriateness of individual items as well as for the instrument as a whole. They were also directed to review the questionnaire for clarity in directions and to state which of the two survey formats they preferred. Results demonstrated a need to rephrase few items like question 3 and question 8 as given to chartered accountants. Five editorial changes resulted from the feedback, and the respondents stated form one provided the greatest clarity, ease of use, and appeared shorter in length. These adjustments were made prior to the administration of the pilot test.

Pilot Test

A pilot test was conducted to test the reliability of the survey instrument. In order to collect the pilot data permission was sought from the chartered accountants and clients through an appointment. The instrument was sent to 50 participants each from clients and Professionals. Conceptually, since the word "satisfaction' exists within the few items, it appeared plausible and it had to be removed.

Data Collection Procedures Approval

The collection of data from both chartered accountants and clients was obtained, through the following method that is Surveys.

Data Analysis Procedures

The data for the entire study was inputted into the microsoft excel program for windows to interpret results. Descriptive statistics were generated for the variables of interest, and a second reliability analysis on the instruments was conducted to ensure the items properly represent each dimension.

The research questions were examined through various data analysis procedures and are individually discussed in further detail.

Questionnaire given to Chartered Accountants

Research Question #1: What is the Experience in Accountancy profession?

This question was primarily asked to find out the years of experience in accountancy profession so that it can be used as a base to compare and make cross classification with other variables.

Research Question #2: What is the major area of your practice?

This question was asked to find out the major areas of specialisation of chartered accountants, as it constitutes the major area of work performed by an accountant.

Research Question #3: Rank the cases according to the number of cases handled by you.

This question was asked to find out the type of cases that are maximum and minimum handled by a chartered accountant to have clarity on the types of cases handled by the accountant.

Research Question #4: Do you define the client groups to be served by you?

This question gives information about the professionals predetermined market for providing his professional services and test his client focus.

Research Question #5: What are the client groups to be served by you?

This question is posed to find out the composition of client groups that are served by the professional, so that the data can be used to identify the potential clients and the amount of business coming from the clients

Research Question #6: Rate the professional skills on the bases of perceived importance while interacting with clients.

This question is asked to find out the importance given by a professional to his professional competencies and skills as they will help him build trust and better professional image.

Research Question #7: Rate the Management skills on the basis of importance to be successful in profession.

This question is asked to find out the professional tactics used by a professional while interacting with the client. As client interaction if becomes successful leads to building more trust and satisfaction and this will in turn reduce the defection rate of clients.

Research Question #8: What are the sources of clientele to your firm?

A Professional has to be aware of the sources of his clients and know where his business is coming from. Therefore, this question is asked to find out the various sources from which business is developing and find out the potential clients who give maximum business to the firm as 80% of the profits of a firm come from 20% if its customers (Pareto's principle).

Research Question#9: What is the importance of referrals?

This is to find out whether the professional is really believing that referrals are important or not as referrals are an important way of gaining the business.

Research Question #10: What are the sources of referrals to your firm?

This question is asked to find out the sources of referrals that help in developing the business further. This question also raises clues about whether the existing clients are passing positive word of mouth communication or not and identify the potential sources of gaining new clients.

Research question#11: Do you have formal system for recording clients?

It is to find out whether the professional is managing the data that he is gaining through business as it will be a source for identifying the major vehicles through which he is getting business

Research Question #12: Rate the following on a three-point scale (ways of gaining new business)

This question is asked to identify the potential ways of gaining new business. The factors that help in acquiring new clients to the chartered accountant.

Research Question #13: What is your view of marketing?

Professionals are perceived to lack a clear understanding on the concept of marketing. This question is asked to find out the professionals understanding of the concept of marketing and find out their view of marketing.

Research Question #14: Is Marketing prevented by your profession?

Professional Accountants are prohibited from marketing by ICAI, INDIA and this question is asked to find out the number of respondents who are aware of this professional restriction.

Research Question #15: Should Advertising be allowed to CA's?

Professional Accountants are prohibited from marketing by ICAI, INDIA and this question is asked to find out whether advertising should be allowed to chartered accountants as the rule against advertising in CA profession has been laid off In many developed countries like USA (Kotler& bloom 2002)

Research Question #16: What is your perception towards ICAI'S role in promoting the profession?

This question is asked to find out the perception of ICAI towards promoting profession. As, ICAI is the National body for controlling the code of ethics for professionals. This is to find out their level of satisfaction with the ICAI's policies.

Research question #17: What are the ways of building public awareness programs?

This is intended to find out the ways and sources through

which a promoting his profession and the different means of communication channels he is opting to promote.

Research question#18 : What is your opinion of satisfaction towards practice?

This question is to find out if professionals are satisfied towards the profession or not

Research Question #20: What is the criteria for selection used by clients as perceived by you?

Every client uses a certain criteria to make a final decision of using the professional services of CA's. To identify the heuristics of decision making as perceived by professionals this question is asked and this would be further used to identify the gap between perceived criteria and actual criteria used by customers.

Research Question #20: Did you notice a change in the practicing environment over years?

Business environment changes according to the changing policies and trends within the society. This question is asked to identify the changing trends if any in the practice over a period of time.

Research Question #21: Which of these marketing strategies are you willing to use In the future?

Marketing helps in a better way of understanding clients and increases client satisfaction, which will ensure enhanced business development for any professional. This question is asked to find out if chartered accountants are willing to use marketing strategies in the future.

Questionnaire given to Clients

Research Question #2: What is your income range?

This question is asked to find out the income range of the clients, as this will greatly influence the client to use the services of a chartered accountant.

Research Question #3: What is the nature of services hired by you?

This question is asked to find out the services used by clients as this gives clarity on the nature of services hired by clients. It also indicates the demand for specific services as rendered by chartered accountants.

Research Question #4: Rate the professional tactics on the basis of an importance scale as felt by you in influencing your service encounter.

This question is asked to find out the professional tactics as perceived by clients. The same question has been asked to chartered accountants as well and therefore a gap analysis is done.

Research Question #5: Rate the service quality (expected and perceived quality) as felt by you.

This question is asked to find out the service quality of the services rendered by chartered accountants. The service quality is the key factor that influences the future relationship with the clients and further loyalty of clients towards the professional. Therefore service quality is analyzed.

Research Question #6: Who are the main sources of referrals?

This question is asked to find out the sources of referrals who help in the process of obtaining service from professionals. This question also raises direct clues about whether the existing clients are passing positive word of mouth communication or not and identify the main sources of referrals who help in business development.

4

Professional's Survey Results

Experience of CA in the Accountancy Profession

The experience of a CA is an important tool to attract the clients. The experience with the professional accountant/firm shows the capabilities and the competency of the professional/firm. In professional services we are dealing with something, which is primarily delivered by people to people. Therefore the purchaser of professional service buys the capabilities of the seller.

Table 4.1
Number of Years of Experience in Accountancy Profession

Experience	*Number of Professionals*	*Percentage*
Below 5	24	16
05-10	38	25.33
10-15	29	19.33
15-20	17	11.33
20-25	20	13.33
25 above	22	14.66

The table 4.1 reveals that there were 24 respondents (16%) having (0-5) years experience; 38 respondents (25.33%) having 5-10 years experience; 29 (19.33%) having 10-15 years experience; 17 (13.33%) having 15-20 years experience, 20 (11.33%) having 20-25 years experience and 22 (14.66%) having above 25 years of experience.

The experience of the professional accountant shows his

technical competence and can be an influential factor from the client's point of view. Therefore, there is need for the professionals to be perceived as having experience, because form clients angle using an experienced professional makes a risky purchase seem less risky. Perhaps experience of the professional accountant attracts the clients at the first meeting when the clients come to the accountancy firms. It is the professional accountant responsibility that first they should study the emotional state and needs of the client and make the client feel at home and relaxed and after that show the unique competence i.e. demonstrate that we have the experience, and knowledge to fulfill their specific requirement, and show a keen interest in client-problem. Thus experience is essential in this profession.

Major area of practice by professional accountants/firm:

The second question what is the major area of your practice was directed to the professional accountants/firms with the objective to find out what were the important service lines which are being opted by the professional accountants. The other objective was also to see whether a generalist approach V/S specialist approach was being practiced by most of the public accountants.

Table 4.2: Major Areas of Practice of Charactered Accountants

Specialisation	*Frequency*	*Percentage*	*Ranking*
Audit Accounts and Finance	145	96	1
Taxation	128	85.3	2
Secretarial and company Affairs	65	43.3	4
Internal Audit and Control	79	52.6	3
Management Serices	65	43.3	4
General Practioner	50	33.33	5

$$\text{Average area of Specialisation} = \frac{\text{cumulativefrequency}}{\text{no. of frespondents}}$$

$$= 532/150 = 3.54$$

Table 4.2 reveals that highest (96%) respondents were dealing with the cases of audit and accounts. They were accepting the cases of audit, accounts but used to restrict themselves for financial cases.

The second highest number of respondents fell in the category of taxation (basically income tax) with 85.33% respondents opting for it. After that followed Internal Audit and Control, Secretarial and Company Affairs, Management Services, and being "general practitioner" with respective percentages of respondents being 52.6%, 43.3%, 43.33%; and 33.33% in descending order of importance.

Since the respondents (professional) accountants) were free to answer as many areas of specializations as were listed and in which they were involved at a particular time when the researcher was interviewing them, it was found that an average respondent (professional accountant) was specializing in three (3) areas of practice as seen from the table no. 4.2. "Specialization" in particular area of practice was preferred over being a general practitioner or adopting a mix range of services. Audit and taxation always remained the dominant area of practice as maximum number of cases was there in those service lines.

Table 4.2.2: Cross-Classification of Arcas of Specialisation and Years of Experience

S.No	*Specification*	*Below 5*	*5-10*	*10-15*	*15-20*	*20-25*	*Above 25*
1	Audit Accounts and finance	22.46	53.59	27.06	19.2	19.7	24.3
2.	Taxation	19.96	47.53	24.06	17.08	17.56	21.65
3.	Secretarial and company Affairs	10.34	24.19	12.2	8.6	8.91	10.9
4.	Internal Audit and Control	12.32	29.4	14.8	10.5	10.8	13.36
5.	Management services	10.14	24.19	12.2	8.6	8.91	10.9
6.	General practioner	7.8	18.6	9.3	6.67	6.86	8.45
	Column total	82.82	197.6	99.62	70.65	72.74	89.56

Note: Total exceeds base as the Respondents have ticked more than one area as their area of specialisation.

The table 4.2.2 reveals that, Audit, Accounts and Taxation always remained the dominant area of practice for all most all-public accountants irrespective of years in practice. But it was also revealed from the table that professional accountant with lesser experience (i.e. having 0-5 years or 5-10 years) or who were new to the profession used to restrict themselves to internal audit of banks etc. or to cases of taxation of small companies, while professional accountants with higher experience (10-20 years, 20-25 years, more than 25 years) were shifting to newer areas of service lines i.e. Company and Secretarial affairs, Management services, going in for International or NRI cases, computerization of facilities and the like, despite Auditing and Taxation remaining their dominant areas of concern. Statistically, also it was seen whether the area of practice vary with years in practice of professional accountants for which Chi2 test was used.

NULL HYPOTHESIS:- The area of practice does not vary with years in practice of professional accountants.

Table 4.2.3: Cross Classification for Showing the Row and Column Totals to use for CHI-Square Test

S. No.	*Specialisation*	*Below 5*	*5-10*	*10-15*	*15-2-*	*20-25*	*above 25*	*Total*
1.	Audit Accounts and finance	24	36	27	17	19	22	144
2.	Taxation	18	30	23	16	18	23	128
3.	Secretariat and company Affairs	3	8	11	10	13	20	65
4.	Internal Audit and control	18	23	18	7	6	7	79
5.	Management Services	0	8	12	13	14	18	65
6.	General Practioner	20	10	9	8	3	Nil	50
	Based of Respondents (150)	24	38	29	17	20	22	532
	Column Total	83	198	100	71	73	90	

Table 4.2.4: Cross Classification for Showing the Row and Column Toals to use for Chi-Square Test (Expected Frequencies)

Specialisaiton	*Below 5*	*5-10*	*10-15*	*15-20*	*20-25*	*above 25*
Audit Accounts and finance	22.46	53.59	27.06	19.2	19.7	24.3
Taxation	19.96	47.63	24.06	17.08	17.56	21.65
Secretarial and company Affairs	10.14	24.19	12.2	8.6	8.91	10.9
General Audit and control	12.32	29.4	14.8	10.5	10.8	13.36
Managment Services	10.14	24.19	12.2	8.6	8.91	10.9
General Practioner	7.8	18.6	9.3	6.67	6.86	8.45
Column Total	82.82	197.6	99.62	70.65	72.74	89.56

Expected Frequency of Cell A =

Row total * column total / Grand Total

Df = (r–1) (c–1) = (6–1) (6–1), 5 × 5 = 25

Table 4.2.5: The Calculation of Chi-Square Test

S.No.	*Of (O)*	*EF (E)*	*)-E*	*(O-E)2*	*(O-E)2/E*
1	24	22-46	1.54	2.3716	0.105592
2	18	19.6	-1.6	2.56	0.130612
3	3	10.14	-7.14	50.9796	5.027574
4	18	12.32	5.68	32.2624	2.618701
5	0	10.14	-10.14	102.8196	10.14
6	20	7.8	12.2	148.84	19.08205
7	36	53.9	-17.9	320.41	5.944527
8	30	47.6	-17.6	309.76	6.507563
9	8	24.19	-16.19	262.1161	10.83572

10	23	29.4	-6.4	40.96	1.393197
11	8	24.19	-16.19	262.1161	10.83572
12	10	18.6	-8.6	73.96	3.976344
13	27	27.06	-0.06	0.0036	0.000133
14	23	24.06	-1.06	1.1236	0.0467
15	11	12.2	-1.2	1.4	0.118033
16	18	14.8	3.2	10.24	0.691892
17	12	12.2	0-0.2	0.04	0.003279
18	9	9.3	-0.3	0.09	0.0009677
19	17	19.2	-2.2	4.84	0.252083
20	16	17.08	-1.08	1.1664	0.06829
21	10	8.6	1.4	1.96	0.227907
22	7	10.5	-3.5	12.25	1.166667
23	13	8.6	4.4	19.36	2.251163
24	8	6.67	1.33	1.7689	0.265202
25	19	19.7	-0.7	0.49	0.024873
26	18	17.56	0.44	0.136	0.011025
27	13	8.91	4.09	16.7281	1.877452
28	6	10.8	-4.8	23.04	2.133333
29	14	8.91	5.09	25.9081	2.907755
30	3	6.86	-3.86	14.8996	2.171953
31	22	24.3	-2.3	5.29	0.217695
32	23	21.6	1.4	1.96	0.090741
33	20	10.9	9.1	82.81	7.597248
34	7	13.36	-6.36	40.4496	3.027665
35	18	10.9	7.1	50.41	3.027665
36	0	8.45	-8.45	71.4025	8.45

$\chi^2 = (O–E)^2/E = 113.994$

where OF = OBSERVED FREQUENCY

EF = Expected Frequency

Df = (r-1) (c-1) = (6-1) (6-1), 5 × 5 = 25

Table value of × 25 and 0.10 level of significance of 99.9% level of confidence = 34.382. Calculated value is than table value thus null hypothesis rejected. So the areas of practice differ with regards to yearsin practice.

χ^2 is given by the formula.

Chisquare $X^2 = (O\text{-}E)^2 / E$

where O = observed frequency

E = Expected Frequency

df = Degrees of freedom and is given as (c-1 (r-1)

c = Column

r = row

Substituting the values in the above formulas we find calculated value of

$\chi^2 = 113.994$ with degree of freedom

$= (6.1)\ (6\text{–}1) = 5 \times 5 = 25$

Also table value of χ^2 at 25 degree of freedom and 0.10 level of significance or 99.9% level of confidence = 34.382, Since the calculated value of x^2 is greater than the table value of x^2, so null hypothesis is rejected. So it is concluded that area of practice do vary with the years in practice of professional Accountants.

As has been said above that those public accountants who are newer to the Profession used to restrict themselves to Internal audit of banks, and cases of taxation of small companies, whereas those with experience used to diversify to newer services of management services, company affairs and others along with audit and taxation remaining their dominant area of concern.

The third question "Rank in order of number of cases handled by you in each following areas of specialization" was related with the different cases dealt by the CAs in their specialized area. Most dealt cases within a particular service line widthwise will indicate the most preferred field within the specialized area of practice. This could give a clear idea of the potential service product offering in our case. *Number of Audit, Accounts and finance cases dealt by the professional accountants.*

The researcher was interested to know what were the specific cases that were being dealt by the public Accountants in the area of audit, accounts and finance. The Researcher was of the view that those cases, which had Top rank, are preferred the most by the public accountants.

Table 4.3: Ranking Assigned to Audit, Acoounts and Finance Cases Dealt by Professional Accountants

S.No.	*Cases Dealt*	*Rank*
1	Audit of Accounts	1
2	Maintenance of Books of A/C	7
3	Installing better Accounting System	2
4	Financial Planning	3
5	Project Reports	3
6	Purchase of New Business	6
7	Raising Capital from FI's	4
8	Advisory Function	5

As the table indicates "Audit of Accounts" and "Preparation of Balance sheet and P & L a/c was ranked Ist. Cases related with "Installing better accounting systems and cost Accounting systems was ranked at 2nd place, followed by cases of "Project Report Preparations" AND "Financial Planning. Purchase of new business etc, "Maintenance of Books of Accounts" were the least dealt cases in the Audit Accounts and Finance cases, being ranked at 6th, 7th.

Cases related with "Raising capital from various Financial Institution", "Investment of surplus Fund" were dealt on an average with ranking of 4th and 5th position.

The researcher came to the conclusion that the cases related with "Audit of Accounts", "Preparation of B/L sheet and P/L a/c", "Project Reports Preparation", "Financial planning" and "Installing better Accounting system and cost Accounting System basically manual" constituted the preferred field in which the public accountants were rendering their services. This is also in accordance with the general observation that traditional statutory audit work is the bread and butter of the profession as a whole

Table 4.3.2: Ranking Given by Chartered Accountants to Taxation Cases Dealt by Them

S.No.	*Cases dealt*	*Rank*
1	Tax Planning	3
2	Preparation of Income Tax	1
3	Presenting cases in assessment	2
4	Tax Clearance Certificates	2
5	Funds	4
6	Appeals	5
7	Tax Consultantion	6

The procedure mentioned in 4.3.1was repeated for 4.3 .2 also. The researcher was again interested to see the RANKING.

When the comparison were done with the cases related by "Taxation aspects", "Preparation of Income Tax, wealth tax returns "was ranked top on the list of 7 cases: followed with "Presenting cases in assessment", getting tax clearance certificates"; "tax planning ; "Refunds & appeals"; and "Consultation on tax matters" at the last on sixth position as revealed from table 4.3.2

The researcher came to the conclusion that cases relating with "preparation of income tax & wealth tax returns "were dealt maximum by public accountant as they could find maximum business in that category. Also it was comparatively easier for the young members to develop their practice in this area because the no. of assesses were increasing day to day and almost all the tax payers now need the help of tax experts. Cases related with "Refunds & appeals" were in the low profile because the professional accountant felt that with the same pay package the client want this activity to be performed when needed which was not possible for them as it called forth for much greater time and effort on their part; so they used to avoid intentionally. Also cases related with "consultation on tax matters" were ranked at the last, as the professionals felt that clients in India are not interested in some peripheral activities but more in concrete activities. So consultation as such formed a part of the category of cases of "Preparation of Income-tax and wealth tax returns."

The table 4.3.3 reveals that cases related with "Preparation of memorandum and articles of Co. formation and prospectus" were ranked Ist , 2ND for cases relating to "preparation of minutes of board meetings and general meeting etc". cases related with "Maintenance of various statutory books as required by Cos. Act "were at IIIrd rank . However, the cases related with "share department and other secretarial work" as well as "Appearance before registrar, company Law Board etc." Were ranked in the last at 5th and 4th position respectively with the researcher came to the conclusions that though cases related with "Secretarial and company matters" are not much popular among the professionals, but still within this category, cases of "Preparations of memorandum and article of company formation and prospectus etc", and "minutes of board meeting etc. "were the most dealt with cases. This was also in light with that area of "co. and Secretarial affairs" is not open for all professionals/and basically experienced professionals with few years of standing only try to enter this area of specialization.

Table 4.3.3: Ranking given by Chartered Accountants to Secretarial and Company Matters Cases dealt by Them

S. No.	*Cases Dealt*	*Rank*
1	Preparation of Memorandum of Association	1
2	Minutes of Board Meeting	2
3	Secretarial Work	5
4	Appearance before Registrar	4
5	Maintenance of Statutory Book	3

Ranking cases dealt by the professionals related with internal audit and control:

Internal Audit and control cases were given more weightages as compared to the company and secretarial affairs cases, as seen from the table 4.3 .4.

Table: 4.3.4: Total Weightage/rank given to Internal Audit and Control cases dealt by the Professional Accountants.

S.No.	*Cases Dealt*	*Rank*
1	Internal Audit	1
2	Physical Verification of Stock	2
3	Physical Verificaton of Cash & investment	3
4	Detectionof Fraud & Error	4
5	Investigation and special Audit	5

The table 4.3.4 shows that in the category of Internal Audit and control, cases related with "Internal audit" were ranked at No. 1., followed with cases of physical verification of stock and inventory at rank 2.; physical verification of cash and investments cases at rank third; cases related with detection of fraud and errors and investigation at rank 4 and special audit was ranked at last place because these were such cases which were dealt with only when proper appointment was given to the professionals to do the same; so the cases related with 'Internal audit and physical verification of stock and inventory were the most dealt with cases in the category of Internal Audit & Control area of specialization.

Ranking given to the various management service cases by the public accountant:

Management services being a newer field, and provide new opportunities for the professionals in this area, weightages given to management services cases were the least as compared to the weightages given to cases for other areas of specialization like - audit, accounts, finance, taxation, internal audit and control; secretarial and company affairs.

The table 4.3.5 projects that cases of Budgeting & budgetary control was ranked at no. 1 ; followed with cost analysis and cost accounting procedures at rank - 2; followed with cases of preparation of accounting manuals at 3rd place; Analysis and interpretation of financial statements cases at 4th rank; profitability studies/

cash flow analysis cases at 5th rank. Cases related with project planning, forecasting, price fixing etc. inter and intra firm comparison and staff selection/training/job evaluation were the least dealt cases in this category. Case related with cash resources management organizational studies were dealt on an average with respective scores of 182 points and 64 points. Thus it can be concluded that cases related with budgeting and budgetary control along with cost analysis and cost accounting procedures and preparation of accounting manuals constituted the potential field within this category of services, since not much awareness was there on the part of clients and lack of expertise of the professionals kept them away from such areas of staff selection, Training, organization studies etc. Which can be considered as future potential areas of practice within the category of management services.

Table 4.3.5: Ranking Given by Chartered Accountants to Management Services Cases Dealt Them

S.No.	*Cases Dealt*	*Rank*
1	Preferation of Accounting Manuals	3
2	Cost Analysis and cost A/c Procedures	2
3	Cash Resources Management	6
4	Material Management	8
5	Budgeting and Budgetary control	1
6	Organisational studies	7
7	Profitability studies	5
8	Job evaluation	11
9	Intra-and inter-firm competition	10
10	Analysis of Financial Statements	4
11	Project plannign, forecasting	9

Ranking given to various miscellaneous cases being dealt by the professional Accountants

It was to be learnt by the researcher, what other miscellaneous cases were being handled by the professionals. The results are tabulated in table 4.3.6.

Table 4.3.6: Ranking Given by chartered Accountants to Miscellaneous Cases Dealt by them

S.No.	*Cases Dealt*	*Rank*
1	Acting as Director	2
2	Arbitrator (on Appointment)	3
3	Liquidator	5
4	Trustee	4
5	Financial Advisor	1

The Table 4.3.6 clearly brings that although miscellaneous cases were not preferred over cases of Audit, Accounts, Finance or Taxation etc. But still within the category of miscellaneous cases, Acting as financial Advisor to their clients was ranked at no. 1 ; followed by acting as Director at 2nd rank; Arbitrator at 3rd place; trustee at 4th rank and liquidator at 5th rank

Thus acting as financial Advisor or 'Director' were the most preferred filed in the category of miscellaneous cases. Also acting as 'Liquidator or Arbitrator were show as least preferred areas because the performance of these roles were not exclusively in the hands of professionals only as Arbitrator or liquidators are appointed by the government or CAG (Controller and Auditor General) or department of direct taxes from among the professionals who have shown their consent to act as such.

Thus it can be concluded that a wide spread awareness of the vital role of accountants has emerged in recent years. Chartered Accountants perform a wide variety of services. Accountancy services are invested with a degree of abstract, trust and creditability. This professional service is different from those of other profession of lawyers, doctors because public accountants seem to be responsible to just about every one relies on their report i.e., stock holders, banking and financial institutions, credit grantors and a multiple of govt. Agencies, (While lawyers are responsible to their clients only: doctors to their patient only) as the world becomes more complex and knowledge revolution continues to accelerate, the breadth of professional services is constantly growing. At the same time, the depth of each single service increases. Their service mix can be shown as below.

Basic Service lines of CA

1. Auditing, Accounts.
2. Taxation and Tax Advisory
3. Management Consultancy.
   a. Management Services
   b. Secretarial & Company

Then within each class-called the width of service line are as shown above in tables 4.3 .1, 4.3.2 , 4.3.3 , 4.3.4 , 4.3.5 etc.

For professional Accountants, Audit and Taxation to some extent are essential service. (Perceptible one). Management consultancy is ancillary (augmented) service, and then is flagship service i.e. of acting as director or financial advisor. As the competition is on the increase, the professionals should think in terms of service mix expansion which includes both line extension to add new package of services (like Agricultural farm Accounting, estate planning, etc.)' or width wise expansion i.e. add one more dimensions of the existing services. It can be a scope of future study, to study the potential in these various viable areas of specialization listed above like estate planning etc. So as to enable the public accountants to diversify their clientele and reduce their dependence on particular set of traditional services. Such a broadening of outlook of professional Accountants can be brought about by greater realization on their part about marketing their services, which is these days, not a consideration but a necessity in the profession. Whether the professionals want to develop a professional practice from scratch or to accelerate the growth of an existing one professionals should learn to market and sell their services in an appropriate way.

Are the type of client groups to be served being segmented by you?

Researcher was of the opinion that in today's increasingly competitive environment, professionals who excel in understanding and satisfying clients will be the survivors and winners. In the broad sense the practice of individual professional in a fee-for service free market economy is being challenged. The best guarantee that professionals in all fields will continue to operate in the free market setting is a satisfied and loyal client. In this sense, the use of marketing by professionals takes on an even greater importance.

The next assessment that accounting firm-s have to make in marketing themselves is who they believe will potentially be using their services. These prospective clients make up a firm target market and must be identified before a firm can satisfy its client's needs. Thus it was to be found out by the researcher, if public accountants were defining such target markets. The results were tabulated in table 4.4. Below.

Table 4.4: Whether the Client Groups are Defined by Profesisional Accountants or Not

Type of Response	*No. of Respondents*	*% Out of 150*
Yes (Segmenting Markets)	28	18.6%
No (Mass Market)	122	81.33%

The Table 4.4 clearly projects that majority of respondents 122 (81.33%) were not using the segmentation approach. They considered the entire market as a single entity. While only 28 (18.06%) of the professional Accountants/Firms were of the opinion that segmentation approach based on some industry characteristics was being adopted by them.

So it can be concluded that undifferentiated target market approach was preferred over differentiated target market approach. A firm that followed an undifferentiated target market approach viewed the entire market as a single entity. Such firms assumed that their firms and their services are acceptable to the entire market without taking into consideration the varying characteristics of the clients in the market. For instance a firm might implicitly offer tax and auditing services to any individual or organizations in the market, regardless of size, location, nature of operations or other, undifferentiating may be a viable approach or other factors.

Undifferentiating may be a viable approach to target market selection as long as the firm realizes it is approaching the market this way and is sure it can effectively serve its clients. While under the differentiated approach, firms try to satisfy the varying needs and wants of several market segments based on geographic, type of clients, demographic characteristics, behavioral characteristics and the like. This gives an increased knowledge of clients and competitors. Thus it has to be realized by the professionals that while the accountant is essentially a generalist and his skills are basic, it is becoming increasingly apparent that a knowledge of industry characteristics is necessary if he has to turn into a competent professional performer and effectively market his services, as there are several benefits to using the segmentation approach for target market selection.

To know what constituted the clientele for the professional Accountant/Firms

To know what were the specific client groups that were being served or what constituted their undifferentiated target market; question 4.5 was asked from the respondents. The table 4.5 reveals that the clientele for public accountants was much diversified ranging from manufacturing firms both Pvt. Ltd and public ltd. to retailers/departmental stores/shop keepers, to various nationalized banks, to educational institution like school/colleges etc. to various charitable hospitals, to exporters, publishers, NRI, transporters to other service agencies as highlighted above. Percentages for Govt. undertakings (72.6%) insurance companies (60% Pts) etc. were less as the auditing of these are allotted by CAG or other Govt. Agencies to the public accountants. However, scores for NRI (foreign clients) 21.3%, is also low being a relatively new area and were being patronized by only a few experienced professionals. real estate clients (66.6%) is a new phenomena due to boom in real estate business not just in visakhapatnam, but across the country.One word of caution here is by Kotler (2002) who rightly remarked that "one of the major marketing errors of "professional firms is to strike out in all direction for possible news clients. They strike out in all direction for possible new clients. clients. This "Total service philosophy is counter-productive. It is inferior strategy to that of service and market specialization.

Table 4.5: Specific Client Groups Served BCA's

S.No.	*Clients Type*	*No. of Respondents*	*Percent-age*
1	Retailers	130	86.6
2	Professional firms (law firms, software)	128	85.33
3	Govt. Undertakings	109	72.6
4	Banks	140	93.3
5	Brokerage Firms	60	40
6	Investment Cl's/Savings Co's	100	66.66
7	Insurance Companies	90	60
8	Hospitals/Health Care	95	63.3
9	Educaitonal Institutions	100	66.6
10	Manufacturing firms (Both Public & Private)	150	100
11	Publishers/Printers	69	46
12	Construction Companies	95	63.3
13	Others (a) Transportation companies	45	30
	(b) Exporters	48	32
	(c) Foreign Clients	32	21.3
	(d) Real Estate	100	66.66
	(e) Service Agencies (beauty parlours, Restaurants, etc.)	90	60

Note: Respondents have indicated that more than one client group is being served.

Professional Tactics as used by Professionals during Service Encounter

The table reveals professional tactics used by professionals while interacting with clients and their importance scales. The question is asked to discover the kind and type of professional tactics used during the process of his interaction with the clients. This is essentially here the service encounter takes place with the client and henceforth is very essential factor in wooing the client for loyalty. A lot of tactics like Uncovering Prospect Problem, Asking good questions, listening all these are considered as crucial factors in the service encounter.

These are some of the most important professional tactics as mentioned by Troy Waugh (2004) in his book called 101 marketing strategies for Accounting, Law, Consulting and Professional firms. The table can be understood easily by looking at the balance of the importance scale as it ranges from extremely important to unimportant.

These are the tactics that professionals feel as either extremely important or unimportant in the process of interacting with the clients. These are the perceptions of the professionals. As the table in the next page indicates, that professionals give extreme importance to Responding to new and existing clients immediately, Asking right questions, trying to understand what clients need and saying the price clearly. And the rest are more or less perceived a unimportant during the interaction process.

The mean ratings of professionals are further compared with the actual perception of the clients, and is tested for rank correlation to see whether the clients and professional tactics are correlated to one another or not.Service encounter, Typically called as the " moments of truth" are the most important aspect to be studied by any type of service provider, as it is at this point of service encounter with the professional that co-production takes place and the client becomes aware of the truth of benefit received by him from the service provider. Therefore, the professional has to use certain tactics to make the service encounter satisfiable to client and influence the overall perception of the service of the professional.

If the mean rating is between 4-5, the professional finds it as extremely important and if it is below 3, he feels it as unimportant. Therefore, the professional gives utmost importance to new and existing clients immediately, without much of the waiting time involved and, asking right questions to know the exact nature of problem of the client and always saying the price clearly as important dimensions that influence the service encounter.

Table showing a list of professional tactics and their subsequent ratings are shown in the next page. According to the weightage given by the professional towards certain professional tactics, the total Weightage given by all the professionals is computed and then the mean rating of the professionals towards the attribute is calculated by the total weightage given to the attribute divided by the total number of respondents.

Table 4.6: Professional Tactics used by Chartered Accountants While Interacting with Clients

S.No.	*Professionals Tactics while Interacting with Client*	*Extremely IMP(5)*	*Very IMP(4)*	*Some what IMP(3)*	*Not IMP but Des 2*	*Un IMP(1)*
1	Fixing Appointments with prospective Clients	0	0	40	60	50
2	Responding to new and existing Clients immediately	70	50	15	15	Nil
3	Trying todress neatly	0	0	130	10	10
4	Keeping the Office clean	0	0	100	30	20
5	Asking right Questions (***???***)	40	110	0	0	0
6	Explaining the Accounting Jargon to clients	0	0	0	30	120
7	To Spend more time Listening to Client than otherwise	0	10	50	80	10
8	Trying to understand what clinets need	40	100	10	0	0
9	Solving the problems of clients	10	75	25	40	0
10	Taking regular feedback from clients	0	20	110	10	10
11	Show Body					

	Language that indicates concern for client	0	0	0	10	140
12	Provide information freely on other services provided	0	0	0	145	5
13	Always saying the Price clearly	130	20	0	0	0
14	Asking Clients for Referrals	0	0	0	140	10
15	Havin well Designed Business Card	0	10	20	30	90

Though the importance given by professions to these areas indicate to the researcher that Chartered Accountants are exhibiting some amount of client sensitivity. Yet the results can be verified only after the mean ratings of the professionals are compared with what the clients feel as important. As Business should always be looked upon not just in the service sector, but in any sector with a client perspective. Hence, the mean ratings are assigned for further evaluation.

As seen in the table 4.6.1 in the next page, importance scales were assigned points with 5 being extremely important and 1 being unimportant. Based on the responses of perceived importance of these factors, the mean ratings are calculated. The data will be further used to find out the gap between professionals perceptions and clients expectations. Mean rating is calculated by:

Total Weighted Values/Total Number of Respondents

Therefore, the importance given to the attributes while interacting with the client is set.

Table 4.6.1 shows the type of Management Skills as used by a Professional in Making a Better Practice. The main aim of the question is to find out the skills used in handling the practice and his profession. These are essential skills to be in the market for a longer run. These are some of the principles of managing which help in handling the business better.Management helps the

Table 4.6.1: Mean Rating of Professional Tactics uses by Chartered Accountants while Interacting with Clients

S.No	*Professionals Tactics while Interacting with Client*	*Mean Rating*
1	Fixing Appoints with Prospective Clients	1.93
2	Rcsponding to new and existing clients immediately	4.166
3	Trying to dress Neatly	2.5
4	Keeping the Office Clean	2.53
5	Asking Right Question	4.26
6	Explaining the Accounting Jargon to Clients	1.2
7	To Spend mroe time Listenign to Client than otherwise	1.86
8	Trying to undertand what clients need	1.8
9	Solvingthe problems of clients	3.36
10	Taking regular feedback from clients	2.93
11	Show Body Language that indicates concern for client	1.96
12	Provide information freely on other services Provided	1.96
13	Always saying the Price clearly	4.86
14	Asking Clients for Referrals	1.92
15	Having Well Designed Business Card	1.66

firms to strengthen the internal environment of the business by doing a careful investigation of the business and planning the efforts of the firm and subsequently use the principles of communicating, Directing, controlling to make sure that the strategic moves are rightly make by an accounting firm. And therefore these are some of the skills that have been picked by the researcher after making a careful review of the literature as mentioned in chapter 2.The scale can be justified as these are the essential skills in one to one business generation. As seen from the tables in the next page, it clearly shows that the main emphasis of professional accountants is on Decision making and planning with a mean rating of 5 and 3.86 respectively. But the most contrasting feature of this that the least rating is given to controlling function which is actually ensuring that the work is done according to the plan. An essential characteristic of a manager is to ensure that he plans and executes his work well. But most of the professionals are not understanding the logic of managing their activities for better client management and this could affect them in the longer run.

Table 4.7: Importance of Management Skills while Interacting with Clients

S.No.	*Management Skills*	*Extremely Important (5)*	*Very IMP (4)*	*Some what IMP (3)*	*Not IMP but Desira-ble (2)*	*Un IMP (1)*	*Rank*
1	Planning & Strategic capabilities are required	8	102	40	Nil	Nil	2
2	Communication Capabilities	15	20	90	25	Nil	3
3	Listening	Nil	10	45	15	80	4
4	Research skills to study client Behaviour	Nil	Nil	Nil	Nil	150	6
5	Setting Skills	Nil	Nil	Nil	140	10	5
6	Decision-making skills	150	Nil	Nil	Nil	Nil	1
7	Implementing Ability	150	Nil	Nil	Nil	Nil	1

Note: The points qlloted are on a scale of 5 being extremely important and being unmportant.

Table 4.7.1: Mean rating of the professional skills to be used while interacting with clients

S.No.	*Management Skills*	*Mean Ratings*
1	Planning & Strategic capailities are required (I plan my work)	3.78
2	Communication Capabilities (I am excellent at convincing others)	2.56
3	Listening (I am a very patient listener)	1.9
4	Research Skills to study client Behaviour (I always try to lookfor information on clients needs)	1
5	Selling Skills (I know how to close a sale)	1.93
6	Decision Making Skills (in good at decision making)	5
7	Controlling (I always make sur ethat I excecute my plan successfully)	1

Sources of Clientele

The question 4.8 is a multiple-choice question. The purpose behind putting this question is to know which source is the most prevalent, through which the public accountants/firms got their business. It was also meant to bring out the percentage of work in approximate figures, which each source contributed for professional growth and enlargement. Results are tabulated in table 4.8.

Table 4.8 shows that the recommendations of existing clients was the most prevalent source of clientele (51.1%) and "Personal contact of partners" which counts for 34.45% of Weightage. The third important source was "Recommendations of friends/Relatives" with a Weightage of 7.46% of work. Fourth source of clientele was the "other professional firms" which counts for 5.52% of Weightage.

So it can be concluded that recommendations of Existing clients pays and constitutive the most important source of clientele for the Professional Accountancy Firm, and not the relations with touts or political party affiliations. Personal contact of partners, as well as relatives and Friends are some viable and considerable sources of clientele also. Thus "existing clients" is the single most important factor in the professional growth. As "satisfied customer" they constitute a formidable group that can promote the accountants interest by recommending him to other clients. The professionals should show their sincere, warm and sympathetic personal interest, for client retention and satisfaction.

Table 4.8: Sources of Clientele as to a Chartered Accountant

S.No.	*Sources*	*No of Respondents opting each source*	*% of work*
1	Recommendatns of Existing Clients	150	51.1%
2	Through Referrals and other professionals	100	5.52%
3	Personal Contacts (family, friends etc.,)	146	34.45%
4	Through Yellow Pages	10	0.33%
5	Through Political Party affiliation	30	1.13%
6	Through Professionals Owned website	0	0
7	Through membership Clubs	0	0
8	ThroughAttending Seminars & Conferneces	130	7.46%
9	Media Appearances	0	0

Accumulating information on sources of potential clients and staying alert to these sources as well to opportunities of service is of course, a typical marketing exercise. Like a driver on a freeway, they must be completely aware of everything that is going on around them.

Importance of Existing Clients. →

------Volume increases of their Business

----- Product lines multiply

----- Geographic locations fan out

------ Brings in more clients who are friends/relatives to them

--------Recommends to others

The most identifiable figures out of the table mentioned above 4.8 is that still the professionals have not taken the digital economy to their stride. It is of striking difference as India is accelerating at a very fast pace in terms of number of Internet users. And this potential is not captured by the chartered accountants mostly. There are very few websites notably and those of which do not at all belong to the chartered accountants of the Visakhapatnam area. Internet has a very huge potential to provide one to one access with anyone across the world.

Therefore, focus of CA's Should also be on the emerging technology that can help at gaining better, faster and speeder access with Clients where generating the leads will be a much easier task for the professional and also the database will be available with the firm to analyze the clients trends.

Importance of Referrals (Inter-Personal Network)

Any accountancy firm, large or small, local or international must learn that sources of leads and referrals are a very important market. And it is one that is often not recognized. According to researcher belief, "Interpersonal network (Referrals) is a vital sources of business for many professional services, including the services of chartered Accountants", for the confirmation of which seventh question was asked:

Table 4.9 reveals that majority of respondents 133 in no. i.e. (88.66%) felt and realized referrals as an important source of business. However only 13 (8.66%) respondent opined in the negative, and 4 (2.68%) felt undecided about the issue under consideration.

Table 4.9. Importance of Referrals

Importance of Referal In Gaining Business Option	*No. of Respondents*	*Percentage*
1 Import Source of Business	132	88.66%
2 Not Important Source	13	8.66%
3 Undecided	4	2.68%

Thus it can be concluded the referrals was considered a vital need to develop referral sources. One of the better ways to reach new clients is to ask present customers whom they know, who have similar problems. The most affective marketing strategy for a professional firm like those of public accountants is the widening and deepening of personal Referral Sources.

Sources of Referals

question was asked because although the chartered accountants consider Referrals as a vital source of such referrals, fail to acknowledge them, and fail to market them. This position was to be made clear from here, as to what are the sources of referrals according to Professional Accountants.

Table 4.10 clearly traces "existing clients/associates" as vital sources of referrals as opined by 133 (100%) respondents. "Other Professionals" was second only to existing clients as a Source of referral scoring 53 points.

Friends and relatives/business contacts were considered as a source of referral at the third place being opted by 47 (35%) of the respondents.

Table 4.10: Sources of Referrals to a Chartered Accountant

Sources of Referrals	*No of Respondents*	*%*
Existing Clients	433	39.8
Other Professionals	53	39.8
Friends, Relatives	47	35.3
Religious Organizations	10	7
Social Service Organisations	8	6.04
Trade associations	25	18.7

Regarding a Formal System for Recording Referrals

Table 4.11 clearly projects that as such no formal system for recording such referrals exists as opined by all 133 (100%) respondents. So the Professional Accountants maintained no formal list of sources of referrals at present in India. Referrals are the best way to get new clients. To get the best referrals, you need more than naturally occurring word of mouth. You need to have a program to actively encourage referrals in multiple ways.

Table 4.11: Opinion of respondent regarding the existence of formal system for recording referrals

Opinion of Respondents	*No. of Respondents (out f 133)*	*Percen-tages*
Yes	Nil	Zero
No	133	100%

One would think that clients would give referrals because they like you or your service. However, it doesn't always happen this way. To have a top practice one must do more than produce good work and wait for referrals to follow.

Troy Waugh (2004) some clients are just more likely to give referrals than are others. When you identify someone who is liberal with their referrals, cultivate them. They will be worth several people who like you just as much but aren't in the habit of giving referrals. While you can't "pay" people for referrals, you can reward them in some ways. One accountant holds an annual dinner for his referral relationships. After dinner, he takes a few moments to thank everyone for sending referrals. A lawyer I work with always sends a letter of appreciation. You certainly should thank them and try to send them referrals in turn, so long as the quality of work and reputation is of high caliber. Or you may be able to do business with them yourself. You can also arrange meetings between clients who might do business with each other.

Thus developing referral sources is an effective marketing strategy which if properly understood by the professional marketer can enable its firm members to provide insight into three questions.

R How to sell prospects?

R How to turn contacts into business opportunities?

R How to obtain more business through clients?

Factors Related with Attracting of the Clients

The Accountancy profession is one of the oldest professions, which is fighting against the commercial barriers. Four P's of marketing mix are the strongest points in the corporate world, while these are the weakest points in the services especially in the professional services of Accountants. The ethics and code of conduct of accountancy profession prevent professionals from advertising about their services or soliciting professional work from others. Personal selling of services is also banned. The cutting of prices are strictly prohibited, and attracting the clients through other channels such as relations which touts/dalals are considered as dirty practice in this profession.

So the basic motive behind the 12th question was to know that in spite of all those barriers, the professional Chartered Accountants were attracting the clients. To get an insight, some physical as well as abstract factors were put in the question. The Accountants/firm members were asked to answer on three points scale of the essential of using the particular factor in attracting the clients.

Table 4.12: Weightage given to different factors used by Professional Accountants to Attract Clients

S.No.	*Factors*	*Total Weightage*	*Ranking*
1.	Lowering fees than others	157	10
2.	Having centrally located office	287	5
3.	Keeping well funished office	293	3
4	Relation with Dalals	153	11
5	Joining as members of clubs	247	8
6	Taking part in social activities	180	9
7	Publishing in social activities	263	6
8	By Hard works	437	1
9	Through personal Apearance	383	2
10	Through educatign public	290	4
11	Throgh public speaking to reach other sections	260	7

Key: very essential = 3
Essential = 2
Not essential = 1

The table 4.12 clearly shows that the professional accountant with the Weightage of 437 points ranked "Hard work, good manner, good deeds" Ist, to attract the client. The next factor considered important by them was "Human personality of its proprietor, partner, their dress etc. "ranked at 2nd place with 383; points followed with "keeping one's office well furnished & decorated "At third place with a weight age of 293 points; "Devoting few hours of time in educating the public on the nuances of tax structure" at 4th rank with a weight age of 290 points. Followed in descending order by factors like "having the office centrally located", "Contribution of articles to journals / magazines" etc. with respective Weightage of 287 and 263 points.

Table also shows that the least important tool was "Relation with dalals/touts "which got only 153 points. "Lowering the fees than other CA's fees "was also not considered an effective tool in attracting the clients.

Other factors, which were not found to be as viable tools in comparison to already listed above, for attracting the clients more "Taking part in performances of Fine arts, painting, music etc. "Joining as member of club/institution", " Public speaking to reach other section of society / public relation campaign" with respective weight age of 180 points, 247 points and 260 pts.Thus it can be concluded that it is the accountant who alone sells the accounting service. Successful marketing of accounting services really become basically a personal marketing activity. Clients often buy "People" rather than services and it is critical for the professional service marketer to pay close attention to how professional are perceived by clients. Marketing emphasis in case of professional services for gaining the clients mean basically giving the client the time and attention, and work he or she wants and deserves. It also means providing the consumer with pleasant surrounding; impress them with a collateral existence of its members, and keeping the waiting time to a minimum. But most of all, it means performing the service better than competitors. A professional accountant who can help people make money and minimize taxes will soon be in demand. Emphasis is on success and performance by hard work, good manners and good deeds.

Price/fees and location of office are relatively minor factor in professionals' service marketing. By definition, people will go out of their way to get such a service and will pay premium price/fees. But they demand satisfaction and set high standard of performance. Relation with touts/dalals was considered as a dirty practice and was not used for gaining business.

Professional's View of Concepts of Marketing

This question is asked to find out the professionals view of Marketing, as many individuals do not have a clarity of what marketing really is and henceforth do not reap the benefits of implementing the concepts in reality. Many view that it as advertising or selling and doesn't have to do anything with an ethical way of doing business. This is to find out the professionals way of understanding the meaning of the word Marketing.

As the table indicates above, nearly 46.6% of the professionals just view marketing as Advertising and because their professional code of conduct restricts them to go for advertising most cf them believe that it is not a useful technique for building business. Nearly 20% of the professionals feel that marketing is desperate selling and it is an aggressive way of approaching the market which they need not actually go for and 13.3% of them think that marketing is Expensive as it involves a lot of monetary commitment from the professional either regarding Advertising or any other promotion.

Table 4.13: Professionals View of Marketing

S. No.	*Professionals view of Marketing*	*No of Professionals Who Opined*	*Percentage*
1.	It is Advertising	70	46.60%
2.	It is Desperate Selling	30	20%
3.	It is Expensive	20	13.30%
4.	It is understnading more about your clients needs	5	3%

What is a striking revelation of this data Is that only 3% of the professionals really think that marketing is understanding clients needs and knowing more about them which is actually true. Being client focused and the profession does not restrict improving the service quality. And hence, this proves that professionals have a total misinterpreted notion of marketing. Researcher was of the opinion that "most professionals probably have a negative reaction when they hear the word "marketing". This negative bias towards marketing is usually an emotional reaction to generalizations and stereotypes the professional associates with the marketing activities, not a reaction based on knowledge or experience. But today's increasingly, well managed and competitive business environment makes this attitude not only inaccurate, but incompetent.

Awareness of the Professionals towards Whether Marketing is Prohibited in their Profession, and by Whom

Many Professions reject tools of Marketing because their use is being severely constrained by the mandatory rules governing standards of practice or ethics. In other to find from the Professional Chartered Accountants if in their profession also this holds true question 14 was asked.

Table 4.14: Opinion of Professionals if Marketing is Banned by their Profession

Opinion of Respondents if Marketing is Banned	*No. of Respondents*	*%*
Yes	150	100%
No	Nil	Zero

By whom prevented: - All 150 Respondents were of the opinion that they are prevented from marketing by ICAI (Institute of Chartered Accountants of India).

Table 4.14 projected that all 150 (100%) respondents were of the opinion that marketing was prohibited in their profession.

When asked part, as to by whom prevented all 150 respondents were of the opinion that they are prevented from marketing by ICAI, Delhi. Thus it can be concluded that all the professionals were aware of the mandatory rules governing their practice, and were adhering to them. In most of the western countries, ban has been lifted on marketing(as quoted by

Kotler,Bloom& Hayes 2002). It gives a larger scope for the development of service orientation of professionals with the clients. But India is still way beyond in applying these strategies in the professional services arena. Marketing empowers the clients and makes them aware of the new service levels that can be enriched by professionals to the clients.

Opinion of the respondents regarding the advertising permission to the Professional Accountants

The objective behind the Q.14 was to reveal the acceptance of advertising in the accountancy profession. The advertising in the accountancy profession is prohibited. So the researcher was of the view that the accountants/firms would also have the same desire of commercializing the services as the companies are commercializing their products. Also, since the ban on professional advertising has been removed in U.S. by the U.S. Supreme Court's decision (1977), many professionals in our country, India, can also

Table 4.15: Charactered Accountants to whether Advertising should be Permitted

Opinion	*No of Respondents*	*Percentage*
Strogly Agree	None	Zero
Agree	27	18%
Not Agree	123	82%

think in that direction, and may impress upon the institute and the government agencies like the competition act 2002, to remove the bans on advertising in the profession. What is the respondents' opinion regarding. Advertising permission can be had from the table given below:-

Basically those in favor are big firms having international association who argue that through advertising we will let know others that we are in services profession, in an cost effective manner. Reasons not agreed for advertising professional services were:

1. Will lead to concentration of power in the hands of few big firms as they have money power, so they will go in for big page advertisements. 2. Not desirable, as it will deteriorate the quality of work. 3.Fight, will be then in terms of gaining of work rather

than performing the work. 4.It is different than other professional as confidentiality and trust has to be maintained which in presence of advertising is not possible.,

The question was form of a statement and the Accountants/ firm members were asked to give answer on the three points scale on the continuum of the agreement. The statement was whether advertising should be permitted to Chartered Accountants and the answer, which the CA's were asked to give, was on the continuum of "Strongly agreed" to "Not agreed".

It was found from Table 4.15, that majority of CA/firm members 123 (82%) were of the opinion that advertising should not be permitted to the Chartered Accountants. However there were 27(18%) respondents who agreed that advertising should be permitted to the Chartered Accountants.

So the researcher concluded that still majority of professionals are opposed to the idea of advertising because of certain "In built fears".

Perception of Professional Accountants Towards the Role Played by Institute of Chartered Accountants of India to Promote the Profession

Q.No 16 is asked primarily to find out the role of ICAI, The concerned governing authority responsible for promoting the profession. In the order of the day where the best pool of talent is attracted towards getting into a software profession or being an MBA in India, Researcher was trying to find out the opinion of professionals regarding whether ICAI is doing enough to promote the profession through creating a unique professional image. Professional services depend on the intellectual asset and there needs a continuous supply of quality professionals to keep the profession at the limelight of public domain.

40% of the professional responded as ICAI is playing an excellent role in promoting the profession and 26.6% opined that ICAI is playing a good role and 13.33 responded that they are satisfied with what the ICAI is doing and 20% felt that it is just fair. And none of the respondents felt that the role of ICAI is poor.

Table 4.16: Rating Regarding the Role of ICAI in Promoting the Profession

S. No.	*Rating of ICAI*	*No. of Respondents*	*Percentage*
1	Excelent	60	40
2	Good	40	26.66
3	Satisfactory	20	13.33
4	Fair	30	20
5	Poor	0	0

ICAI is doing a phenomenal role in promoting the profession and is desperately working towards attracting the best pool of talent into the profession. It has made itself accessible to every student or prospective student by providing complete access to the information on its official website www.icai.org. It is in fact going for strategic tie ups with many institutes and is campaigning massively to promote the chartered accountancy as a very lucrative profession. Recently it has also released its logo to change its professional image which it wants all its members to follow. Therefore, it is trying to brand itself by creating an identity to the profession. The logo is as below.

Source: Downloaded from official website of ICAI (www.icai.org) 2007

This is a branding attempt done by the Institute to even recoup the long felt need to have a separate identity of their own. The details of the logo are enclosed in Appendix 3

Ways of Building the public awareness and professional image among clients

There are professional and ethical constraints placed upon the use of certain promotional methods. Still a practicing Chartered Accountant should be able to acquire the necessary quantum of work to keep him self going, for which he needs to employ various techniques for enhancing their self image and make their services known to the public. To know the ways employed by the professionals for building public awareness and professional image, Q.17 was asked.

Table 4.17: Ways of Building the public awareness and professional image among clients

S. No.	*Activities Employed*	*No. of Respondents*	*%*
1	Personal Contact	150	100
2	Brochures	0	0
3	Press Releases	6	4
4	Media Appearances	0	0
5	Advertising with clubs/institutes	75	20
6	Exhibitions	0	0
7	Sponsorships	0	0
8	Awarding merit scholarships to students	10	7
9	Publication of Articles	25	17
10	Name Plates	0	0
11	Business cards	50	33
12	Gifts	3	2
13	Greeting on important dates	113	75
14	Advertising	0	0
15	Direct Mail	0	0
16	E-mails	15	10
17	Website	2	1
18	Signage's	0	6
19	Location of Occice	90	60

The highlighted rows in blue in the table mentioned in the next page shows the top three promotional activities that professionals have to undertake to build public awareness and professional image

The question 17 was a multiple choice question in which the respondent were asked to tick the various promotional activities employed by them for improving their image among client and for public awareness

Note: Respondents were asked to tick as many promotional methods as they were using as mentioned in the Table 4.17.

The Table 4.17 portrays that among the various techniques listed, majority 150 (100%) of the respondents ranked "Personal Contact" at No.1. Next method of communication adopted as the "Use of Other preferred medium used for highlighting the accountancy firms ranged from "Membership of association/ Club/ Institutions, business cards, Participation in professional contests ";" Publication of articles ";" Press interviews etc. "with respective respondents opining in their favor being 80 (53.3%); 60(40%); 53(35.33%); 10(6.66%); and 6(4%).

Greeting for important dates like birthdays etc. as opined by 113 (75.3%) respondents at place 2: followed by the location of office opted for by 90 (60%) respondents.

Thus it can be concluded from above that personal contact was considered to be the most important and best approach to communication. Other medium of communication/promotion were also found favorable like sending of greetings, or use of seminars, published articles, or use of speeches to get publicity. Brochure, or newsletters sent to the existing clients also carry message and communicate with clients in the form of reminding them about the professional. Communication can be internal as well external. In internal communication large firms keeps the clients informed about the important developments in the tax field, or changes in various other laws etc. that enhances the image of professional in the eyes of clients. In external communication personal contact with the prospective client through meeting etc. assumes importance. This gives an opportunity to the professional whose services being essentially intangible, to provide tangible evidence of the quality, skill, concern and experience which they possess to the prospects by demonstrating - i.e. (outlining procedures), and showing literature concerning how their Audit, tax, and management services staff works. Not only this, as has been brought out in question 8 above, that prospects are pre sold through the courteous, polite behavior of the staff and professional, which was ranked at no. 1. Atmospherics too are important for client retention which include office locations, layout, décor, sound and light level, professionals personality, dress, language, individual office furnishings and the like, as shown in question nos. which was ranked at no. 2. and 3. Thus it can be inferred that accounting firms constantly communicate with present and prospective clients, often unintentionally. Client "read" and receive messages from many sources other than traditional communication media of personal contact, publicity, promotional tools). Items such as office furnishing and stationary letter heads as well as the dress and attitudes of members of the firm send out messages to clients. Office location and fees also send out messages through not that important, all of which can be critical to a firm's marketing strategy.

Opinion of the Professional Accountants regarding Satisfaction with their Practice

To know whether the professional accountant in practice were satisfied with their practice or not, question 18 was asked "Do you feel satisfied with your practice " to which the respondents were asked to give their opinion in the form of 'Yes' or 'No'.

Table 4.18: Satisfaction of clients as perceived by professionals

Perceived client Satisfaction	*No. of Respondents*	*Percentage*
Yes	127	84.67
No	17	11.33
Undecided	6	4

Table 4.18 clearly shows that majority 127 (84.67%) respondents felt satisfied with their practice while 17 (11.33%)

respondents were found to be not satisfied with their practice and only 6 (4%) felt undecided as they told that it is very difficult to answer it.Thus majority of respondents were found satisfied with their practices.

Perceived Importance of Accountant Selection Criteria according to CA/Firms under consideration

Since the professional accountants were consistently interacting with their clients, therefore, professional accountants must be having considerable information on the bases by which they are being selected by clients with this objective in mind, the said question "what in your opinion are the selection criteria adopted by your clients in selecting you is asked?. Every client uses certain heuristic principles for deciding on the professional, and therefore, this question has been asked to find out if the professionals are aware that their clients have a certain criteria for selecting them and this helps to understand the professionals knowledge regarding the selection criteria which in turn could be used for the comparison with clients way of assessment.

Table 4.19 reveals that 'Quality of work performed / advertising capacity' is the most important criteria ranked at no. 1 with total weight age of 418 points, by the professional accountants; followed with. "Technical competence' at rank 2, with a weight age of 405 points reputation/integrity of firm at rank 3 with weight age of 382 points; experience/years in practice', at rank 4 with a score of 318 points; promptness of service at rank 5 with a score of 289 points; personal acquaintance at 6th rank with weight age of 265 points.

The question itself contained 13 selection criteria's. Professional Accountants/Firms were asked to selection criteria's their clients most often used the felt. They were then asked to rate the criteria based upon how important each should be when selecting a public accountant. Rating were provided along a these point Likert scale with and points labeled 3 = very important = important and 1= Not Important. Results can be seen from the table.

Table 4.19: Perceived Importance of Accountant Selection Criteria according to CA/Firms under consideration

S.No.	*Selection Criteria*	*Total Weightage use P/ACC*	*Rank*
1	Overall Reputaiton	382	3
2	Technical Competance	408	2
3	Quality of work performed	418	1
4	Past Experience	318	4
5	Meeting Deadlines on work	289	5
6	Costof Accountign Services	209	11
7	Recommendations by Friends	238	8
8	Convenience of Office Hours	163	12
9	Personal Acquaintance	265	6
10	Listing in Official Directory	150	13
11	Collateral Appearances	244	7
12	Location of office	228	9
13	Repuation	218	18

However, their location of office, or fees charged, convenience of office hours, or listing in yellow pages are such factors for which the client do not much bother (in the opinion of respondents) as they were placed at respective ranks of 9th, 11th 12th and 13th. To certain extent the 'Collateral appearance and behavior of the professionals' as well as 'Recommendations of friends and relatives' were considered essential selection criteria in the eyes of professional accountants as they were placed at 7th and 8th ranks with respective weightages being 244 points and 238 points.

Thus it can be concluded that according to professional accountants perception, "Quality of work, Technical Competence, Reputation/Integrity of firm, and experience of the professional / firm were the important selection criteria's employed by their clients in selecting them.

Fees charged, listing in yellow pages, convenience of office hours, or location were relatively minor factors in professional selection and as perceived by professional accountants Firms. According to them, for such special services, people/clients will go out of their way to get such a service and will not mind in paying a premium price provided the work is done satisfactorily for which high standards of performance are being set.

Opinion of respondents that changes have come in practicing environment

To have an idea whether the practicing professional accountants have also started feeling changes in practicing scene. Q. 20 are asked from the respondents. The question was: 'over the years of practice have you felt any changes in the environment or market place? 'The respondents were asked to answer as "Yes" or "No". The purpose was to know whether the professional accountants were keeping pace with the changes in the social, technological, economic, legal and competitive environments, and what means were adopted to cope with such changes.

Table 4.20: Opinion of CA's Regarding the Changes in Practising environment Over Years

S. No.	*Opinion Regarding Changes in Practising Environment*	*Respondents*
1	Yes	137
2	No	13
	Base	150

As evident from the table above, nearly 137 respondents felt that there are changes in the practicing environment and nearly 13 respondents felt that there are not changes in the practicing environment.

Adapting the concepts of Marketing

Marketing is usually thought of in terms of selling, advertising, and promotion or distribution. But these all are aspects of marketing and the total concept is considerably bigger than the sum of these. Marketing function alone can expand volume and profits of professional service scene by ascertaining the needs and demands of clients, and satisfying them. But there is a general reluctance, on the part of the professional firms, to practice marketing consciously, although they are doing so unconsciously. A conservative professional attitude continues to prevail. So to have an idea of some type of marketing practices being adopted by the professional accountancy firms the Q.21 was asked. The question was divided into six categories covering the various activities of marketing related to 1. Service offerings 2. Communication Mix 3. Location decision 4. Fees structure 5. Market research. 6. Marketing-Orientation, and the respondents were asked to indicate their answer as 'yes' OR 'NO' against each activity listed in each of the above categories made. This was related to the degree to which firms were committed to the overall concept of marketing

Table 4.21: Opinion of professionals regarding the embracing of the Marketing concept is given in the next page.

S.No.	*Services*	*Yes*	*No*	*% of Professionals Using these*
1	Peridically reexamine services	90	60	60
2	Create New Services to offer	120	30	80
3	Estimate number of clients for new services	60	90	40
4	Determine share of market for Present services	47	103	31.33
5	Establish written goals and policies	53	97	35.3
6	Define specific client groups	30	120	20

S.No.	*Communication Mix*	*Yes*	*No*	*% of Professionals Using these*
1	Develop overall information approach to reach clients	23	127	15.33
2	Create internal brochers and attend seminars	38	117	22
3	Develop public Relations programmes	27	123	18

S.No.	*Location decision*	*Yes*	*No*	*% of Professionals Using these*
1	Analysis locations for new officer	60	90	40
2	Evaluate volume and trend s of existign locations	27	123	18

S.No.	*Fee Policies*	*Yes*	*No*	*% of Professionals Using these*
1	Evaluate fee policies on systematic basis	133	17	88.67
2	Evaluate volume and trends of existing locations	30	120	20

Hint: (Total percentage of firms performing the activities divided by number of the marketing practices highlighted = 1103/ 22=50. 14 or say 50% approx.

S.No.	*Marketing Research*	*Yes*	*No*	*% of Professionals Using these*
1.	Collect information on clients needs	142	8	94.36
2.	Study client behaviour	51	99	34
3.	Study the decision influences	60	90	40
4.	Collect regular feedback	120	30	80
5.	Determine fim image among clients public	60	90	40

S.No.	*Marketing Orientation*	*Yes*	*No*	*% of Professionals Using these*
1.	Firms activities ensuring customer satisfaction	147	3	98
2.	Involving customers in creatign new services	113	37	75.33
3.	Identifying dissatisfied customers	74	76	49.33
4.	Initiating customer retention of lost customers	60	90	40

Eighty percent of the firms reported that they were periodically re-examining the services offered and regularly determining which new services to offer. Similarly round 89% of the firms reported that they regularly evaluate fee policies and 95% approx. Reported to have regularly evaluated client needs. 80% of the firms were also found to be conscious to the need for training and motivating firm members for showing courteous attitudes towards clients. 98% of the firms also reported having their all activities coordinated to provide customer satisfaction. But only 50% reported having a methodological approach to identifying major potential users of their services and adopting means of reaching them. Similarly analysis of potential locations for new offices was being practiced by only 40% of the firms (As few reported that it is difficult to find good new locations in these days of scarcity and appreciation of land in Visakhapatnam).

Thus it can be concluded that practically all firms had adopted some types of marketing practices but 50% commitment to the various 22 marketing practices enumerated was there. The field of marketing professional services though in existence is still in its infancy. One should realize that the future of professional service marketing would surely see a more pronounced tendency towards the increased use of marketing. Service marketers like accountants are beginning to overcome disdain for commercialism, increasingly adhering to the provision of they codes of ethics and are incurring marketing expenses like:

1. The careful redecoration of office to make it convent and attractive to clients is a marketing expense.
2. The membership of husband and wife in local clubs or organizations is a marketing expense.
3. Information bulletins/speeches for community development education on tax laws is a marketing expense. An accountant fixing a brass nameplate to his front door is a marketing expense. Thus professionals do market but their marketing expenses are normally absorbed under the categories/heads of practice management of administrative expenses. Thus there should be a common agreement of professionals with the researcher that the broad principles of marketing are applicable

to marketing of their professional services with the only understanding that the key to the successful marketing of professional services is services performed by people and for people.

The centrality of customer should always remind professionals that in their zeal for customer satisfaction they should not loose sight of being marketing-oriented. This is what the future time also demands from the professionals, which enable them to survive and grow.

5

Discussion Related to the Professionals' Survey

Times have changed and so have man's needs, wants and requirements. It is, therefore, more appropriate, economical and convenient to buy services from professionals than to create them within the organization. And it is thus in the recent years that professional services have started adopting marketing ideas, but are yet to go a long way to get along the road to a true marketing orientation. Many professional services of accountants, lawyers, doctors etc. are severely constrained by the mandatory or voluntary rules governing standards of practice or ethics. Not only this many professionals, as observed by the researcher, reject tools of marketing considering them not only unrealistic but distasteful, and incompatible with their self-images,

A discussion of the results presented in chapter IV follows.

Experience as a Variable

Experience as an attribute was taken as a variable of study by the Researcher to bring meaningful insights relating to review of clients and to know top-of-mind attitude of professionals towards the word 'marketing' accordingly, the chartered accounts i.e. respondents of the study were classified into six groups on the basis of experience. Marketing of professional services being the marketing of intangibles, so the experience is an indicator of the competence of the professionals. From clients point of view, using an experienced professional makes a risky purchase seems less risky. Also 'experience' attracts the clients at the first meeting when they come for the purchase of professional service of an accountant.

In the studies by Raimond, (1983); Bloom, (1984); Parasuraman, Zeithaml and Berry, (1985); Helgeson and Birrer, (1986); Kotler and Bloom (1983); Denney (1983); Smith & Meyer (1980), and Wood & Ball (1978), similar observation has been made.

Generalist vs Specialist Approach Orientaton

The results of the study brought about that specialization in a particular area of practice was preferred over being a General practitioner as opined by MAJORITY Also, it was found that an average respondents (Professional Accountant) was specializing in three areas of practice, with Audit and taxation comprising their principle offerings. Further, it was revealed form the study that public accountants with lesser experience (having 0-5 or 5-10 years of experience) used to restrict themselves to internal Audit of Banks etc. or to cases of taxation of small companies, while professional accountants with higher experience (10-15, 15-20 and above experience class) were shifting to newer areas of service lines being of management services, secretarial and company Affairs, NRI cases handling, EDP facilities etc. with Auditing and Taxation remaining their dominant areas of concern. Chi2 Test further supported the above results.

These results are supported by Studies and observations of Bhandari, (1971); Chakraborty, (1971), Mahon, (1978); Wilson (1972); and Wheatley (1983). As Wheatley comments, "There is one principle, however, that I believe that we as professionals, can agree upon. I'm referring to the Principle of specialization". Further Kotler & Connor, (1977) also commented that "specialization offers two distinct advantages to the Professional Firm:

1. ... a preferred position placing it automatically in contention for potential clients seeking that kind of expertise.
2. ... permits a greater profit on volume because the firm develops "cutting-edge" expertise and low cost procedures for handling recurrent situation."

Implications for Professionals

They need to specialize which can be effectively used in their marketing Strategy of Market positioning. Specialization can be service wise, as well as market-type with lable to Accountancy firms as construction specialists. Retail specialists and the like which can further enhance their scope of operation.

Service Mix & Potential of the Professional Services

The results of the study showed that most of the Professional Accountancy Firms were multiservice firms. The service mix comprised of basic line services and a number of other services constituting the width of the service line (see table 5.3). Further the results showed that there was a constant service Mix expansion which included both line extension in the form of adding new package of services as well as width wise expansion i.e. to add one more dimension of the existing service.

The width of these line services can be seen from the question No. 3 of the study. However, within each line services, the respective potential fields highlighted by the study, and in use by the C.A.'s were as follows.

Table 5.3: Showing the Service Mix for Professional Accountants

Line Services	*Width Wise Services*
1. Auditing, Accounts and finance	Audit of Accounts at Rank 1
2. Taxation	Preparation f incoe Tax, Wealth Tax and Other returns at rank 1.
3. Secretariat & Company Affairs	Preparation of Memorandum & articles of Company formation, prospectus etc. at rank 1.
4. Internal Audit and Control	Internal Audit at Rank 1.
5. Management Services	Budgeting & Budgetary Control at Rank 1
6. Miscellaneous	As Financial Adviser at Rank 1

Areas within these line services to which the professional accountants could expand were also brought about by the study. Like within Management Services are, the width wise expansion could take place towards rendering of services like those of organizational studies, materials Management and Installation etc.

Implications for Professionals

1. Professional Accountants need to expand and diversify to reduce their dependence on a particular set of traditional services. Potential areas need to be highlighted and can be further uncovered through future research.

2. Use market information to decide and answer the question, "What to sell, how and whom to sell", services be modified and improved based on market information and answering of the following questions.

a) What services are in Demand?.

b) What type of services prospective clients will require.

c) Are any of our service outdated?.

d) Whether balance of resources and capabilities of firm with respect to factors like 'variety', Quality.

e) Whether the service is being provided from the clients angle?

f) Appropriate consideration of the above mentioned questions will lead to a type of service mix innovation that will ensure marketing success of the Professional Accountants. Such need for service mix innovation has been highlighted by Helgheson & Eirrer (1986), Kotler and Bloom (1983); Parikh, (1971); Raimond (1983); Dirsmith and Covaleski, (1987); Bateson (1977); Eiglier and Langeard, (1981); Sassar, Olsen & Wyckoff (1978); Wilson (1972) and Shostack, (1982).

Target Marketing

After having understood the significance of service mix and its composition from the clients point of view, the next assessment that accounting firms need to make in marketing themselves is who they believe will potentially be using their services. These prospective clients make up the Firm's target market and thus need to be identified before the firm can satisfy their needs.

The results of the study showed that Professional Accountants, viewed the entire market as a single entity and believed in offering their services to 'whosoever comes' as was opined by 82% respondents. No approach to segmentation of the market was used. This was mainly because the market for Professional Services of Accountants was more of "Statutory Nature" rather than being of 'well being' nature. Professionals, especially Accountants were being hired by clients-Individual, institutional and other professional-more for official business purpose of Auditing and Taxation rather than for consultations on Real property etc. If the attest function of Accountant would not have been important and obligatory, the existence of the professional Accountant was under doubt (as brought out from the results of client survey-Question 1 and 2. This undifferentiated approach as was being practices by professional accountant may be a viable short term approach to target market selection as long as a firm realizes it is approaching the market this way. However, such an approach to target marketing is not tenable from the long term point of view.

There are several benefits of using the segmentation approach to target market selection as given below:

1) Firms can gain increased knowledge of their clients and therefore are better able to satisfy, their needs. Mahon (1978); remarked "Organizing the practice by Industry will give Industry competence.

2) Firms can more easily identify potential clients because target markets are defined precisely.

3) Firms can more readily identify their competitors and assess the relative competitive strengths and weaknesses. As Cooke (1970) pointed out that "in competitive situations service organizations need to differentiate their offerings, which is possible through their employees and through emphasizing the quality of interactions between clients and employees, possible when one have industry/client specializations."

Implications for Professional Accountant

(i) Professional Accountants may gradually adopt differentiated approach to target market selection because of the diversity of Industry characteristics and to reap all benefits of segmentation highlighted above.

(ii) Organize the practice by industry, to give the clients a personalized approach as essentially a service is ultimately an interaction between people, to ensure true marketing success. Similar observations have been made by Gulvarjani, (1987) Parikh (1971), Ingram (1984); Sevinyard (1977).

Client Profile

The next marketing activity is that of making clients profile. The clients for Professional Accountants included wide diversity ranging from Manufacturing Organizations both public and Pvt. Ltd. Commercial Firms, Banks, Government undertakings, Colleges, Schools, Exporters, Retailers, Departmental Stores etc. as could be seen from the results of Question No. 4(b). Majority of clients from professional Accountants comprises of manufacturing organizations both Public and Pvt. Ltd. as opined by respondents. Thus there is a need for maintaining a list of client profile by the chartered Accountants/firms, which in itself is a step in their marketing programme. Similar observation has been made by Denney (1983).

Client ReviewProgrammes

Another activity that can contribute to the marketing success of the firm is that of 'Client Review'. By undertaking such clients review programs, professional images can be projected. This in turn also gives the clients an impression that the firm is really interested in how its clients feel they are being served. A sense of belongingness and pride is inculcated in the minds of the existing clients. Also misunderstandings, if any, can be understood and uncovered at this stage to further enhance the client's loyalty towards the professional firm.

The results showed those majorities were engaged in client review regularly but in an informal manner. It showed the lack of marketing significance of such a critical activity among the professional Accountants.

The main reasons given for having informal client review were

a) Keeping upto date knowledge of client needs

b) Developing more work, and

c) Keeping good relationship with the clients.

Further Chi2 test employed projected that Review of Client was more pronounced among professional Accountants with experience that in the case of new entrants.

Implications for Professional Accountants

1.Answer to the question, "Who makes the decisions on the selection of accountancy service", i.e. D.M.U. (Decision Making Units) needs to be obtained on a systematic basis, for which client review activity becomes a necessity. Also undertaking of such favorable Awareness program is the most effective marketing strategy for a Professional Firm.

2.Greater realization has to be brought on the part of Professional Accountants that real road to marketing success is the Review of Clients. This will lead to greater client acceptability, confidence and loyalty. The need for client review by professional service providers as a part of marketing programme has been suggested by Raimond (1983), Davis (1985); Kotler & Connor (1977); Gummesson (1979); Kubr (1976); Wilson (1972); Bloom (1984); Kotler & Bloom (1983); Denney (1983); Mahon (1978); Davidson (1978); Denney (1981); Bernstein (1978); Maister (1982); George & Barksdale (1974), and Vdalakis (1961).

Sources of Clients

Results showed that "Recommendations of the existing Clients" was the most prevalent source of business contributing an average of 51% of the total work. "Personal / Business Contacts of Partners" was the next source of clientele contributing for 34.45% of the total work, followed with Recommendations of Friends/Relatives comprising approximately 7.46% of the work. However, websites were not considered a source of clientele by all the (100%) Professional Accountants covered. This shows that existing clients form a formidable group who can bring business by recommending the existing professional Accountants to others as well as by rehiring them in future:

Recommendations

(1) Information on sources of clientele needs to be accumulated on a constant basses. This will enable them to remain alert to

these sources and make it feasible for professional accountants to tap them when need arises. Further expanding service to existing clients can be the most effective strategy for a Professional Firm of Accountancy.

2.Also this activity be performed by the professional himself so as to give a personalized touch, which assumes importance from marketing perspective. Studies supporting these results are by Kotler and Bloom (2002), Kotler and Connor (1977), Denny (1981), Armstrong (1980) and Mahon (1978).

Importance of Referrals

Majority of respondents - Professional Accountants felt and realized referrals as an important source of business. Respondents also considered "Existing Clients/Associates" as a vital source of referrals. "Other professionals' like lawyers. Doctors and other accountants" were considered at the third place. However, no formal system existed for keeping record of such referrals by the Professionals Accountants, and was considered more of an informal activity than a formalized one (as opined by 53.38%) of Professional Accountants).

Thus Accountancy Firms, large, or small, local or international must learn that sources of leads and referrals constitute a very important market. Developing referral sources is an effective marketing strategy which can help professional Accountants to answer, "How to obtain more business through existing clients".

Recommendations

(1) Every Professional Accountant need to develop referral sources and that too on a more 'formalized bases'. Widening and deepening of Personal Referral sources can prove to be the most effective marketing strategy for a professional Firm.

(2) Existing clients being the largest source of referral, efforts of Accountant be directed to make the existing clients more satisfied, by offering them timely, accurate, distinctive and well-packed, service and through their collateral appearance.

Studies supporting the results are:

Raimond (1983), Mahon (1978),d Kotler and Connor (1977),

Bloom (1984), Helgeson & Birrer (1978), Wheatley (1983), Kotler & Bloom (1983), Wilson (1972), Gummesson (1979), Denney (1983), Kotler (1979), Stall (1978) and Wittreich (1966)..

Factors for Client Attraction/Retention

Four 'p's of the marketing mix being the strongest points in goods marketing in the corporate world, are seen to be the weakest points in the professional services of Accountants, because of the self-regulation of profession. But, inspite of all these barriers, there is a need to attract and retain clients, who are influenced by the professional accountant skills and physical and abstract factors like those being brought out by the study.

Recommendations

(1) There is a need for tangibalize the intangible elements of professional service of an Accountant, to build client visibility and inspire confidence in their minds. (Intangible elements being of quality, skill, concern, competence etc So for this, Accountants can outline their procedures. Wheatley (1978) also remarked that "Demonstration, slide presentation, use of comparative case examples, Telescoping dramatization, etc. can be the various ways for providing tangile evidence to the intangible elements of professional services".

(2) Demonstrate and improve upon the following activities helpful in attracting and retaining of clients:

a) The personal appearance of the professional and members of the staff.

b) The state of maintenance and decoration of its office.

c) The courtesy with which clients are received.

d) The efficiency demonstrated by switchboard staff.

e) The General behavior of the Practitioner. It was revealed that 'meetings' (at rank 1) was found to be the most preferred way of maintaining the contact with potential clients. Hence it can be said that meetings may provide an opportunity to Professional Accountants to tangibalize the intangible elements of the professional services (according to the needs and tastes of prospects) through practical demonstration. The studies supporting the above results are by :

Barker (1968),d Belk (1975), Hall (1959), Nord & Peter (1980), Berry (1975), Eiglier & Langeard (1977),d George (1977), particularly is arrived at by the consumer mostly through a process of deduction, based on the total impression that the tangible evidence creates."

Similar observations are reported in the studies of Levitt (1981), Wheatley (1983), Mahon (1978), Wilson (1972), Armstrong (1980), Raimond (1983), Uhl & Upah (1983), and Bhandari (1971).

Top of mind attitude of Professionals towards the word "Marketing"

Realization that marketing plays an increasingly more important role in their overall success was not there on the part of most of the Accounting Firms, as Professional Accountants had a negative attitude towards "Marketing". They were found to be guided by their emotional feelings only and equated marketing with advertising, selling or other promotional activities. They considered it to be unprofessional to use certain marketing practices because of their code of ethics. They used to think of themselves as producers of services and not as marketers of services, and therefore, were opposed to the idea of marketing.

But increased competition from clients, greater consumer selectivity and the rapid changes taking place both within the profession and in business, government and society, and competitive business environment makes this attitude not only inaccurate but dangerously unproductive. Already the professionals in their professional fields have started feeling the pangs of this fear . So there is a need on the part of the professionals to reconsider their attitudes and base their reactions towards 'Marketing' on knowledge of what marketing is and their experiences. Marketing is not advertising, not selling, not promotion only but, these and many other are the elements of marketing. Marketing is much broader than all these elements of marketing, as has already been clarified in the conceptual framework of the study.

Recommendations for Professionals

(1) Professional Accountants need to correct their attitudes towards the word 'Marketing' and adopt the marketing concept a consumer-oriented philosophy that views profits and clients satisfaction as outcomes of satisfying client wants and needs. There is a need for the professionals to convert themselves from 'Doers' into 'Sellers'.

2. Many professional Accountants may not realize the importance of marketing under today's economic conditions when they are making enough profits from their practice, but should realize about the future, when there will be a 'Future Shock' for all of us as pointed out by Alvin Toffler (1984) then marketing will become a necessity not a consideration. So instead of being overpowered by tomorrow's environment why not start thinking or using marketing in today's conditions of economic prosperity to be safer in the future, periods. Such observation has also been made by Helgeson & Birrer (1986), Uhl and Upah (1983), Majaro (1982), Cowell (1984), Shostack (1982), Shostack, Zaltman & Bonoma (1979), Lovelock (1979), Borden (1965), Kotler (1975), George & Barksdale (1974), Langeard, Lovelock, Bateson and Young (1977), Wilson (1972), Davis (1985), Denney (1981), Kotler & Bloom (1983), Wheatley (1983), Mahon (1978), Denney (1981), Kotler & Connor (1977), Bloom (1984), Turner (1969).

Regarding 'Advertising' Permission

While many professional Accountants realized the importance of Advertising (as they were seen commenting, "since hospitals and Doctors in India have started using Advertising, although it is also banned in the professions of Doctors then why not-----") but they did not say it openly with regard to their profession because of certain 'Built-in-Fears'.

But as has been brought elsewhere in the research study that the intangibility of professional services leads to pre-purchase anxiety among potential clients about the professional firm's ability, capabilities, integrity etc. for which they look for better and more sources of information, besides consulting influencers. However it is advertising only as means of communication, which can reduce the tension and anxiety, be providing information to the clients about professionals. Thus in future, research needs to be undertaken to demonstrate to the Professional Accountants, that the most effective means of disseminating information to clients regarding the explosion in accounting developments, Tax changes, new methods of doing the work, (one that being of applicability of data processing equipments) and converting the attitude of clients towards professional service providers, is through advertising".

Recommendations

1) There is a need for the practicing Professional Accountants to understand the benefits of advertising. (Future Area of Research).

2) The institute of Chartered Accountants of India, Delhi can recommend to Govt. of India to relax provisions of Competition act 2002 regarding Advertising provisions for professionals.

Ban on Advertising should be lifted. It may be mentioned here that ban on advertising of professional services has already been lifted in America in 1977. Such an approach has also been advocated in the studies by Smith & Meyer (1980), Bloom, (1984), Kotler & Connor (1977), Baird (1977), Cunningham, & Isabella (1976); Philip & Ford (1977), Tiffany & Smoth (1978), Brian & andreasen (1972); Desster (July 1981), Newell (1982): Bernstein (1978); Maister (1982); Shimp & Dyer (1978); Shostack (1977); Anderson et al (1976); George and Berry (1981); King and Label (1979).

Techniques Employed for Enhancing Profesional Image

The Ethics and Code of Conduct for Professionals

In India prevent them from Advertising their services or soliciting professional work from others. In such a situation what are the various techniques that can be employed by a practicing chartered accountant to acquire the necessary quantum of work to keep himself going was brought out by the results of this study. It was opined that 'personal contact' was the most effective way used for promoting the practice. Next promotional tool used for enhancing the professional image among the existing clients was the "use of Birthday Greetings, Diwali Greetings, and other type of Greetings". Next in order was the 'Use of Internal circulars to the clients' and so on as can be seen from results of the study. Use of Advertising in Radio/T.V. or 'Direct Mail was not preferred at all, being restricted by the self-regulation of the profession.

Thus accounting firms were found to be constantly communicating with present and prospective clients unintentionally. Clients read and received messages from many sources e.g. personal contact and publicity and other promotional tools (like firm's letterhead, business Cards, nameplates, notepads, calendars, files, broachers etc.

Important thing to note here is that the tools used by a professional firm and the image and the information they convey should be consistent with the target market and market position chosen by the firm.

Recommendations for Professionals

(1) Understand consciously that communicating, results in confidence in clients, and communicating is the key to develop a professional practice and professional image.

(2) Younger C.A.'s can gain greater visibility among prospective clients by becoming active members of their Regional Bodies.

(3) Socialize: Become visible in the Organizations and perform other activities that allow you to meet people e.g through seminars, conferences, awarding fellowships, writing articles, books, meeting etc. Studies supporting the above results are by Driscoll (1985), Helgeson & Birrer (1986), Davis (1985), Wilson (1972), Kotler & Conner (1977), Kubr (1976), Bennion (1969), Williams (1985); Wittreich (1966), Paul Raimond (1983), Chakraborty (1971).

Levinson (1987), Wheatley (1983), Mahon (1978), Denney (1983), Kotler (1973), Kotler (1980), Majaro, (1982).

Opinion of the Respondents Regarding Satisfaction of the Clients

93.33% of the respondents professional accountants felt that their clients were satisfied with their work and thus 'satisfaction of clients' was considered important by them. Factors like Hard work, Good, Timely, proper, Honest work was found to be the most helpful factor in bringing about desired satisfaction. Other factors considered important were: "Professional Competence, perfect Auditing, Accuracy of work etc."

Thus it can be interpreted that the 'Hard-work and Quality work of Professional Accountants, consistent with Genuine Fee package, good staff, personal attention and other factors can bring about the desired client-satisfaction in the professional scene. But a word of caution is that in their zeal for client-satisfaction, professional Accountants lack market-orientation. They offered the services which they could perform and discharge in a way convenient to them, i.e. by posing I am the expert without hearing to and answering client queries and complaints. This makes them self-centered rather than being client-oriented, which is an in appropriate thinking on their part and need to be changed.

Recommendations

Professional Accountants in their zeal for client-satisfaction, should always be market-oriented, so as to bring continued success in their profession. This is possible by doing and performing all their activities from the view point of clients. Similar observation has been made by Cowell (1984), Wilson (1972), Kotler & Connor (1977), Bloom (1984), Turner (1969), Gummesson (1979), Davies (1985),d Mahon (1978), Wheatley (1983), Kotler and Bloom (1983), and Denney (1983)

Satisfaction with their Practice

Almost 84.67% professional Accountants opined as being satisfied with their practice. The satisfaction came to them as they felt they were earning worth their efforts. Factors that helped them to satisfy their ego and build their practice over period of years of their practice were, performing good, hard, honest and sincere work at rank I with 100% Weightage given to it, Followed with personal contacts with 31.5% of respondents favoring it, updating of the knowledge, Induction of Qualified and knowledgeable staff etc. However, the factor of undertaking extensive promotional work was not opted by any one of the professional accountants.

Thus we can interpret from the above results that the essence to practice development and client attraction is performing hard and sincere work. But professionals should understand that in their zeal to perform quality and sincere work, they should not forget the clients needs, rather the work be performed consistent to the needs and wants of the clients to nurture long-term client loyalty and remain market-oriented.

Recommendations

(1)The Professionals should demonstrate their technical competence, a primary priority in service and audit all the areas to come out with those areas in with they have capabilities.

Further new horizons of service in which the professionals could diversify and demonstrate their capabilities, highlighted by the study were those of computer and Electronic Data Processing, Management services, International tie-ups to become Liaison representatives, Human resources Development services, Agricultural farm Accounting, Estate Planning and the like. But further studies be conducted to show and demonstrate the potential in the above listed areas, before the professionals can think of entering them (further area of Research).

The above results are being supported by works of Hise, (1977), Rathmell, (1974),d Kotler (1975), Carman & Langeard (1979), Wilson (1972), Ansoff (1968), Eiglier & Langeard (1981), Stanton, (1981), Mahon, (1978), Wheatley (1983), Kotler & Connor (1977), Wittreich (1966), Levitt (1960) and Shostack, (1982).

Embracing the Marketing Concept

The degree to which firms of Professional Accountants were committed to the overall concept of Marketing, (in spite of the fact that they were having negative attitude towards the word marketing: and advertising /sales promotion as marketing activities being banned in their profession an indirect question was asked to bring out the same from the professional firms of chartered accountants. Unconsciously these firms covered were found to be performing a number of activities, which truly qualified them to be having a Marketing Orientation. 50% commitments to the 23 marketing practices marketing namely (i) service offerings

(ii) communication, (iii) place location, (iv) fee structure, (v) Market (vi) Clients-orientation, was found among the professional Accountants Firms. Like 80% of the firms reported periodically re-examining the service offered and determine which new services to offer. Around 89% of the firms reported having regularly evaluating fee policies and 95% approx. Reported to have regularly evaluated client needs. 80% of the firms were also conscious of the needs for training and motivating firm members for showing courteous attitudes towards clients. 98% of the firms reported having their all activities coordinated to provide customer satisfaction.

Although all these activities brought above were being reported to be performed by the professional firms of the accountants however not in a formal manner. Here the observation of Markin (1982) may be taken note of according to whom "the future of service marketing will surely see a more pronounced tendency towards the increased use of marketing in a wide range of professional service organizations as professionals not longer simply equate marketing with selling and are reconsidering the promotions of their codes of ethics"

Recommendations

The professionals need to embrace marketing concept in their practice or management as also suggested by Mahon (1978), wheatly (1983), Kotler & Bloom (1983), Denney (1983), Markin (1979) Kotler & Connor (1977), Kotler (1980), Helgeson, (1987), Gummesson (1977).

Change in Practicing Environment

Majority respondent firms reported having felt changes in the practicing scene and environment. They were of the opinion that what environment existed at the time of starting their practice was not the same as of today. So to say that changes in environment have come and are more pronounced for young members of profession, and less for experienced one's will be wrong. It was equal for all changes that had come in the practicing scene were enumerated like:

1. Clients have become more demanding.

2. Client have become be informed. So engages in shopping around.
3. Tax laws have changed.
4. Downtrend of the profession is there because of the practice of fee cutting and commission tactics.
5. Technological shits have called for professionals to up date their knowledge.
6. Personal attention to clients have become more demanding because of compliant base for each professional has become limited.
7. Accountants are not rendering their professional services but are doing liason job between various government agencies and the client.
8. Work culture has changed.
9. Sincerity towards profession has decreased.

Recommendation

1. The professional accountants have to keep pace with these changes in he environment by remaining with in their professional code of conduct and constantly doing situational/environmental Analysis-to keep abreast of changes in the environment.

2. Further the professional Accountants also needs to be dynamic in their approach by keeping sight of client needs and wants. This and only this approach can guarantee success to time. Studies supporting the results are:

Mahon (1978), Wheatley (1983), Kotler & Connor (1977), Turner (1969); Kotler & Bloom (1983), Denney (1983), and Gummesson (1979).

Perceived Importance of Chartered Accountants Selection Criteria

93% of the professional Accountants perceived that "quality of work/Advising capacity was the most important criteria which clients use in their selection being ranked at No. 1 followed with such factors like technical competence of the firm at rank 3, Experience year in practice at rank 4 and so on, as can be seen from the results of the study. Spearman rank order correlation co-efficient test performed at a later stage (Client survey part) showed a high degree of similarity between selection criteria that consumers report using and those that accountants perceive their clients to be using with value.

Thus the factors, which are of importance from the professional's point of view to ensure them client - centeredness is the real understanding of the importance of 4 ps as brought out below:

1. (p):- People: Professional services are performed by people, for people and therefore there is a need for client - orientation.

2. (p):- Product Service offerings: Tangibalizing the intangible 'components of services like competence, quality, integrity, promptness etc. to gain client visibility. Also included is the control of services from clients angle.

3. (p):- Processes: It includes how of service delivery. Here good manners, qualified staff, facilities and equipments to discharge the services have to be there.

4. (p):- Physical Evidences: The importance of atmosphere and collateral appearance - like furnishing, light and sound, dress etc. in the performance of professional services.

Lesser Importance be given to following 3p's:

5. (p):- Price: (Fee charged: They are immaterial in the light of above 4 p.s. but still Genuine fees be charged, with scope for negotiations.

6. (p):- Place (Location): Location is immaterial. So professionals can be established at far off place. But still as far as possible. Location be accessible and convenient to reach, with adequate parking facility.

7. (p):- Promotions: (Advertising, and other forms): The best form can be Personal Contact or personal Recommendations.

The adoption of this expanded marketing mix will result in considerable satisfaction of the clients for the professional services.

Recommendations for Professionals

There is a need to adopt this revised marketing mix comprising of 7 p's by chartered Accountants to become market oriented and to ensure long term client satisfaction. The same observation has been made in the studies by Cowell (1984), McDonald & Gattorna (1980), Thomas (1978), Langeard, Bateson, Lovelock and Eiglier (1981), Borden (1965), Kotler (1975), Booms & Bitner (1981): and Davidson, (1978).

Suggestions given by Professional Accountants

The suggestions were aimed at both the Institute side as well as towards their fellow professionals:

Role of Institute is improving the practicing scene: -

1) Minimum fees to recommended below which no Auditing work be accepted depending on the number of partners in the firm.

2) Allocation of Audit work be made through rotation, so that even the junior members in practice could avail of the opportunity rather than being monopolized by select few experienced or influential ones. Govt. Audit and other work be uniformly distributed among members of profession.

3) Institute should also see that professional Accountants in service be not allowed part-time practice instead, non-practicing allowance be recommended.

4) Before giving certificate of practice (COP), experience certificate from qualified C.A. from where he has taken training be asked to ensure that non-competent C.A. may not join the practice.

5) Regular changes in course curriculum of Institute of Chartered Accountants of India, Visakhapatnam is there.

6) So, far, only Pvt. Ltd. Companies are having statutory Audit, therefore, recommending to the Govt. to make statutory Audit of the partnership firms as compulsory, can provide further extension of opportunities for the C.A. in practice.

7) Constant follow-ups be there on the part of institute to better ensure that professionals in practice stick to code of conduct.

Other suggestions related with fellow Professionals were:

1. Training be imparted to article clerks be modified and upgraded to meet with the changing environments.
2. C.A. with good financial background and family status should only join practice to ensure early success.
3. New entrants to practice to ensure who are under-employed can take up other lines of practice time those of
   a. Hire-purchase financing.
   b. Consultancy
   c. Specialized management Audit and the like.
4. Increase in Ability and competence on the part of professionals be there.
5. Regular updating of knowledge should be a necessary on their part rather than a consideration.
6. Sanctity of the profession is maintained by adopting ethical means in practice development.
7. Unethical and unjust bowing before clients be avoided to maintain the sanctity and reputation of the profession.

Overview

The professional firms of Accountants have to meet the challenges of marketing professional services. These professional firms of Chartered Accountants must be increasingly marketing oriented in the future and be aware of the changes that are taking place in the professional practice scene. Their future success and well-being will largely be a function of their understanding of clients needs and embracing. Marketing concepts, as has been brought about in the foregoing discussion. The success brought about by the adoption of such marketing concept can be evaluated by cases, earning billings or expected profit of the professionals. So need for marketing of professional Accounting services in today and tomorrow's changing environment social, economic, technological, competitive etc. can not be consideration on the part of professionals but becomes of necessity as brought about in foregoing discussion. How to adopt such marketing -orientation in their need to bring desired satisfaction to their clients had also been discussed at length in the foregoing paragraphs.

Though the idea of marketing professional services may still be debatable in India yet many changes in the environment as already highlighted in the study call forth a timely recognition of applying marketing approach to the services provided by professional chartered accountants. In other words, a proactive rather than reactive approach to professional services scene in future is advocated.

6

Results of Clients' Survey

The first part of the questionnaire was related with the Personal Data - to find out the type of client - user or non-user, its specific type, and their income range to be of user in experimental data part:

Type	*Users*	*Non users*
Professional services of CA Firms	200	200

Sampling was done in such a manner that there be 200 users and 200 non-users of professional services.

For knowing the specific type (of these clients, both users and Non users of the services of CA, respondents were asked to indicate their nature of ticking the options given. Space was provided for respondents to enter any other not highlighted in the list of options given.

Table 6.1: Classification of users and Non-users of Professional Accountants according to the nature of Business

Individual Clients

Individual Clients	*Users*	*Nonusers*
Contractors	4	7
Transporters	8	12
Retailers	38	34
Retailers	38	34
Agency Holders	9	4
Personal Services	11	18
Schools/Colleges	10	19
Financiers	4	3
Lodging Places/Hotels	10	7
	94	104

2. Institutional Clients

Institutional Clients	*Users*	*Non-users*
manufacturing Organizations	58	30
Commercial Firms	8	10
Exporters	6	8
Brokerage Firms	4	6
Business Services Firms	12	18
	88	72

3. Other Professionals

Other Professionals	*Users*	*Non-Users*
Doctors	10	12
Engineers	5	7
Architects	3	5
Total	18	24

The above table clearly shows that among users and Non-Users of Professional Services of Accountant/CA Firms, three type of respondent groups were there:

- Individual Clients,
- Institutional Clients
- Other professionals.

Among users category, the distribution of 200 respondents were like individual clients being 94 in number, Institutional clients being 88 and other professionals being (18) in number. Similarly, in the non-users category, 200 respondents were distributed as; 104 individual respondents, 72 Institutional respondents, and 24 other professionals. In both the categories of Users and non-Users, the individual respondents included were such individuals like contractors, transporters, Retailers, Agency Holders, discharger of personal services like Beauty Saloons, Dry cleaners etc. Financers, owners of lodging places etc.; whereas the Institutions/Organizations covered ranged from the Manufacturing Organizations. Commercial firms, like publishing Houses etc.; and other professionals included Doctors, Engineers/ valuers, and Architects.

Classification of Respondents according to their income range and their Nature

The above Table 6.2 clearly depicts the distribution of respondents according to the respective income range. Among individual respondent in the users (user of professional services of CA) category, out of the total of 94,82 belonged to income range of Rs. 80,000/- and above and for balance 12 individuals the same was not declared; while in the non-users category the distribution was like, 58 were belonging to income range of less than Rs. 20,000/-, 18 were in the range of Rs. 20,000/- but less than 50,000/- 4 belonged to the class of Rs. 50,000/- but less than 80,000/- and for the balance 24 individuals the same was not declared. Similarly, in the case of Institutional clients, the income distribution pattern in the Users category was like, all 88 respondents belonged to income class of Rs. 80,000/- and above, while for non-users category out of 72 types of organizations covered, 14 belonged to Income range of less than Rs. 20,000/- 22 belonged to the range of Rs. 20,000/- but less than Rs. 50,000/-, 24 belonged to income class of Rs. 50,000/- but less than Rs. 80,000/- and for the balance 12 the same was not declared.

Table 6.2: Income range of the various respondents

S.No.	*Annual Revenue*	*1. User*	*1 non-user*	*2 user*	*2non user*	*3. user*	*3 non user*
1	Less than 20,000	Nil	58	Nil	14	Nil	4
2	Rs. 20,000-50,000	Nil	18	Nil	22	Nil	4
3	Rs. 50,000-80,000	Nil	4	Nil	24	Nil	4
4	80,000 & above	82	Nil	88	Nil	16	Nil
5	Not Available	12	24	Nil	12	2	8

1 = INDIVIDUAL USER

2 = INSTITUTIONAL USER

3 = OTHER PROFESSIONALS

In case of other professionals out of 18 users of CA services, 16 were belonging to the range of Rs. 80,000/- and above and for 2, the same was not declared; while for 24 non-users, the picture was much different with 4 belonging to the class of less than Rs. 20,000/- 8 in the income range of Rs. 20,000/- but less than Rs. 50,000/- and for the balance 8, the income was not disclosed.

From the above income distribution pattern of the various respondents, it can be concluded that people /organizations who were using the services of professional Accountants were most often people/organizations with higher incomes, ranging from Rs. 80,000/- and above. Thus the usage of Accountancy services by individual's organizations /professionals was positively related to their income range.

To learn from the users of professional accountant's the nature of services for which they were being hired, an open ended question was asked in which the respondents were asked to specify the nature of services for which professional Accountants were being hired.

Table 6.3 showed that among individual clients Institutional clients and other professionals; Auditing and taxation services computed majority of the requirement for which professional Accountant were hired. In case of individual clients and time services were patronized by 88 (93.62%) respondents for taxation purpose by 92 (97.87%) individuals while in the case of Institutional clients 88(100%) were using professional accountants for Auditing as well as taxation purpose and in case of other professionals in the picture was different with 6(33.33%)respondents using Auditing services and majority 12(66.67%) using the services of Professional Accountant for taxation purpose. On the total, 182(91%) users were found hiring the CA's for Auditing requirement and 192(96%) for taxation purpose.

Other type of services for which Professional Accountants were hired were principally by Institutional clients for their requirements in Management services area with 22(25%) opting for it; secretarial and company Affairs with 28(31.82%) respondents; other miscellaneous needs of Estate Planning, EDP etc. by 14(15.9%0 respondents. However, 20(21.28%) individuals also went in for hiring CA services for secretarial and company affairs purpose.

Thus it can be concluded from above that the most important fields of professional work for which users hired professional accountants comprised of Auditing and tax Representation. Other growing fields of Professional work where their importance had

Table 6. 3: Clients needs (users) for professional Services for which the Professional Accountants were hired

S.No.	*Nature of Services*	*IC*	*IC per*	*Inst CLI*	*Inst CLI Per*	*Op*	*Op Per*
1	Auditing	88	94	88	100	6	33
2	Taxation	92	98	88	100	12	67
3	Management services	Nil	Nil	22	25	Nil	Nil
4	Secretarial service	20	21	28	32	Nil	Nil
5	Information systems Audit	Nil	Nil	Nil	Nil	Nil	
6	Miscellaneous	8	9	14	16	Nil	Nil

Note:

IC = INDIVIDUAL CLIENTS

IC PER= INDIVIDUAL CLIENTS PERCENTAGE

INST CLI = INSTITUTIONAL CLIENTS

INST CLI PER = INSTITUTIONAL CLIENTS PERCENTAGE

OP = OTHER PROFESSIONALS

OP PER =OTHER PROFESSIONALS PERCENTAGE.

started being realized are the areas of Management Services, Secretarial and Company affairs, Estate Planning, handling NRI's Foreign Nationals/Firms Liason work in India and the like. This finding is very much in accordance with the belief that "the main and the most well-known role of a Charted Accountant is the a tested function incase of Auditing, which is the very lifeline or the backbone of corporate organization of business.

Rate the tactics on the basis of your perceived importance as used by professionals

Question No 4 is asked to find out the perceived importance of the tactics as used by professionals and the client's view of the important tactics that attracts them towards a professional. Every successful professional is successful because his clients like him. The response to this question gives a clue of the variables that are felt as most important traits exhibited by a professional.

Table 6.4.1: Importance of the type of Tactics as perceived by Users of Individual Clients

Professionals tactics while Interacting with	*EXT IMP*	*Very Imp*	*Some What*	*Not Important Desirable*	*Un But*	*Total Imp*
Accountant Fixing an appointment With you	40	40	12	2	0	400
Giving an immediate Response to your Need	94	0	0	0	0	470
Dressing sense of the professional	0	14	80	0	0	296
A neat office environment of Professional	24	30	40	0	0	360
Asking Right Questions (** ???***)	20	170	8	0	0	804
Explaning the Accounting Jargon to you	10	80	4	0	0	382
To Spend more time Listening to You than otherwise	0	24	30	40	0	266
Trying to understand what you need	90	2	2	0	0	464
Providing Right Solutions	92	2	0	0	0	470
Taking regular feedback from You	0	0	20	74	0	208
Show Body Language that indicates concern for You	5	30	50	9	0	313
Provide information freely on other services Provided	0	6	40	40	8	232
Always saying the Price clearly	94	0	0	0	0	470
Professional Asking Referrals	0	0	0	0	94	94
Professional's Business Card Quality	14	30	50	0	0	340

- Extremely important(EXT IMP) =5
- Very important = 4
- Somewhat important =3
- Not important but desirable
- Unimportant -=1 Total number of Respondents = 94

Q.No 4 is an importance scale which lists down the tactics as used by a professional. The scale is rated with 5 being extremely important and 1 being unimportant. The data that will be a result of this question will be further split according to the status of the user (user/ non-user) as their choice of importance might vary. The Researcher is very keen to find out the difference in user and nonuser's perception of the importance.

Based on the responses given by the respondents who are individual clients, institutional clients and other professionals, the data is compiled according to the user status (user/ non user). Mean ratings are computed to find out the difference between clients (both users and non-users) perception and professionals perception. Professionals were also asked the same question which is tabulated in table 4.6 in chapter 4.

The total number of respondents in each case is considered with the responses given and mean rating is subsequently computed. The tables concerning the users and non users of all the individual clients, institutional clients and other professionals are given next.

Based on the option ticked by the respondents, the weights are assigned accordingly.

- Extremely important = 5
- very important =4
- somewhat important=3
- Not important but desirable =2
- unimportant =1

Basing on this, the weights are calculated accordingly.

All the values in the comparison of the individual clients rating with professional rating clearly indicate negative figures except about two tactics i.e. taking feedback and asking for referrals. This shows that the professional is not able to meet up to the expected tactic levels of clients. There is a huge gap in all the dimensions taken by the researcher between the individual clients and professionals. Especially regarding the asking of questions, as the professionals method of asking right questions will help the client in responding accordingly. The researcher is interested to know if there is any correlation between perception of professional towards professional tactics and the expected performance of professional tactics.

Table 6.4.2: Comparison of Mean Ratings of the type of Tactics as Perceived by Users who are individual clients with professional perceived mean rating

Professionals tactics while Interacting with Client	*CMR*	*PMR*	*Difference*
Accountant Fixing an appointment with you	4.26	1.93	-2.33
Giving an immediate Response to your need	5.00	4.17	-0.83
Dressing sense of the professional	3.15	2.80	-0.35
A neat office environment of Professional	3.83	2.53	-1.30
Asking Right Questions (***???***)	8.55	4.26	-4.29
Explaining the Accounting Jargon to you	4.06	1.20	-2.86
To Spendmore time Listening to you than otherwise	2.83	1.886	-0.97
Trying to understand what you need	4.94	1.80	-3.14
Providing Rights Solutions	5.0	3.36	-1.64
Taking regular feedback from you	3.33	1.06	-2.27
Provide information freely on other services Provided	2.47	1.96	-0.51
Always saying the Price clearly	5.00	4.86	-0.14
Professional Asking Referrals	1.00	1.93	0.93
Professional's Business Card quality	3.62	1.66	-1.96

Note: Mean rating is calculated by the total importance scale of an attribute divided by number of respondents.

Overall experience = perceived levels- expected level

(N=94)

This has been tested separately for all the different types of clients, individual, institutional and other professionals(both users and non-users)

Table 6.4.3: Rank Correlation of Professional and Individual Clients (Users)

S.no.	*Professionals tactics while interacting with client*	*PT weig1ht Imp*	*Ind CLI WEI*	*R1*	*R2*	*d=R1 R2*	*d2*
1.	Fixing Appointment s with Prospective Clients	290.00	400.00	11	6	5	25
2.	Responding to new and existing clients immediately	290.00	470.00	11	3	8	64
3.	Trying to dress Neeatly	420.00	296.00	6	11	-5	25
4.	Keeping the Office clean	380.00	360.00	7	8	-1	1
5.	Asking Right Questoins	640.00	804.00	2	1	1	1
6.	Explaining the Accounting Jargon to Clients	180.00	382.00	14	7	7	49
7.	To Spend more time Listening to Client than otherwise	360.00	266.00	8	12	-4	16
8.	Trying to understand what clients need	630.00	464.00	3	5	-2	4
9.	Solving the problems of clients	505.00	470.00	4	3	1	1
10.	Taking regular feed-back from clients	440.00	208.00	5	14	-9	81
11.	Show Body Language that indicates concern for client	160.0	313.00	15	10	5	25
12.	Provide information freely on other services provided	295.00	232.00	9	13	-4	16
13.	Always saying the Price clearly	730.00	470.00	1	3	-2	4
14.	Asking Cliens for Referrals	290.00	94.00	11	15	-4	16
15.	Having Well Designed Business Card	250.00	340.00	13	9	4	16

$$P = 1 - 6\ [\Sigma d^2 + m\ (m2-1)]$$

$$12$$

$$\overline{\qquad\qquad} \text{ where } \Sigma d^2 = 309$$

$$\frac{}{n\ (n^2-1)}$$

$$= 1-6\ [309+2+2]$$

$$15\ (225-1)$$

$$= 1-0.55 = 0.45$$

Since ? =0.86 so there exist positive correlation between individual client users and Professionals regarding the professional tactics to be used during the service encounter or Moments of truth.

Table 6.4.4: Importance of the type of Tactics as Perceived by Non-Users of Individual Clients

Professionals tactics while interacting with client	*Ext Imp*	*Very Imp*	*Some what imp*	*Not imp but desirable*	*Un imp*	*Total*
Accountant Fixing an appointment with you	0	0	0	4	100	108
Giving an immediate response to yourneed	104	0	0	0	0	520
dressing sense of the professional	0	4	20	80	0	236
A neatoffice environment of Professional	24	30	40	10	0	380
Asking Right Question	104	0	0	0	0	520
explaining the Accounting Jargon to you	10	90	4	0	0	422
To Spend more time Listening to You than otherwise	0	0	20	74	10	218
Show Body Language that indicates concern for you	5	40	50	9	0	353
Provide information freely on other services provided	0	16	40	40	8	272
Always saying the price clearly	104	0	0	0	0	520
Professional Asking Referrals	0	0	0	0	104	104
Professional's Business Card Quality	14	30	60	0	0	370

Notes: The procedure mentioned above is repeated here for non-users of individual clients.

N=104

Therefore, it is true that perception of professionals towards the use of professional tactics during service encounter are correlated to the expectations of individual client users towards the same.

Now, the same process that has been followed above is repeated For Non-users of individual clients to prove the same. This is done separately for users and non-users as the researcher felt that users and non-users have different expectations towards the use of professional tactics during the "moments of truth".

Table 6.4.5: Comparison of Mean Ratings of the type of Tactics as Perceived by Non-users who are individual Clients with Professional Perceived mean Rating

Professionals tactics while interacting with client	*CMR*	*PMR*	*DIFF*
Accountant Fixing an appointment with you	1.04	1.93	0.89
Giving an immediate Response to your need	5.00	4.17	-0.83
Dressing sense of the professional	2.27	2.80	0.53
A neat office environemnt of Professional	3.65	2.53	-1.12
Asking Right Questions (***???***)	5.00	4.26	-0.74
Explaining the Accounting Jargon to you	4.06	1.20	-2.86
To Spend more time Listenign to you than otherwise	2.65	1.86	-0.79
Trying to understnad what you need	5.00	1.80	-3.20
Providing Right Solutions	5.00	3.36	-1.54
Taking regular feedback from your	2.10	2.93	0.83
Show Body Language that indicates concern for you	3.39	1.06	-2.33
Provide information freely on other services Provided	2.62	1.96	-0.66
Always saying the Price clearly	5.00	4.86	-0.12
Professional Asking Referrals	1.00	1.93	0.93
professional's Business Card Quality	3.56	1.66	-1.90

N=104. the mean ratings show differences in many areas highlighted above.

Table 6.4.6: Rank Correlation of Individual Clients who are nonusers and Perception of Professionals towards Professional Tactics

SNo	*Professionals tactics while Intarscting with Client*	*PT Weig Imp*	*Non users CLI WEI*	*R1*	*R2*	*d-R1 R2*	*d2*
1.	Fixing Appointments with Prospective Clients	290.00	108.00	11	14	-3	9
2.	Respondin to new and existing clients immediately	290.00	520.00	11	3	8	64
3.	Trying to dress Nealty	420.00	236.00	6	12	-6	36
4.	Keeping the Office clean	380.00	380.00	7	7	0	0
5.	Asking Right Questions (***???***)	640.00	520.00	2	3	-1	1
6.	Explaining the Account Jargon to Clients	180.00	422.00	14	6	8	64
7.	To Spend more time Listening to Client than otherwise	360	276.00	8	10	-2	4
8.	Trying to understand what clients need	630.00	520.00	3	3	0	0
9.	Solving the problems of clients	505.00	520.00	4	3	1	1
10.	Taking regular feedbak from clietns	440.00	218.00	5	13	-8	64
11	Show Body Language that indicates concern for client	160.00	353.00	15	9	6	36
12.	Provide information freely on other services Provided	295.00	272.00	9	11	-2	4
13.	Always saying the Price clearly	730.00	520.00	1	3	-2	4
14.	Asking Clients for Referrals	290.00	104.00	11	15	-4	16
15.	Having well Designed Business Card	250.00	370.00	13	8	5	25
							328.00

$$P = 1 - \frac{6\,[\Sigma d^2 + m\,(m2-1)]}{\frac{12}{n\,(n^2-1)}} \quad \text{where } \Sigma d^2 = 328$$

$$= 1 - \frac{6\,[328+12+2]}{15\,(225-1)}$$

$$= 1 - 0.6107 = 0.38$$

Since ? =0.38 so there exist positive correlation between individual client Non-users and Professionals regarding the professional tactics to be used during the service encounter or Moments of truth.

Table 6.4.7: Importance of the type of Tactics as Perceived by Users of Institutional Clients

S.No.	*Professionals tactics while Interacting with Client*	*Extre mely imp*	*very Imp imp*	*some whatimp*	*Not important but desirable*	*Un imp*	*Total*
1	Accountant Fixing an appointment with you	60	18	10	0	0	402.00
2	Giving an immediate Response to your need	88	0	0	0	0	440.00
3	Dressing sense of the professional	30	38	0	0	0	462.00
4	A neat office environment of Professional	80	8	0	0	0	432.00
5	Asking Right Questions (***???***)	88	0	0	0	0	440.00
6	Explaining the Accounting Jargon to you	0	10	30	48	0	226.00
7	To Spend more time Listening to you than other wise	25	50	18	0	0	379.00
8	Trying tounderstand what you need	88	0	0	0	0	440.00
9	Providing Right Solutions	88	0	0	0	0	440.00
10	Takign regular feedback from you	10	50	28	0	0	334.00
11	Show Body Language that indicates concern for you	0	0	10	30	48	138.00
12.	Provide information freely on other services provided	20	40	18	0	0	314.00
13.	Always saying the Price clearly	0	88	0	0	0	352.00
14.	Professional asking Referrals	0	0	0	80	8	168.00
15.	Professionals Business Card Quality	18	60	10	0	0	360.00

Therefore, it is true that perception of professionals towards the use of professional tactics during service encounter is correlated to the expectations of individual client Non-users towards the same.

Now, the same process is repeated for institutional client users and non-users and professionals.

Table 6.4.8: Comparison of Mean Ratings of the type of Tactics as perceived by Users who are Institutional Clients with Professional Perceived Mean Rating

S.No.	*Professionals tactics while interacting with Client*	*CMR*	*PMR*	*DIFF*
1	Accountant Fixing an appointment with you	4.57	4.17	-2.64
2	Giving an immediate Response to your need	5.00	4.17	-0.83
3	Dressing sense of the professional	4.11	2.80	-1.31
4	A neat office environment of Professional	4.91	2.53	-2.38
5	Asking Right Questions (***???***)	5.00	4.26	-0.74
6	Explaining the Accounting Jargon to you	2.57	1.20	-1.37
7	To Spend more time Listening to you than other wise	4.31	1.86	-2.45
8	Trying tounderstand what you need	5.00	1.80	-3.20
9	Providing Right Solutions	5.00	3.36	-1.64
10	Takign regular feedback from you	3.80	2.93	-0.87
11	Show Body Language that indicates concern for you	1.57	1.06	-0.67
12.	Provide information freely on other services provided	3.57	1.96	-1.67
13.	Always saying the Price clearly	4.00	4.86	0.86
14.	Professional asking Referrals	1.91	1.93	0.02
15.	Professionals Business Card Quality	4.09	1.66	-2.43

Mean ratings again show a difference in various attributes as perceived by professionals and as expected from user(institutional clients).

Table 6.4.9: Correlation between Professionals and Institutonal Client Users

SNo	*Professionals tactics while Intarscting with Client*	*PT Weig Imp*	*Non users CLI WEI*	*R1*	*R2*	*d-R1 R2*	*d2*
1.	Fixing Appointments with Prospective Clients	290.00	402.00	11	6.0	5	25
2.	Respondin to new and existing clients immediately	290.00	440.00	11	2.5	9	72
3.	Trying to dress Nealty	420.00	362.00	6	8.0	-2	4
4.	Keeping the Office clean	380.00	432.00	7	5.0	2	4
5.	Asking Right Questions (***???***)	640.00	440.00	2	2.5	-1	1
6.	Explaining the Account Jargon to Clients	180.00	226.00	14	13.0	1	1
7.	To Spend more time Listening to Client than otherwise	360	379.00	8	7.0	1	1
8.	Trying to understand what clients need	630.00	440.00	3	2.5	1	0
9.	Solving the problems of clients	505.00	440.00	4	2.5	2	2
10.	Taking regular feedbak from clietns	440.00	334.00	511.0	-6	6	36
11	Show Body Language that indicates concern for client	160.00	138.00	15	15.	0	0
12.	Provide information freely on other services Provided	295.00	314.00	9	12.0	-3	9
13.	Always saying the Price clearly	730.00	352.00	1	11.0	-9	81
14.	Asking Clients for Referrals	290.00	168.00	11	14.0	-3	9
15.	Having well Designed Business Card	250.00	360.00	13	9.0	4	16
							261.00

P = 1– 6 [Σd² + m (m²–1)]

12

——————— where $\Sigma d^2 = 261$

n (n²–1)

= 1–6 [261+5+2]

15 (225–1)

= 1–0.478 = 0.522

Since ? =0.522 so there exist positive correlation between institutional client users and Professionals regarding the professional tactics to be used during the service encounter or Moments of truth.

Therefore, it is true that perception of professionals towards the use of professional tactics during service encounter is correlated to the expectations of institutional client users towards the same.

The same procedure followed above is now again repeated for the institutional client nonusers and professionals.

Table 6.4.10: Importance of the Type of Tactics as Perceived by Non-Users of Insitutional Clients

Professionals tactics while Interacting with	*EXT IMP*	*Very Imp*	*Some What*	*Not Important Desirable*	*Un But*	*Total Imp*
Accountant Fixing an appointment with you	0	0	0	60	12	132.00
Giving an immediate Response to your Need	72	0	0	0	0	360.00
Dressing sense of the professional	0	38	20	14	0	240.00
A neat office environment of Professional	20	30	22	0	0	286.00
Asking Right Questions (** ???***)	72	0	0	0	0	360.00
Explaning the Accounting Jargon to you	5	60	7	0	0	286.00
To Spend more time Listening to You than otherwise	12	50	10	0	0	290.00
Trying to understand what you need	72	0	0	0	0	360.00
Providing Right Solutions	72	0	0	0	0	360.00

Taking regular feedback from You	0	10	30	30	30	126.00
Show Body Language that indicates concern for You	0	0	12	30	30	126.00
Provide information freely on other services Provided	10	20	42	0	0	256.00
Always saying the Price clearly	0	72	0	0	0	288.00
Professional Asking Referrals	0	0	0	70	2	142.00
Professional's Business Card Quality	10	60	2	0	0	296.00

Table 6.4.11: Comparison of Mean Ratings of the type of Tactics as Perceived by Non-users who are Intitutional Clients with Professional Perceived Mean Rating

S.No.	*Professionals tactics while interacting with Client*	*CMR*	*PMR*	*DIFF*
1	Accountant Fixing an appointment with you	1.83	1.93	0.10
2	Giving an immediate Response to your need	5.00	4.17	-0.83
3	Dressing sense of the professional	3.33	2.80	-0.63
4	A neat office environment of Professional	3.97	2.53	-1.44
5	Asking Right Questions	5.00	4.26	-0.74
6	Explaining the Accounting Jargon to you	4.03	1.86	-0.17
7	To Spend more time Listening to you than other wise	5.00	1.80	-3.20
8	Trying tounderstand what you need	5.00	1.80	-3.20
9	Providing Right Solutions	5.00	3.36	-0.89
10	Takign regular feedback from you	2.67	2.93	-0.26
11	Show Body Language that indicates concern for you	1.75	1.06	-0.69
12.	Provide information freely on other services provided	3.56	1.96	-1.60
13.	Always saying the Price clearly	4.00	4.86	0.86
14.	Professional asking Referrals	1.97	1.93	0.04
15.	Professionals Business Card Quality	4.11	1.66	-2.45

Table 6.4.12: Rank Correlation for the above

SNo	Professionals tactics while Intarscting with Client	PT Weig Imp	Non users CLI WEI	R1	R2	d-R1 R2	d2
1.	Fixing Appointments with Prospective Clients	290.00	132.00	11	14.0	-3	9
2.	Respondin to new and existing clients immediately	290.00	360	11	2.5	9	72
3.	Trying to dress Nealty	420.00	240	6	11.0	-5	25
4.	Keeping the Office clean	380.00	286.00	7	8.5	-2	2
5.	Asking Right Questions	640.00	360.00	2	2.5	-1	0
6.	Explaining the Account Jargon to Clients	180.00	286.0	14	8.5	6	30
7.	To Spend more time Listening to Client than otherwise	360	290	8	6.0	2	4
8.	Trying to understand what clients need	630.00	360.00	3	2.5	1	0
9.	Solving the problems of clients	505.00	360	4	2.5	2	2
10.	Taking regular feedbak from clietns	440.00	192.00	5	12.0	-7	49
11	Show Body Language that indicates concern for client	160.00	126.00	15	15.0	0	0
12.	Provide information freely on other services Provided	295.00	256.00	9	10.0	-1	1
13.	Always saying the Price clearly	730.00	288.00	1	7.0	-6	36
14.	Asking Clients for Referrals	290.00	142.00	11	13.0	-2	4
15.	Having well Designed Business Card	250.00	296.00	13	5.0	8	64
							299.00

$$P = 1 - \frac{6\,[\Sigma d^2 + m\,(m^2-1)]\quad 12}{n\,(n^2-1)} \quad \text{where } \Sigma d^2 = 299.50$$

$$= 1 - \frac{6\,[299.50+5+0.522]}{15\,(225-1)}$$

$$= 1-0.5482 = 0.4518$$

Since ? =0.4518 so there exist positive correlation between institutional client Non-users and Professionals regarding the professional tactics to be used during the service encounter or Moments of truth.

Therefore, it is true that perception of professionals towards the use of professional tactics during service encounter is correlated to the expectations of institutional client Non users as well towards the same.

Table 6.4.12: Importance of the type of tactics as perceived by users who are users (other professionals) with professional perceived mean rating

Professionals tactics while Interacting with	*EXT IMP*	*Very Imp*	*Some What Imp*	*Not Important Desirable*	*Un Imp*	*Total*
Accountant Fixing an appointment With you	0	18	0	0	0	72
Giving an immediate Response to your Need	18	0	0	0	0	90
Dressing sense of the professional	4	14	0	0	0	76
A neat office environment of Professional	0	14	4	0	0	68
Asking Right Questions	18	0	0	0	0	90
Explaning the Accounting Jargon to you	0	14	4	0	0	68
To Spend more time Listening to You than otherwise	0	0	14	8	0	58
Trying to understand what you need	18	0	0	0	0	90
Providing Right Solutions	18	0	0	0	0	90
Taking regular feedback from You	0	0	16	2	0	52
Show Body Language that indicates concern for You	0	3	15	0	0	57
Provide information freely on other services Provided	0	0	18	0	8	62
Always saying the Price clearly	18	0	0	0	0	90
Professional Asking Referrals	0	0	0	0	18	18
Professional's Business Card Quality	0	13	5	0	0	67

Now the procedure is used for finding out regarding the other professionals as well. The same one mentioned above is followed for this.

Mean ratings: except in one variable in all the rest there is a difference in perception between professionals and clients who are professionals.

Table 6.1.13: Comparison of mean ratings of the type of Tactics as Perceived by Users (other Professionals) Who are other Professionals with Professional Perceived Mean Rating

S.No.	*Professionals tactics while interacting with Client*	*CMR*	*PMR*	*DIFF*
1	Accountant Fixing an appointment with you	4.00	1.93	-2.02
2	Giving an immediate Response to your need	5.00	4.17	-0.83
3	Dressing sense of the professional	4.22	2.80	-1.42
4	A neat office environment of Professional	3.78	2.53	-1.25
5	Asking Right Questions	5.00	4.26	-0.75
6	Explaining the Accounting Jargon to you	3.78	1.20	-2.58
7	To Spend more time Listening to you than other wise	3.22	1.86	-1.36
8	Trying tounderstand what you need	5.00	1.80	-3.20
9	Providing Right Solutions	5.00	3.36	-1.61
10	Taking regular feedback from you	2.89	2.93	0.04
11	Show Body Language that indicates concern for you	3.17	1.06	-2.17
12.	Provide information freely on other services provided	3.44	1.96	-0.48
13.	Always saying the Price clearly	5.00	4.86	-0.48
14.	Professional asking Referrals	1.00	1.93	0.93
15.	Professionals Business Card Quality	3.72	1.66	-2.06

Table 6.4.14: Rank Correlation between other Professionals and Professionals

SNo	*Professionals tactics while Intarscting with Client*	*PT weight Imp*	*Users Other Proof*	*R1*	*R2*	*d-R1*	*d2*
1	Fixing Appointments with Prospective Clients	290.00	72.00	11	7.0	4	16
2	Responding to new and existing clients Immediately	290.00	90.00	11	3.0	8	64
3	Trying to dress Neatly	420.00	76.00	6	6.0	0	0
4	Keeping the Office clean	380.00	68.00	7	8.5	-2	2
5	Asking Right Questions	640.00	90.00	2	3.0	-1	1
6	Explaining the Accounting Jargon to Clients	180.00	68.00	14	8.5	6	30
7	To Spend more time Listening to Client than otherwise	360.00	58.00	8	12.0	-4	16
8	Trying to understand what clients need	630.00	90.00	3	3.0	0	0
9	Solving the problems of clients	505.00	90.00	4	3.0	1	1
10	Taking regular feedback from clients	440.00	52.00	5	14.0	-9	81
11	Show Body Language that indicates concern for client	160.00	57.00	15	13.0	2	4
12	Provide information freely on other services Provided	295.00	62.00	9	11.0	-2	4
13	Always saying the Price clearly	730.00	90.00	1	3.0	-2	4
14	Asking Clients for Referrals	290.00	18.00	11	15.0	-4	16
15	Having Well Designed Business Card	250.00	67.00	13	10.0	3	9
							248.50

$$P = 1 - \frac{6\,[\Sigma d^2 + m\,(m^2-1)]}{12} \over n\,(n^2-1)$$ where $\Sigma d^2 = 248.50$

$$= \frac{1-6\,[248.50+10+0.5+2]}{15\,(225-1)}$$

$$= 1-0.56 = 0.54$$

Since ? =0.54 so there exist positive correlation between other professional users and Professionals regarding the professional tactics to be used during the service encounter or Moments of truth.

Table 6.4.15: Importance of the type of Tactics as Perceived by Non-users (Other Professionas) who are other Professionals with Professional Perceived Mean Rating

Professionals tactics while Interacting with	*EXT IMP*	*Very Imp*	*Some What Imp*	*Not Important Desirable*	*Un Imp*	*Total*
Accountant Fixing an appointment With you	0	15	9	0	0	87
Giving an immediate Response to your Need	24	0	0	0	0	120
Dressing sense of the professional	0	14	10	0	0	86
A neat office environment of Professional	0	20	4	0	0	92
Asking Right Questions	10	14	0	0	0	106
Explaning the Accounting Jargon to you	10	14	0	0	0	106
To Spend more time Listening to You than otherwise	0	10	14	0	0	82
Trying to understand what you need	24	0	0	0	0	120
Providing Right Solutions	24	0	0	0	0	120
Taking regular feedback from You	0	4	20	2	0	76
Show Body Language that indicates concern for You	0	20	4	0	0	92
Provide information freely on other services Provided	0	15	9	0	8	87
Always saying the Price clearly	24	0	0	0	0	120
Professional Asking Referrals	0	0	0	0	24	24
Professional's Business Card Quality	4	20	0	0	0	100

Therefore, it is true that perception of professionals towards the use of professional tactics during service encounter is correlated to the expectations of other professionals who are users as well towards the same.

Now the procedure is repeated for other professional nonusers and professionals. The important criteria for the researcher in finding the correlation is to check if each type of user is looking out for various factors while interacting with client and is there any correlation between the perception of professional and the other clients.

Keeping this motive in mind, the researcher has taken this approach to find out the extent of correlation between different types of clients and professionals.

Table 6.4.16: Comparison of the mean of the type of Tactics as Perceived by Non-users in Other Professionals with the Professionals Perception

Professionals tactics while interacting with Client	*CMR*	*PMR*	*DIFF*
Accountant Fixing an appointment with you	3.63	1.93	-0.70
Giving an immediate Response to your need	5.00	4.17	-0.83
Dressing sense of the professional	3.58	2.80	-0.78
A neat office environment of Professional	3.83	2.53	-1.30
Asking Right Questions	4.42	4.26	-0.16
Explaining the Accounting Jargon to you	4.42	1.20	-3.22
To Spend more time Listening to you than other wise	3.42	1.86	-1.56
Trying tounderstand what you need	5.00	1.80	-3.20
Providing Right Solutions	5.00	3.36	-1.84
Taking regular feedback from you	3.17	2.93	-0.24
Show Body Language that indicates concern for you	3.83	1.06	-2.77
Provide information freely on other services provided	3.63	1.96	-1.67
Always saying the Price clearly	5.00	4.86	-0.14
Professional asking Referrals	1.00	1.93	0.93

DIFF = CMR- PMR (CLIENT MEAN RATING- PROFESSIONALS MEAN RATING)

Mean ratings again indicate variations in perception and expectations between other professionals and professionals.

Table 6.4.17: Rank Correlation between other Professional Clients who are nonusers and Professionals

S.No	*Professionals tactics while Interacting with Client*	*PT*	*Non*	*R1*	*R2*	*d=R1-R2*	*d2*
1	Fixing Appointments with Prospective Clients	290.00	87.00	11	10.5	1	0
2	Responding to new and existing clients Immediately	290.00	120.00	11	2.5	9	72
3	Trying to dress Neatly	420.00	86.00	6	12.0	-6	36
4	Keeping the Office clean	380.00	92.00	7	8.5	-2	2
5	Asking Right Questions	640.00	106.00	2	5.5	-4	12
6	Explaning the Accounting Jargon to Clients	180.00	106.00	14	5.5	9	72
7	To Spend more time Listening to Client than otherwise	360.00	82.00	8	13.0	-5	25
8	Trying to understand what clients need	630.00	120.00	3	2.5	1	0
9	Solving the problems of clients	505.00	120.00	4	2.5	2	2
10	Taking regular feedback from clients	440.00	76.00	5	14.0	-9	81
11	Show Body Language that indicates concern for client	160.00	92.00	15	8.5	7	42
12	Provide information freely on other services Provided	295.00	87.00	9	10.5	-2	2
13	Always saying the Price clearly	730.00	120.00	1	2.5	-2	2
14	Asking Clients for Referrals	290.00	24.00	11	15.0	-4	16
15	Having Well Designed Business Card	250.00	100.00	13	7.0	6	36

Table 6.5.1: Expected Service Levels by Individual Clients

S.No.	*Type of Service*	*1*	*2*	*3*	*4*	*5*	*6*	*7*	*Expected quality scores*	*Mean Rating*
1	Have up to date Equipment	0	0	0	2	40	50	2	522	5.55
2	Physical Facilities shoudl be visual appealing	0	0	4	10	20	30	30	542	5.77
3	Employees should be well Dressed	0	0	4	90	0	0	0	372	3.96
4	Appearance of Phy Facilities shluld be kept with service promised	0	0	0	4	30	50	10	536	5.70
5	Will Fulfil promises when professionals promise to do	0	0	0	0	0	0	94	658	7.00
6	When clients have problems firms should be sympathetic & reasouring	0	0	0	0	0	4	90	654	6.96
7	Professionals should be Dependable	0	0	0	0	0	0	94	658	7.00
8	Provide service at the time promised	0	0	0	0	0	0	94	658	7.00
9	Keep Records Accurate	0	0	0	0	0	0	94	658	7.00
10	Professionals shoudl tell clients when work will be completed	0	0	0	0	0	0	94	658	7.00
11	Employees shoudl given prompt service	0	0	0	0	0	0	94	658	7.00
12	Professionals should always be willing to help clients	0	0	0	0	0	0	94	658	7.00

13	Professionals are never too tired to respond to you	0	0	0	0	0	0	94	658	7.00
14	Professionals should instill confidence in clients	0	0	0	0	0	0	94	658	7.00
15	You will feel safe in their transactions	0	0	0	0	0	0	94	658	7.00
16	Professionals front office staff should be Polite	0	0	0	4	30	50	10	536	5.70
17	Professional should give adequate support to the office staff	0	0	0	24	10	10	20	346	3.68
18	Professionals should give Individual attention	0	0	0	0	0	4	90	654	6.96
19	Should have convenient operating hours	0	0	20	10	10	9	45	308	5.55
20	Professionals fron office staff should give personal attention	0	0	0	0	45	40	9	528	5.62
21	Professional should have customers best interests at heart	0	0	0	0	0	4	90	654	6.96
22	Professionals should understnad to your specific needs	0	0	0	0	0	4	90	654	6.96

Table 6.5.2: Perceived Service by Individual Clients

S.No.	*Type of Service*	*1*	*2*	*3*	*4*	*5*	*6*	*7*	*Expected quality scores*	*Mean Rating*
1	Have up to date Equipment	0	48	50	4	0	0	0	262	2.79
2	Physical Facilities shoudl be visual appealing	35	40	19	0	0	0	0	172	1.83
3	Employees should be well Dressed	0	0	34	60	0	0	0	342	3.64
4	Appearance of Phy Facilities shluld be kept with service promised	0	30	30	20	14	0	0	300	3.10
5	Will Fulfil promises when professionals promise to do	0	20	15	30	20	5	4	363	3.86
6	When clients have problems firms should be sympathetic & reasouring	0	80	8	6	0	0	0	208	2.21
7	Professionals should be Dependable	0	0	0	0	34	60	0	530	5.64
8	Provide service at the time promised	0	4	10	60	20	0	0	378	4.02
9	Keep Records Accurate	0	0	0	0	4	90	0	560	5.06
10	Professionals shoudl tell clients when work will be completed	2	2	90	0	0	0	0	276	2.94
11	Employees shoudl given prompt service	90	4	0	0	0	0	0	276	2.94

12	Professionals should always be willing to help clients	0	0	0	60	34	0	0	410	4.36
13	Professionals are never too tired to respond to you	0	20	30	30	10	2	2	326	3.47
14	Professionals should instill confidence in clients	0	0	0	0	0	14	80	644	6.85
15	You will feel safe in their transactions	0	0	0	0	4	10	80	640	6.81
16	Professionals front office staff should be Polite	4	20	70	0	0	0	0	264	2.70
17	Professional should give adequate support to the office staff	0	14	50	30	0	0	0	206	3.17
18	Professionals should give Individual attention	0	0	0	0	40	50	4	528	5.62
19	Should have convenient operating hours	0	0	0	30	14	30	20	510	5.43
20	Professionals fron office staff should give personal attention	0	4	10	30	50	0	0	408	4.34
21	Professional should have customers best interests at heart	0	0	0	0	2	12	80	642	6.8322
22.	Professionals should understnad to your specific needs	10	70	14	0	0	0	0	192	2.04

Since ? =0.3 so there exist positive correlation between other professional Nonusers and Professionals regarding the professional tactics to be used during the service encounter or Moments of truth.

Therefore, it is true that perception of professionals towards the use of professional tactics during service encounter is correlated to the expectations of other professional who are non-users as well towards the same.

Comparision of the Correlation Coefficients between all the Clients and Professionals:

The correlation coefficients of all the clients is as follows

Individual Clients Users and Professionals:	0.45
Individual Clients Nonusers Professionals:	0.38
Intitutional Clients Users and Professionals:	0.522
Institutional Client Nonusers & Professionals :	0.4518
Other Professional Users and Professionals:	0.54
Other Professional Nonusers and Professionals:	0.3

From the data above it can be inferred that there is close relationship between expectations of other professionals who are users and institutional clients who are users.

There is also close relationship between individual client nonusers and professionals and other professional client nonusers and professionals. There fore, it can be deemed to be thought that both the above-mentioned categories show similar expectations towards the service encounter.

It can also be inferred that there is very low positive correlation between individual client non-users and other professionals.

Service Quality as Expected by Clients

Q.No 5 is asked to find out what clients expect while they go through a service encounter. Every client expects a certain level of service from the professional. And most of the times the professional may not be aware of the clients needs, which has been rightly pointed out through the question that has been asked above (q.no4). The response to the question above has shown that in almost many of the areas surveyed, the responses of the clients

Table 6.5.3: Difference in Service Quality with Respect to Individual Clients

S.No.	*Type of Service*	*Perceived Mean*	*Expected Mean*	*DIFF*
1	Have up to date Equipment	2.79	5.55	-2.76
2	Physical Facilities should be visual appealing	1.83	5.77	-3.94
3	Employees should be well Dressed	3.64	3.96	-0.32
4	Appearance of Phy Facilities shluld be kept with service promised	3.19	5.70	-2.51
5	Will Fulfil promises when professionals promise to do	3.86	7.00	-3.14
6	When clients have problems firms should be sympathetic & reasouring	2.21	6.96	-4.73
7	Professionals should be Dependable	5.64	7.00	-1.36
8	Provide service at the time promised	4.02	7.00	-2.98
9	Keep Records Accurate	5.96	7.00	-1.04
10	Professionals should tell clients when work will be completed	2.94	7.00	-4.06
11	Employees should given prompt service	1.04	7.00	-5.96
12	Professionals should always be willing to help clients	4.36	7.00	-2.64
13	Professionals are never too tired to respond to you	3.47	7.00	-3.53
14	Professionals should instill confidence in clients	6.85	7.00	-0.15
15	You will feel safe in their transactions	6.81	7.00	-0.19
16	Professionals front office staff should be Polite	2.70	5.70	-3.00
17	Professional should give adequate support to the office staff	3.17	3.68	-0.51
18	Professionals should give Individual attention	5.62	6.96	-1.34
19	Should have convenient operating hours	5.43	5.55	-0.12
20	Professionals fron office staff should give personal attention	4.34	5.62	-1.28
21	Professional should have customers best interests at heart	6.83	6.96	-0.13
22.	Professionals should understnad to your specific needs	2.04	6.96	-4.92

Table 6.5.4: Expected and perceived service levels of institutional clients

S.No.	*Type of Service*	*1*	*2*	*3*	*4*	*5*	*6*	*7*	*Es*	*EM*
1	Have up to date Equipment	0	0	0	0	0	8	80	608	6.91
2	Physical Facilities should be visual appealing	0	0	0	0	0	18	70	598	6.80
3	Employees should be well Dressed	0	0	0	0	8	20	60	580	6.59
4	Appearance of Phy Facilities shluld be kept with service promised	0	0	0	0	8	50	30	550	6.25
5	Will Fulfil promises when professionals promise to do	0	0	0	0	0	0	88	616	7.00
6	When clients have problems firms should be sympathetic & reasouring	0	0	0	0	0	0	88	616	7.00
7	Professionals should be Dependable	0	0	0	0	0	0	88	616	7.00
8	Provide service at the time promised	0	0	0	0	0	0	88	616	7.00
9	Keep Records Accurate	0	0	0	0	0	0	88	616	7.00
10	Professionals shoudl tell clients when work will be completed	0	0	0	0	0	0	88	616	7.00
11	Employees shoudl given prompt service	0	0	0	0	0	0	88	616	7.00
12	Professionals should always be willing to help clients	0	0	0	0	0	0	88	616	7.00

13	Professionals are never too tired to respond to you	0	0	0	0	0	28	60	588	6.68
14	Professionals should instill confidence in clients	0	0	0	0	0	0	88	616	7.00
15	You will feel safe in their transactions	0	0	0	0	0	0	88	616	7.00
16	Professionals front office staff should s be Polite	0	0	0	0	0	28	60	588	6.68
17	Professional should give adequate support to the office staff	0	0	0	0	0	18	70	598	6.80
18	Professionals should give Individual attention	0	0	0	0	0	0	88	616	7.00
19	Should have convenient operating hours	0	0	0	0	0	0	88	616	7.00
20	Professionals fron office staff should give personal attention	0	0	0	0	0	0	88	616	7.00
21	Professional should have customers best interests at heart	0	0	0	0	0	0	88	616	7.00
22.	Professionals should understnad to your specific needs	0	0	0	0	0	0	88	616	7.00

Table 6.5.5: Perceived Service by Institutional Clients

S.No.	Type of Service	1	2	3	4	5	6	7	Es	EM
1	Have up to date Equipment	0	0	58	8	6	4	12	344	3.91
2	Physical Facilities should be visual appealing	0	30	50	8	0	18	0	242	2.75
3	Employees should be well Dressed	0	0	18	60	10	20	0	344	3.91
4	Appearance of Phy Facilities shluld be kept with service promised	0	18	70	0	0	50	0	246	2.80
5	Will Fulfil promises when professionals promise to do	0	20	8	30	30	0	0	334	3.80
6	When clients have problems firms should be sympathetic & reasouring	0	18	30	40	0	0	0	286	3.25
7	Professionals should be Dependable	0	0	18	20	60	0	0	434	4.93
8	Provide service at the time promised	0	8	30	50	50	0	0	306	3.48
9	Keep Records Accurate	0	0	0	8	40	0	0	452	5.14
10	Professionals shoudl tell clients when work will be completed	0	0	0	30	20	0	4	422	4.80
11	Employees shoudl given prompt service	0	0	0	4	0	20	4	484	5.50
12	Professionals should always be willing to help clients	0	0	0	50	0	4	8	416	4.73
13	Professionals are never too tired to respond to you	0	80	0	0	60	40	0	168	1.91

14	Professionals should instill confidence in clients	0	0	0	0	0	10	8	536	6.09
15	You will feel safe in their transactions	0	0	0	0	60	0	8	476	5,41
16	Professionals front office staff should s be Polite	0	0	0	0	0	80	8	536	6.09
17	Professional should give adequate support to the office staff	0	0	0	0	30	40	18	516	5.86
18	Professionals should give Individual attention	0	0	0	0	20	60	18	586	6.66
19	Should have convenient operating hours	0	0	0	25	23	20	20	4765	5.40
20	Professionals fron office staff should give personal attention	0	0	0	40	28	10	8	416	4.73
21	Professional should have customers best interests at heart	0	0	0	80	8	0	0	360	4.09
22.	Professionals should understnad to your specific needs	0	0	0	0	20	60	8	516	5.86

(only users) has shown that the professional is unaware of the expectations of the customer. Quality of the service is an important dimension of Professional service as, quality is considered as the most right factor for making successful business. The data has been compiled according to the category to which the clients belong(users only). The results of the question are shown in the next page.

Therefore the researcher from the perspective of has observed the concept of service quality:

Users in individual clients (Expected and perceived quality)

Users in institutional clients (Expected and perceived quality)

Users in other professionals.(Expected and perceived quality)

Only users have been selected for this question as, the users of professional services have gone through the "Moments of truth" and will therefore be able to provide the data which will be an unbiased projection of the service quality. Service quality as mentioned in chapter 2, is one of the most research areas in services marketing.

The question is a Likert scale where the respondent has to indicate dimension of service quality on a scale of 1 to 7 with 7 being highest and 1 being lowest. A 22 Dimensional service quality scale has been adapted to find out the quality of services as perceived and expected by Clients (users).

Overall satisfaction score of individual clients =

Total of Mean Rating = -50.44

By calculating the sum of the quality scores, it is evident that the perception of overall service quality by individual users is negative.

The data has been specific only to the clients who are users, as the non-users cannot assess the quality of service as understood through the review of literature.

Therefore by finding out the mean ratings of the individual clients towards service quality, the overall perception of service quality has been proved to be negative. Which may lead to dissatisfaction towards the quality of service received from the professional.

Satisfaction of the clients is very important for the loyalty of the clients and for retention. Therefore, professionals have to make sure that they consider these alternatives while interacting with the client and give an overall delighted service levels to the clients.

The same process is repeated for institutional clients and other professionals as well.

Table 6.5.4 shows the expected and perceived service levels of institutional clients

The researcher is of the opinion that each type of client will have Separate set of needs towards service quality and hence, this form of separate analysis has been chosen. Every type of client may have unique set of needs and therefore, it is to be analyzed whether it is true or not.The perception of the institutional clients towards the service quality exhibited by the professional and the expected service levels are computed in the next page.

The data once gain reveals that the overall satisfaction score towards service is negative. Institutional clients are perceiving that in all the dimensions that have been asked for, there is a huge gap in expected and perceived quality of service levels of the clients.

The overall satisfaction score is -50.60 which shows huge difference between service quality perceptions and service quality expectations

The data extensively reveals that there are high expectations on service quality rendered to institutional clients but the perception of clients towards the service quality is low.

The professionals have to understand the unique set of needs of the institutional clients and thereby offer the benefits to the institutional clients so that they will continue using the services of the professionals without any attrition. Retaining the existing clients and attracting new clients can be done through strong service quality and therefore, it should be in the intent of the professional to do the same to ensure that they provide a better service quality to them.

Table 6.5.6: Difference in Service Qulity with Respect to Institutional Clients

S.No.	*Type of Service*	*Perceived Mean*	*Expected Mean*	*DIFF*
1	Have up to date Equipment	3.91	6.91	-3.00
2	Physical Facilities should be visual appealing	2.75	6.80	-4.05
3	Employees should be well Dressed	3.91	6.59	-2.88
4	Appearance of Phy Facilities shluld be kept with service promised	2.80	6.25	-3.45
5	Will Fulfil promises when professionals promise to do	3.80	7.00	-3.20
6	When clients have problems firms should be sympathetic & reasouring	3.25	7.00	-3.75
7	Professionals should be Dependable	4.93	7.00	-2.07
8	Provide service at the time promised	3.48	7.00	-3.52
9	Keep Records Accurate	5.14	7.00	-1.88
10	Professionals should tell clients when work will be completed	4.80	7.00	-2.20
11	Employees should given prompt service	5.50	7.00	-1.50
12	Professionals should always be willing to help clients	4.73	7.00	-2.27
13	Professionals are never too tired to respond to you	1.91	6.67	-4.76
14	Professionals should instill confidence in clients	6.09	7.00	-0.91
15	You will feel safe in their transactions	5.41	7.00	-1.59
16	Professionals front office staff should be Polite	6.09	6.69	-0.69
17	Professional should give adequate support to the office staff	5.86	6.80	0.36
18	Professionals should give Individual attention	6.66	7.00	-0.34
19	Should have convenient operating hours	5.435.40	7.00	-1.50
20	Professionals fron office staff should give personal attention	4..73	7.00	-2.27
21	Professional should have customers best interests at heart	4.73	7.00	-2.91
22.	Professionals should understnad to your specific needs	5.86	7.00	-1.14

Total of Mean Rating = - 50.60

Table 6.5.7: Expected Service Levels by other Professionals

S.No.	Type of Service	1	2	3	4	5	6	7	ES	EM
1	Have up to date Equipment	0	0	0	10	8	0	0	80	4.44
2	Physical Facilities should be visual appealing	0	0	0	0	12	4	2	98	5.44
3	Employees should be well Dressed	0	0	0	0	10	8	0	98	5.44
4	Appearance of Phy Facilities shluld be kept with service promised	0	0	0	0	0	13	5	113	6.28
5	Will Fulfil promises when professionals promise to do	0	0	0	0	0	0	18	126	7.00
6	When clients have problems firms should be sympathetic & reasouring	0	0	0	0	0	0	18	126	7.00
7	Professionals should be Dependable	0	0	0	0	0	0	18		7.00
8	Provide service at the time promised	0	0	0	0	0	0	18	126	7.00
9	Keep Records Accurate	0	0	0	0	0	0	18	126	7.00
10	Professionals shoudl tell clients when work will be completed	0	0	0	0	0	0	18	126	7.00
11	Employees shoudl given prompt service	0	0	0	0	0	0	18	126	7.00
12	Professionals should always be willing to help clients	0	0	0	0	0	0	18	126	7.00
13	Professionals are never too tired to respond to you	0	0	0	0	0	0	18	126	7.00

14	Professionals should instill confidence in clients	0	0	0	0	0	0	18	126	7.00
15	You will feel safe in their transactions	0	0	0	0	0	0	18	126	7.00
16	Professionals front office staff should s be Polite	0	0	0	0	0	0	18	126	7.00
17	Professional should give adequate support to the office staff	0	0	0	0	0	0	0	98	5.44
18	Professionals should give Individual attention	0	0	0	0	0	0	18	126	7.00
19	Should have convenient operating hours	0	0	0	0	0	0	18	126	7.00
20	Professionals fron office staff should give personal attention	0	0	0	0	0	0	18	126	7.00
21	Professional should have customers best interests at heart	0	0	0	0	0	0	18	126	7.00
22.	Professionals should understnad to your specific needs	0	0	0	0	0	0	18	126	7.00

ES = Expected Service Level
EM = Expected Mean of Service Level

Table 6.5.8: Perceived Service Levels by Other Professionals

S.No.	*Type of Service*	*1*	*2*	*3*	*4*	*5*	*6*	*7*	*PS*	*PM*
1	Have up to date Equipment	0	0	8	10	0	0	0	64	3.56
2	Physical Facilities should be visual appealing	4	8	6	0	0	0	0	38	2.11
3	Employees should be well Dressed	0	0	10	8	0	0	0	62	3.44
4	Appearance of Phy Facilities shluld be kept with service promised	0	4	14	0	0	0	0	50	2.75
5	Will Fulfil promises when professionals promise to do	0	0	3	15	0	0	0	69	3.83
6	When clients have problems firms should be sympathetic & reasouring	0	5	10	3	0	0	0	52	2.89
7	Professionals should be Dependable	0	0	0	0	0	0	18	126	7.00
8	Provide service at the time promised	0	0	0	14	4	0	0	76	4.22
9	Keep Records Accurate	0	0	0	0	13	3	2	97	5.39
10	Professionals shoudl tell clients when work will be completed	0	0	0	12	3	3	0	81	4.50
11	Employees shoudl given prompt service	0	0	0	9	6	3	0	84	4.67
12	Professionals should always be willing to help clients	0	0	0	10	6	2	0	82	4.56

(contd.)

S.No.	Type of Service	1	2	3	4	5	6	7	PS	PM
13	Professionals are never too tired to respond to you	0	0	0	4	10	4	0	90	5.00
14	Professionals should instill confidence in clients	0	0	0	0	0	0	18	126	7.00
15	You will feel safe in their transactions	0	0	0	0	0	2	16	124	6.89
16	Professionals front office staff should s be Polite	0	2	10	6	0	0	0	58	3.22
17	Professional should give adequate support to the office staff	0	0	10	4	4	0	0	66	3.67
18	Professionals should give Individual attention	0	0	0	0	12	6	0	96	5.33
19	Should have convenient operating hours	10	8	0	0	0	0	0	26	1.44
20	Professionals fron office staff should give personal attention	0	0	8	8	2	0	0	66	3.67
21	Professional should have customers best interests at heart	0	0	0	0	8	6	4	104	5.78
22.	Professionals should understnad to your specific needs	0	0	0	0	0	12	6	114	6.33

PS = Perceived Service Level PM = Perceived Mean Rating

If quality is ignored, business is ignored by the professional, which in marketing language it is called as marketing myopia.

The difference in the perceived and expected service levels shows again a negative value. It shows that the other professionals are also not satisfied with the service levels that the professionals are rendering. There is a gap between the perceived quality and expected quality.

Therefore, it is to be noted that with almost all the various types of clients, there is a gap in the perceived and expected service quality.

Table 6.5.9: Differences in mean rating by other professionals

S.No.	*Type of Service*	*Perceived Mean*	*Expected Mean*	*DIFF*
1	Have up to date Equipment	3.56	4.44	-0.88
2	Physical Facilities should be visual appealing	211	5.44	-3.33
3	Employees should be well Dressed	3.44	5.44	-2.00
4	Appearance of Phy Facilities shluld be kept with service promised	2.78	6.28	-3.50
5	Will Fulfil promises when professionals promise to do	3.83	7.00	-3.17
6	When clients have problems firms should be sympathetic & reasouring	2.89	7.00	-4.11
7	Professionals should be Dependable	7.00	7.00	0.00
8	Provide service at the time promised	4.22	7.00	-2.78
9	Keep Records Accurate	5.39	7.00	-1.61
10	Professionals should tell clients when work will be completed	4.50	7.00	-2.50
11	Employees should given prompt service	4.67	7.00	-2.33
12	Professionals should always be willing to help clients	4.56	7.00	-214
13	Professionals are never too tired to respond to you	5.00	7.00	-2.00
14	Professionals should instill confidence in clients	7.00	7.00	0.00
15	You will feel safe in their transactions	6.89	7.00	-0.11

16	Professionals front office staff should be Polite	3.22	5.44	-2.22
17	Professional should give adequate support to the office staff	3.67	7.00	-3.33
18	Professionals should give Individual attention	5.33	7.00	-4.67
19	Should have convenient operating hours	1.44	7.00	-5.56
20	Professionals fron office staff should give personal attention	3.67	7.00	-3.33
21	Professional should have customers best interests at heart	5.78	7.00	-4.22
22.	Professionals should understnad to your specific needs	6.33	7.00	-0.87

The overall satisfaction score =

Total Mean Rating = - 48.76

The researcher is interested to find out if there is any close relationship between the expected service quality levels of all the different types of clients. Therefore, rank correlation is done to all the users of different types of clients- individual, institutional and other professionals.

Table 6.5.10: Expected service levels of all the three different types of clients.

S.No.	*Type of Service*	*Ind exp.*	*Inst. exp.*	*Other exp.*
1	Have up to date Equipment	522	608	80
2	Physical Facilities should be visual appealing	542	598	98
3	Employees should be well Dressed	372	580	98
4	Appearance of Phy Facilities shluld be kept with service promised	536	550	113
5	Will Fulfil promises when professionals promise to do	6588	616	126
6	When clients have problems firms should be sympathetic & reasouring	654	616	126
7	Professionals should be Dependable	658	616	126
8	Provide service at the time promised	658	616	126
9	Keep Records Accurate	658	616	126

10	Professionals should tell clients when work will be completed	658	616	126
11	Employees should given prompt service	658	616	126
12	Professionals should always be willing to help clients	658	616	126
13	Professionals are never too tired to respond to you	658	616	126
14	Professionals should instill confidence in clients	658	616	126
15	You will feel safe in their transactions	658	616	126
16	Professionals front office staff should be Polite	536	588	126
17	Professional should give adequate support to the office staff	346	598	98
18	Professionals should give Individual attention	654	616	126
19	Should have convenient operating hours	308	616	126
20	Professionals fron office staff should give personal attention	528	616	126
21	Professional should have customers best interests at heart	654	616	126
22.	Professionals should understnad to your specific needs	654	616	126

Ind exp = individual clients expectations;

Inst exp= institutional clients expectations

Other exp= other professionals expectations.

When ranks are repeated the formula for spearman rank difference correlation coefficient become:-

i) Correlation for Individual and institutional clients:

?= 1- 6[?d2 + m(m2-1)]

$$\frac{\frac{\quad}{12}}{n(n2-1)}$$

where ?d 2 =697

$$= \frac{1- 6[697+7.5+5+0.5+42+0.5+0.5]}{22(484-1)}$$

= 1- 0.42 = 0.58.

Since ? =0.58 so there exist positive correlation between individual and institutional clients expected service quality levels.

ii) Correlation between individual and other professionals:

$$? = \frac{1- 6[?d2 + m(m2-1)]}{12}$$

$$\frac{\qquad}{n(n2 -1)} \qquad \text{where } ?d\ 2 = 515$$

$$= \frac{1- 6[515+11+2+7.5+5+0.5]}{22(484-1)}$$

$$= 1- 0.31 = 0.69$$

iii) Correlation between institutional and other professionals:

$$?= \frac{1- 6[?d2 + m(m2-1)]}{12}$$

$$\frac{\qquad}{n(n2 -1)} \qquad \text{where } ?d\ 2 = 301$$

$$= \frac{1- 6[301+42+0.5+0.5+7.5+5+0.5]}{22(484-1)}$$

$$= 1- 0.21 = 0.79$$

correlation values of the clients and their expected service levels are as follows

Individual and Institutional Clients = 0.58

Individual and Other Professionals = 0.69

Institutonal and other Professionals = 0.79

The values mentioned above show high correlation between institutional and other professionals and they show that all the clients are almost having a close relationship in expected service levels.

It can also be derived that all the clients have similar expectation levels and therefore they could be treated on the same lines .

Table 6.5.11: Ranked Correlation between all the Different types of Clients and Their expected service quality levels.

S.No.	Type of Service	R1	R2	R3	X=R1 R2	Y=R1 R3	Z=R1 R3	X2	Y2	Z2
1	Have up to date Equipment	19.0	16.0	22.0	3.0	-3.0	-6.0	9.00	9.00	36.00
2	Physical Facilities should be visual appealing	15.0	17.5	20.0	-2.0	-5.0	-2.5	6.25	25.00	6.25
3	Employees should be well Dressed	20.0	21.0	20.0	-1.0	0.0	1.0	1.00	0.00	1.00
4	Appearance of Phy Facilities shluld be kept with service promised	16.5	22.0	18.0	-5.5	-1.5	4.0	30.25	2.25	16.00
5	Will Fulfil promises when professionals promise to do	5.5	8.0	9.0	-2.5	-3.5	-1.0	6.25	12.25	1.00
6	When clients have problems firms should be sympathetic & reasouring	12.5	8.0	9.0	4.5	3.5	-1.0	20.25	12.25	1.00
7	Professionals should be Dependable	5.5	8.0	9.0	-2.5	-3.5	-1.0	6.25	12.25	1.00
8	Provide service at the time promised	5.5	8.0	9.0	-2.5	-3.5	-1.0	6.25	12.25	1.00
9	Keep Records Accurate	5.5	8.0	9.0	-2.5	-3.5	-1.0	6.25	12.25	1.00
10	Professionals shoudl tell clients when work will be completed	5.5	8.0	9.0	-2.5	-3.5	-1.0	6.25	12.25	1.00
11	Employees shoudl given prompt service	5.5	8.0	9.0	-2.5	-3.5	-1.0	6.25	12.25	1.00
12	Professionals should always be willing to help clients	5.5	8.0	9.0	-2.5	-3.5	-1.0	6.25	12.25	1.00

S.No.	Type of Service	R1	R2	R3	X=R1 R2	Y=R1 R3	Z=R1 R3	X2	Y2	Z2
13	Professionals are never too tired to respond to you	5.5	19.5	9.0	-14.0	-3.5	10.5	196.00	12.25	10.25
14	Professionals should instill confidence in clients	5.5	8.0	9.0	-2.5	-3.5	-1.0	6.25	12.25	1.00
15	You will feel safe in their transactions	5.5	8.0	9.0	-2.5	-3.5	-1.0	6.25	12.25	1.00
16	Professionals front office staff should s be Polite	16.5	19.5	9.0	-3.0	7.5	10.5	9.00	56.25	110.25
17	Professional should give adequate support to the office staff	21.0	17.5	20.0	3.5	1.0	-2.5	12.25	1.00	6.25
18	Professionals should give Individual attention	12.5	8.0	9.0	4.5	3.5	-1.0	20.25	12.25	1.00
19	Should have convenient operating hours	22.0	8.0	9.0	14.0	13.0	-1.0	196.00	169.00	1.00
20	Professionals fron office staff should give personal attention	18.0	8.0	9.0	10.0	9.0	-1.0	100.0	81.00	1.00
21	Professional should have customers best interests at heart	12.5	8.0	9.0	4.5	3.5	-1.0	20.25	12.25	1.00
22.	Professionals should understnad to your specific needs	12.5	8.0	9.0	4.5	3.5	-1.0	20.25	12.25	1.00
					0.0	0.0	0.0	697.	515.0	301.0

RI = Individual Client users, Rs = Institutional, R3 = Other Professionals

Sources of Information from Clients Point of View

"What are the sources of Information from where you came to know of CA/Firm" was a multiple choice question used for the Users clients to know about information sources for choosing Professional Accountants. In the absence of advertising which is banned in the profession by code of ethics, as well as lack of information about the capabilities of the accountant/firm, buyer uncertainty increases, and in that situation which information source dominates in the choice of professional accountant was to be clearly brought about from the abovfe question. The information sources (complied from previous studies, literature and from consultations with various knowledgeable people, including several chartered accountants) were dived into five categories of (i) official Organisational sources. (ii) Personal Sources, (iii) Promotional Sources, (iv) Daily contacts, and (v) Referral Sources. Respondents were asked to indicate among each of the 15 information sources, the one which they had used while choosing a chartered accountant/firm by putting a tick-mark against each.

It is obvious that 'personal information sources' were considered most important by 108 clients opted Business acquaintances, in selecting chartered accountants/firms, followed by friends and family with 92 Clients opting it as a source of information to them 19 clients opted that information sources are existing clients and other user recommendations were opted by 17 users. Business cards interestingly has been opted by 27 clients which meant that they became the source of information to them. Promotional sources, however had little importance in the eyes of clients white selecting professional service providers with only 0 respondents being disposed towards it.

To have a better picture of the overall information sources used by the clients in selecting professional accountants, the various information sources can be considered one by one.

Table 6.6: Information to Clients

S.No.	Sources	Individual Clients	Institutional Clients	Other Professionals	Total
1	Chambers of Commerce	Nil	Nil	Nil	0
2	Professional Councils	Nil	Nil	Nil	0
3	Professioinal Associations	Nil	Nil	Nil	0
4	Friends family	21	63	8	92
5	Business Acquaintances	62	37	9	108
6	Yellow Pages	Nil	Nil	Nil	0
7	Advertisements of Shifting Locations	Nil	Nil	Nil	0
8	Membership Clubs	Nil	6	1	7
9	Sponsorphips	Nil	Nil	Nil	0
10	Existing Clients	Nil	19	Nil	19
11	Other User recommendations	11	6	Nil	17
12	Accountants own Websie	Nil	Nil	Nil	0

Clients way of searching the Professional Accountants

"Did you select a Chartered Accountancy Firm randomly?" was the next question asked from the respondents so as to know whether they had some predetermined idea about selecting a CA Firm or they select the CA Firm as they just went to the place of work like Taxation office/other offices. The question was a dichotomous one in which the respondents were asked to indicate their answer in the form of 'yes' or 'no.' The findings are given in table.

Table 6.7

S.No:	Type of.Pesponse	Ind Clients	Inst Clients	Other Prof.
1	Random Selection	4(4.2%)	0(0)	0(0)
2	Not Random Selection	90 (95.7%)	88 (100%)	18 (100)
	Base	94	88	18

Table 6.5 clearly depicts the clients decision while hiring a professional accountant. The table shows that only 4(4.2%). Individual clients, 0(0%) of Institutional clients, none of other professionals had given the response 'yes' However, 90(95.7%) Individual clients, 88(100%) Institutional clients and 18(100%) of other professionals had given the response No. i.e. they do not choose the professional accountant randomly. They had some predetermined idea while selecting a chartered Accountant/Firm.

After knowing from the User clients that majority of them had some predetermined idea in mind, it was important to know as to what were those pre-decision attributes considered important in selecting a CA Firm.

Weighted ranking of different attributes of selection criteria assigned by users and non-users of Professional Services

To determine what criteria consumers have used or will use in selecting professional accountants, the question, Rank in order of importance, the following professional Accountants selection criteria's by putting a tick mark along the important continuum was asked from users, as well as non-users. The question contained 13 selection criteria's complied from literature. All respondents, 200 users and 200 non-users were then asked to rate the criteria's based upon how important each should be when selecting a professional Accountant. Ratings were provided along a three-point Likert scale with and points labeled: 3=very important to 1= not important.

The different attributes of professional accountants/Firm were assigned rank, according to the weightage/score given to each attribute by the users as well as non-users, as can be seen from the tables. Table 6.8 In the next page reveals that among users, Technical competence was the most sought for attribute while selecting professional Accountants ranked at no. 1 with a total weightage of 558 points; followed by Quality of work/Service at rank 2 with a weightage of 540 points 'Overall Reputation/ integrity of CA' at rank 3 with a weightage of 510 points; past Experience of CA/firm' at rank 4 with a score of 408 points and so on as can be seen from the table.

Table showing weighted Ranking of Different Attributes as Assigned by Users

Key: Very Important = 3,
Important = 2,
Not Important = 1

However, the "cost of Accountancy Services" Location of office' as well as 'Listing in yellow pages' were not considered important attributes in the case of Professional selection, as they were ranked at 11, 12 and 13 position with a weightage of 265 points, 219 points and 200 points respectively. Importance of their 'Collateral Appearance' personal Acquaintance and 'recommendations by Friends / relatives cannot be overlooked as these attributes are placed at 6th, 7th and 8th rank with respective weightages being 358, 330 and 318 points 'Convenience of office Hours' was also not considered an important attribute being ranked at 9th position.

i) Individual clients: When results were further analyzed according to the type of users, it was found that among individual clients, most sought after attribute in Professional Selection was "quality of work" at rank 1 with a score of 273 points, followed by 'technical Competence' at rank 2 with a total weight age of 262 points; Overall Reputation / integrity of CA /firm at rank with a score of 225 points, 'Experience in the practice at rank 4, promptness of service at rank 5 with a score of 172 points and so on. Attributes not considered important were 'Fees Charged', 'Location on Office', and 'Listing in yellow pages' which were ranked at 11th, 12th and 13th position.

ii)Among Institutional Clients, the picture was slightly different, with the attribute of "Technical Competence' being ranked at no. 1 with weightage of 258 points; followed by attributes, like 'Overall Reputation / Integrity of CA firm' at rank 2 with a score of 249 points ; Quality of work /Service' at rank 3 with weightage of 219 points, 'Experience in the Industry' at rank 4 with a score of 190 points, 'Promptness of Service' at rank 5 with score of 179 points similar to that in case of individual clients. Attributes not considered important were the same as were in case of individual clients as can be seen from the table.

(iii) Among Other Professionals attributes considered

important were like this "Quality of work" at rank 1 (score 48 points), 'Technical Competence and Promptness of service' bracketed at rank 2 with score of 38 points each, 'overall reputation /Integrity of CA firm' and collateral Appearance' bracketed at rank 3 with a score of 36 points each, 'Personal Acquaintance' at rank 4 with a score of 32 points. Attributes not considered important were the same as were in the case of individual and Institutional clients.

Table 6.8: Weighted Ranking of Different Attributes as assigned by non-users

S.No.	*Sel Cri*	*Ind Cli (Wel Avg)*	*Rankby Ind cli*	*Inst Cli*	*Rank by Inst Clip*	*Other Prof.*	*Rank by Prof*
1	Overall Reputation of CA Firm	225	3	249	2	36	3
2	Technical Competence	262	2	258	1	38	2
3	Quality of work performed	273	1	219	3	48	1
4	Past Experience of CA	188	4	190	4	30	5
5	Meeting Timelines	172	5	179	5	38	2
6	Fee	124	11	121	11	20	8
7	Recommendations by Clients	148	8	142	8	28	6
8	Convenience of working hours	144	9	138	9	22	7
9	Personal Acquaintances	14	7	147	7	32	4
10	Location of Office	151	12	96	12	20	8
11	Listingin Yellow Pages	101	13	88	13	18	9
12	Behaviour and Appearance	94	6	160	6	36	3
13	CA's Reputation within Profession	162	10	130	10	28	6

Thus it can be concluded that a set of attributes considered important while selecting a professional Accountant in descending order of importance were 'Technical Competence' Quality of work', Overall Reputation / Integrity of CA firm', and 'Experience on the Industry /years in practice' with a slight variations in their importance, as seen from the analysis above.

Table 6.8.1meant for non-users, i.e. those respondents who

have not engaged the Professional Accountant so but in future may use them.

The table 6.8.1 clearly shows that attributes considered most important while selecting a professional.

Table 6.8.1: Weighted Ranking of Different Attributes as Assigned by non-users

S.No.	*Sel Cri*	*Ind Cli (Wel Avg)*	*Rankby Ind cli*	*Inst Cli*	*Rank by Inst Clip*	*Other Prof.*	*Rank by Prof*
1	Overall Reputation of CA Firm	299	2	212	1	60	2
2	Technical Competence	305	1	206	2	54	4
3	Quality of work performed	272	3	184	3	68	1
4	Past Experience of CA	229	4	169	4	47	6
5	Meeting Timelines	223	5	160	5	58	3
6	Fee	166	10	87	11	32	9
7	Recommendations by Clients	174	7	154	7	47	6
8	Convenience of working hours	168	9	123	10	58	7
9	Personal Acquaintances	220	6	156	6	32	5
10	Location of Office	114	11	83	12	47	10
11	Listingin Yellow Pages	104	13	74	13	24	11
12	Behaviour and Appearance	110	12	136	9	54	4
13	CA's Reputation within Profession	170	8	142	8	39	8

All reputation /Integrity of CA Firm's at rank 1 with a score 1 points followed with 'Technical Competence' at rank 2 with a of 565 points, quality of work' at rank 3 (score 524 points); past sentence of CA' at rank 4 with weightage of 445 points; promptness of service' at rank 5 with weightage being 441 pts and. They were also nut much worried about such attributes as 'Convenience of office hours', collateral appearance', cost of Accounting service, Location of Office' and 'Listing in the yellow pages' as these were ranked at 9th, 10th, 11th, 12th, and 13th place.

The difference among users and non-users were not much concerned about the collateral appearance of the Professional, which was ranked at 10th position in contrast to users, who had ranked the same attribute at rank 6th. This was basically as one respondent (non-user) replied, "we are not worried about the dress etc. but we want our work to be got done in time. "So presently the factor, of collateral appearance was immaterial for non-users.

When seen form Type of Respondents Category, the picture was like this:

1) In case of Individual respondents, attribute considered important was ranked as "Technical Competence" at No. 1 score 305 points; Overall Reputation / Integrity of CA' at, rank 2 with Weightage of 299 points 'Quality of services' at rank 3 with a Weightage of 272 points, 'Experience of CA' at rank 4th with score being 238 points, and as on. Collateral Appearance'. 'Cost of accounting service location of office, listing in yellow pages were not considered important attributes by the non-users in selection of professional service providers as they were ranked at 10th, 11th, 12th, and 13th position.

2) Among Institutional Clients first and the foremost attribute sought was overall reputation / Integrity of CA Firm' at rank 1 with a score of 210 points followed by 'Technical Competence' at rank 2 with weightage of 206 points, 'Quality of work' at rank 3 with weightage being 169 points and soon. Attributes not considered important were the same as in the case of individual respondents.

3) Among other Professionals, it was 'Quality of work' which was ranked at No. 1 with a score of 68 points; 'Overall Reputations / Integrity of CA' at No. 2 rank with a score of 60 points; "Meeting of Deadlines on Work" at rank 3 with Weightage of 58 points; 'Technical Competence and Collateral Appearance" bracketed at rank 4 with a Weightage of 54 each and so on.

However, 'Experience and Recommendations by Friends / Relatives' were considered simultaneously at rank 6th with a score of 47 points each. Attributes not considered important were 'Fee Charged', 'Location of Office and 'Listing in Yellow Pages'.

Table 6.8.2: Ranks assigned by users and non-users to different attributes related with the selection criteria of Individual Clients

	Criteria	*Indivudla Clients*			
		R1 Users	*R2 Users*	*D=R1 -R2*	*D2*
1	Reputation /Integrity	3	2	1	1
2	Technical Competence	2	1	*1	*1
3					
4	Experience of CA	4	4	0	0
5	Promptness of work	5	5	0	0
6	Cost of Accountancy Service	11	10	1	1
7	Recommendation Friends	8	7	1	1
8	Convenience of office hours	9	9	0	0
9	Personal acquaintance	7	6	1	1
10	Location of Office	12	11	1	1
11	Listing in yellow pages	13	13	0	0
12	Collateral Appearance	6	12	-6	+36
13.	Their Reputation in the profession	10	8	2	4

Since R=0.86 so there exist positive correlation between users and non-users as regards selection criteria.

Among non-users, also the set of attributes considered important in their future selection of professional Accountant were the same as those of the actual users of Professional Accountant, those being in descending order of importance as "Overall Reputation / Integrity of Firm", Technical Competence' quality of Services, Experience of CA'. While Technical Competence' was ranked at No. 1 in case of users, 'Overall reputation/Integrity of firm was ranked at No. 1 in case of non-users.

To determine the consistency in response patterns among users and non-users regarding attributes considered important in selection professional Accountants, the Spearman rank order correlation coefficient formula was used and applied for all types of respondents individual, institutional and other professionals:-

Table 6.8.3: Institutional Clients Ranking Correlation

	Selection Criteria	*Users Rank R1*	*N-Users Rank R2*	*D=R1-R2*	*D2*
1	Reputation /Integrity	2	1	1	1
2	Technical Competence	1	2	–1	1
3	Quality of work	3	3	0	0
4	Experience of CA	4	4	0	0
5	Promptness of work	5	5	0	0
6	Cost of Accountancy Service	11	11	0	0
7	Recommendation Friends	8	7	+1	1
8	Convenience of office hours	7	6	1	1
9	Personal acquaintance	9	10	-1	1
10	Location of Office	12	12	0	0
11	Listing in yellow pages	13	13	0	0
12	Collateral Appearance	6	9	–3	9
13.	Their Reputation in the profession	10	8	2	4

$$R = 1 \quad \frac{6Ed2}{n(n\ 2-1)} = 1 \quad \frac{6*\ 18}{13*\ 168} = 0.9506$$

So, high degree of correlation exists between users and non-users (Institutional clients) regards attributes preferred in case of the selection criteria.

Table 6.8.4: Professional Clients

	Selection Criteria	Users Rank R1	N-Users Rank R2	D=R1-R2	D2
1	Reputation /Integrity	4.5m2	2	2.5	6.25
2	Technical Competence	2.5 ml	4.5 m5	-2	4
3	Quality of work	1	1	0	0
4	Experience of CA	7	7.5m6	–5	–25
5	Promptness of work	2.5	3	–5	–25
6	Cost of Accountancy Service	11.5 m4	11	–5	–25
7	Recommendation Friends	8.5 m3	7.5m6	1.0	1
8	Convenience of office hours	10 7	9 6	1.0 1	1 1
9	Personal acquaintance	6	6	0	0
10	Location of Office	11.5 m4	12	–5	–25
11	Listing in yellow pages	13	13	0	0
12	Collateral Appearance	4.5 m2	4.5m5	0	0
13.	Their Reputation in the profession	8.5m3	10	–1.5	2.25
				Σd^2	15.50

When ranks are repeated the formula for spearman rank difference correlation coefficient become:-

= P = 1– 6Σ[d2 + m(m2–1))]

12

———— where Sd2 = 15.50

n(n2 –1)

M = No. of ranks which are repeated

n = Total No. of observations

R = 1 1-6 (15.50+ 1/12 (2 3-2) +1/12 (2 3-2) + 1/12(2 3-2)+

1/12(23 –2) +1/1/12(23 – 2) (23+1/12(23–2)

———— = R = 0.9492

2184

OR R = +0.95 High degree of correlation exists in case of other professionals among users and non-users.

Since there was a significant correlation between the users and non-users perceptions regarding the attribute while choosing a professional accountant, so researcher came to the conclusion that the two groups of user and non-users demonstrated considerable consistency in response patterns.

Weighted ranking of the perceived importance and use of professional Accountant /Firm selection criteria

The question No. 19 of Professional Accountants Survey part, revealed the perceived importance of various attributes on the bases of which Professional Accountants are being selected by the clients. The question No. 5 (a) of this survey part high lighted the users experiences of the attributes they actually considered important while making a professional choice. So the Professional Accountants perception and users experience could be compared for seeing the consistency in response pattern and supplying some cross-validations.

Table 6.8.5: Ranks given by professional and user to various selection criterions in selecting professional accountants / firm.

	ection Criteria	*Rank R1*	*Professional Rank R2*	*D=R 1-R2*	*Ed2*
1	Reputation /Integrity	3	3	+0	0
2	Technical Competence	1	2	–1	1
3	Quality of work	2	1	1	1
4	Experience of CA	4	4	0	0
5	Promptness of work	5	5	0	0
6	Cost of Accountancy Service	11	11	0	0
7	Recommendation Friends	8	8	0	0
8	Convenience of office hours	9	12	–3	9
9	Personal acquaintance	7	6	1	1
10	Location of Office	12	13	1	1
11	Listing in yellow pages	13	7	6	36
12	Collateral Appearance	6	9	–3	9
13.	Their Reputation in the profession	10	10	0	0
				Ed2	–58

The table shows that there is high degree of similarity between the ranks given to selection criteria by user clients and Professional Accountants. The Spearman's Rank Order Correlation co-efficient between these two groups was calculated to see the consistency in response patterns of the two.

Spearman Rank diffeence co-efficient of correlation

$$R=1-\frac{6Ed2)}{n(n2-1)} \qquad 1-6\ \frac{6*58}{2184} = 1\text{-}0.1593$$

$$R= +0.84 \qquad\qquad = 0.84$$

Thus high degree of correlation exists in the response pattern of the two groups of users and Professional Accountants regarding importance of selection criteria in selection of Professional Accountants.

The Significance Test:- Null Hypothesis

There is no consistency in the response pattern of the two groups.

$$\sqrt{\frac{n-2}{1-r2}} \text{ for df= (n-2) = T=.84 } \sqrt{\frac{13-2}{1-(.84)}} = 5.135$$

at df = 11 value of t = 3.106 (Table at 0.01%) and df=11. Since the calculated value of t=5.135 than the table value of t at df= (n-2) =11; is 3.106, so the null hypothesis is rejected. So there is a considerable degree of consistency in the Response pattern of the two groups (Professionals and user clients as regards selection criteria).

7

Discussion Related to Client Survey

The foundation of any effective marketing program is as through an understanding as possible of what clients want, identification of target markets, understanding the needs of clients, the bases they use in the choices they make, and how they seek and purchases the service. Thus if professionals had a complete answer to all these questions and are both qualified and flexible, a marketing mix could be designed by them in the best possible manner. But client behavior may be inconsistent, clients may not have sufficient knowledge or understanding to make a fully informed or intelligent search; and clients may not be able to correctly evaluate the qualifications of competing professionals. Thus to have a through understanding of customer needs and desires-their functional requirements and emotional needs in buying professional services of accountants, a client survey or market analysis of this type was done. The method of market analysis adopted is the same as is being used for goods, as there is a consensus on this issue. Cooke, (1970), for example, suggested that, "In so far as logical and procedural considerations are considered, there is no meaningful and substantive difference to be drawn between the process of defining and analyzing a market for a product and a market for a service."

Staton (1981), confirms, "Market Analysis is essentially the same whether a firm is selling a product or a service". This is because analyzing the market is essentially concerned with human needs and wants. So marketers of professional services they want, motives underlying their purchases, attributes of Professionals affecting their behaviour and choices in their selection, sources of information they look into while making a purchase decision, degree of client loyalty, difference in user and non-user behaviour and the like, and on the basis of which clients behaviour Models can be made which can guide the professionals in their approach to marketing of Professionals services. Such Models of consumer behaviour in existence are of :

Konard, (1968); Green & Tull, (1974); McDermott, (1978):

Chisnall (1981); Engel, & Blackwell, (1982); Sasser, Olsen, & Wyckoff, (1978); Fisk; (1981); Zeitmall, (1981), Langeard, Bateson, Lovelock, & Eioliear; (1981); Fox and Wheatley (1978).

Client Uncertainty

This part of the study presents an important insight into what clients of professional accountancy services, really want.

One important conclusion that can be derived from the results of the study is that Today's consumer of Professional Services are more informed, more aggressive, most cost-concious, and probably engages in more comparative shopping than ever before. Some examples to illustrate it are given below:

1) As one client's objection to professional was, "your fee seems high. I can engage the 'X' firm at half the price".
2) Another prospect's objection was, "you are handling my competitor's work".
3) Another client query related to professional was "How can you possibly justify such a charge for what we have asked you to do"

These and many other statements by clients show the

Increased awareness among the clients. Therefore, the clients want other things besides benefits that stem from the outcome of the application of the Firm's skills. Clients buy security and service. No doubt, as brought about in the study that all type of clients -individual, Institutional and other professionals hire accountants for professional work of Auditing and Tax representation, and for other newer areas where they have started feeling needs like those of Secretarial and Company affairs, Management Services, EDP, Estate Planning and the like.

Therefore, the purchase of professional service by the client was the purchase of uncertainty reductions. Therefore, high degree of emotionalism was built in the purchase of professional services, essentially intangibles, and often the clients used to ask the question in their minds consciously or unconsciously that, "If I buy this service will my current unease be replaced by an acceptable feeling of comfort". For example, if some problem comes before the client relating to company affairs, then he will, start searching here and there the professional accountant who can help him to be free of that worry and get the work accomplished. This is true for individuals as well as institutional client which leads to inference that client often buys 'people' i.e. "Professional Providers" rather than services which is critical for the professional service marketer to understand. The above conclusions of the researcher are supported by studies of Witt Reich (1966), Stapleton (1980); Wilson (1972); Denney (1983); Kotler & Connor, (1977); Mahon (1978); Wheatley (1983) Bloom & Kotler (1983); Deardan and Kiser, (1981); Co well (1984).

Implications

The foregoing discussion suggests the following:

1) Professional Accountants should survey their local markets to determine potential accountancy needs of the area. Wilson (1972) says, "it is truly surprising how rarely well organized and managed firms have failed to audit all the areas in which they have capabilities.

2) Real understanding of the clients problems and the real understanding of the Organizations professional resources be there, to ensure client satisfaction.

3) Widespread awareness of their usefulness, be demonstrated to reduce the client uncertainty and enable them to answer themselves the question, "whether we have made the right choice of Professional Accountant or not". This is possible by uncovering all objections of the clients, and paying close attention to their problems.

4) Based on survey as recommended in (1) above, specialties can be developed and promoted, e.g. one professional accountant advertised about his experience in handling liaison work for NRI's

Foreign Nationals/Firms and Individuals in India. (Hindustan Times, March 1988). This will ensure increased use of specialized Accountancy Services by many clients.

The results are supported by many studies available from review of literature like Wilson (1986), Deardan, Deardan & Kiser (1981); Hal Lauer (1972); Deborah Rankin, (1977); Kotler & Bloom (1983); Mahon (1978); Dirsmith (1987); Helgeson and Birrer (1986); Wittreich (1966); Eiglier and Langeard (1981); Levitt (1960). Shostack (1977), Levitt, (1981), Wheatley (1983); Denney (1983); Parikh (1971); Bhandari (1971);

Sources of Information and Client Uncertainty

Clients of professional accountancy services, buy an expectation of a result. They cannot know in advance what they will receive. Reputation, experience or long association with a particular firm does not guarantee that the quality, efficiency and speed of a service will replicate itself. Professional services are people based and people are unpredictable even when operating within standard practices, procedures and precepts. The inability to know, positively, just what will be received is a major source of uncertainty.

Furthermore, there are many things about which clients are uncertain and will not or cannot specify. Some of these are: -

(a) Unsure-ness of their own needs.

(b) Lack of confidence of the profession itself.

(c) Which firm to deal with.

(d) Ignorance about usefulness of the professional for special service.

(e) Value for money assessment.

(f) Unspecified or open-ended cost commitment.

(g) Rejection of liability by the professional services providers (i.e. no insurance. Liability exists in our country given by the professionals to clients).

Because of all the uncertainties, prevailing in the professional market place, clients look to varied sources of information for reduction of uncertainty. Many sources available for goods promotion are restricted for professional service because of self-regulation e.g. professional services cannot advertise. Still within these constraints, it was found from the study that personal information sources dominated the selection process for service providers of Accounting and inter about his quality and integrity form his/her behavior, with 50% users, (individual), institutional and other clients opining in its favor. Referral sources and Daily Contacts were next only to Personal Information Sources being consulted opted by approx. 8.5% user respondents. Personal Information Sources comprised mainly of family members, self, friends relatives, coworkers and the like, while referral sources comprised of existing clients, other professionals; and Daily Contacts comprised of other Users recommendations. The results are very much in line with the work of Bloom,Kotler and Hayes(2002): who remarked "in and effort to reduce the great uncertainty experienced in buying professional services, people tend to seek large amount of information from others like family members, friends, co-workers and other trusted sources."

Results are further supported by works of Wilson (1986); Kotler & Connor (1977); Kuehl & Ford (1977); Feldman & Spenser (1975); Smith & Meyer (1980); Deardan, Deardan & Kiser (1981); Word, Scott (1974); Bloom, (1977); Kotler (1980); Sarkar & Saleh, (1974); Wittreich, Warren (1966) ; Uhl & Upah (1980); Kotler & Bloom (1983).

Recommendations for professional can be that:

1) In an atmosphere of great uncertainty, clients do not want to feel uncertain about the Professionals them will be working with form, which they should employ personal Contact strategy, which alone will be the best approach to communication in such professional setting where other means of communication like advertising etc. are banned.

2) Accountants could widen their personal social circles by becoming members of clubs etc. which can provide an opportunity to have access to non-users i.e. potential clients.

Selection Criteria

The study revealed that clients/users were having some

predetermined idea in their mind before they went in for the selection of Professional Accountants, as opined by majority 90-100% clients in various categories Individual clients and other Professionals (94.68% and 100% respectively). As compared to institutional clients (88.63%) were found to be having more pre-decisive criteria's for professional service providers.

Form among the different attributes of the professionals highlighted (compiled for literature and discussion), Technical Competence was found to be the most sought for attribute in professional choice selection by the users ranked at No. I with weightages of 558 pts i.e. 93%, followed with Quality of Work/ Service at rank 2 with corresponding percentage of 90% "overall reputation/Integrity of CA at rank 3 with percentage of 85%; Experience of Account at rank 4 with a 68% respondents.

Among non-users category, attributes considered important were ranked category, attributes considered important were ranked as; overall reputation/ integrity of CA Firm at rank I, with percentage 95%; Technical Competence at rank 2 with percentage 94%; quality of work at rank 3 with percentage being 87% and Experience of CA at rank 4 with 74% respondents. Thus while technical competence was ranked at No. 1 in case of users, non-users were more inclined for the 'overall reputation/integrity of Firm ranked at No. 1 in case of users, non-users were more inclined for the overall reputation/integrity of Firm ranked at No. 1. Thus, the users of Professional Service buy the capabilities of the seller. Spearman Rank Order correlation co-efficient ('R') further showed that considerable degree of consistency existed in the response pattern of the two groups- users and non-users.

The results of the study further revealed that the selection criterion that users were using and those that the professional accountants perceived their clients to be using were quite similar. The Spearman rank order correlation co-efficient, between these twos groups demonstrated considerable consistency in response patterns.

It is important to note here that the most important attributes of Professional service Provider i.e. Technical competence, quality, integrity and experience correlated with the expected satisfaction of users and non-users, therefore adequate information required to generate reliable inferences of quality, integrity, competence, experience be made available to the clients before they make their choice. But such information are not made available or inferred from external sources either because of (1) difficulties involved in assessing quality, competence and integrity of professionals (clients definition/may be different from those of Professionals definitions) by the client, and secondly (2) advertising as means of mass communication, is prohibited in the profession as a result of which much information is not made available to client. Because of these reasons clients frequently turn to personal information sources like personal acquaintances and friends/relatives advice to select a Professional Accountant.

Other reported studies also support these findings such as Anderson et al (1976); Sarkar & Saleh (1974); Smith & MEYER (1980); Wood & Ball (1978); Kuehl & Ford (1977); Bloom (1984); Uhl & UPHA (1983); Wittreich (1966); Helgeson (1986); Denney, (1981); Kotler and Bloom (1983).

Recommendations for Professionals

(1) Professionals should provide tangible evidence to the intangible elements - (particularly human skills and aptitudes) of their service, to build consumer confidence before they are being selected.

(2) Use personal means of communication more pronouncing like personal contact etc. For attracting the customers, and demonstration of their capabilities of providing better service than their competitors, like one commented providing "value-added Audit".

(3) Provide for a better environmental and collateral evidence, to instill confidence in the clients, which include things like dress, manner, premises etc.

Necessity of Professional Accountants for different Type of Cases

Users, ranked the necessity of a chartered Accountant for 'Business Taxation' and Auditing' work at rank 1 and 2 with respective weightages being 594 points and 569 points respectively. Other spheres where necessity of CA was felt by users were for 'consultations' at rank 3 followed with attestation of Financial Reports for arranging 'Bank Loans' at rank 4 and so on. This was true for all type of user clients -Individual. Institutional and other professionals.

Among non-users, the necessity of a CA was felt for 'Business Taxation', Auditing, Attestation of Financial Reports for arranging Bank Loans, consultations', Preparing Project Reports' etc. at rank 1,2,3,4 and 5 respectively. Less need for CA was realized for cases, similar to those of users' i.e. for staff recruitments, Appearance before Registrar or monopolies cases, Functional Organisational studies, Amalgamation/Merger cases being ranked at 12th, 13th, and 14th positions respectively.

Thus it can be interpreted from above that Auditing and Tax representation being the predominant area where maximum cases are being currently handled, will continue to remain as predominant areas of practice in future times to come, with number of assesses on the increase as well as number of companies being floated on the increases and statutory audit remaining important function of C.A.'s. However, greater scope also lies in newer area where cases can be found by the practicing C.A.'s in greater numbers (future area of research). However, to tap business in these newer area calls forth for the experience and skills which needs to be learnt and nurtured by these professional accountants to fully exploit the potentiality that lies in these newer areas of practice.

Implications for Professionals

(1) Necessity for Professional Accountants has to be seen from the client's angle and not from the angle of the performer i.e. provider of services so as to come out with innovations according to the clients expectations.

(2) Constant Audit of Service lines be done to keep track of the newer areas of practice and match the capabilities of the firm with these opportunities. Staying alert and aggressive from client's angle is advocated. This is key to remain Market-oriented i.e. client-centered.

Studies that support the above conclusions are by Mahon, (1978); Wheatley, (1983); Denney, (1981); Denney, (1983); Turner,

(1969); Kelter and Connor (1977); Kotler and Bloom, (1983) and Bloom, (1984).

Service Quality and Client Satisfaction

The study revealed that although complete satisfaction of client can only be there from the results of professional services provider, which shows up only after the service is performed, but still when the case is in process, factors like 'behavior of CA/Firms members; service provided as regards accuracy, timeliness, promptness; Fee charged; and personal attention, become the attributes of a professional Accountant on which the satisfaction depends. If the clients rate the intensity of satisfaction on any one of these attributes as low, then the level of dis-satisfaction will increase and as a result of which clients will not repurchase or rehire the services of that particular Professional Accountant the next time.

The result of the study showed that clients were not so much satisfied with these 22 items that have been taken for measuring service quality i.e. "their behavior"; personal attendance; fee package charged, service provided as regards accuracy, Timeliness and promptness."

Implications

Thus to ensure the client loyalty for future repurchase, like is there in case of goods marketing; professionals should demonstrate good behavior, timely, accurate and prompt service, personal attention to clients, and reasonable fee package.

The results helped to conclude that the great uncertainty and consequent tension and anxiety - which many clients experience in buying professional services discourages 'shopping around' and encourage loyalty, like brand loyalty for products.

However, this is not to say that thus there is no need for the professionals to exert or make efforts. But results without serious effort may not well equate with the client view of skill, utilized time, involvement, care, or fees charged by the Professionals. So efforts that need to be done on the part of professionals cannot be overlooked. Findings are supported by studies done by; Wilson (1986); Kotler & Bloom (1983); Cooke, (1970); Wilson, (1972); Denney, (1981), & Kotler (1980);

Clients and Professionals: What they want from their Accountant?

The total study clearly projects that there is a need to fully understand what clients and prospects want from their accountants, so as to enable them to market their services effectively. A partial list would include the following:

1. Help in solving problems. Understand and reduce uncertainties facing them.
2. Help in preventing problems.
3. Need to be perceived as having experience & competence
4. Attention
5. Availability.
6. New ideas and new services
7. Timeliness
8. Confidence/Integrity or peace of mind.
9. Quality of work according to client's requirements as have been brought in the conceptual framework.
10. Follow-up.
11. Personal counsel
12. Value for their money.
13. More and better information to help in professional choice and selection.
14. The right chemistry i.e. work is got accomplished.
15. Project 'effort and activity'.
16. Project 'Environmental & 'Collateral' evidence i.e. of dress, manners, politeness, premises etc to instill confidence in the minds of clients and prospects.

The above list is not an exhaustive one, and further studies can be undertaken to uncover more consumer insights with regards to professionals.

8

Summary and Conclusion

Marketing of Professional Services as an area of investigation is one of the rapidly expanding fields of marketing and is of growing interest for research and investigation by academicians, intellectuals and professionals too. Marketing Professional Services in an important addition of modern practice of management. Besides being intellectually stimulating for the academic researcher, it is of considerable value for professionals and firms in practice or for those just entering the profession by helping them to modify their attitude towards "Marketing" by bringing about greater realization of today's increasingly well-managed and competitive business environment as well as providing the tools to better integrate "Marketing" into their practice of management.

Times have changed and so have man's needs, wants and requirements. It is, therefore, more appropriate, economical and convenient to buy services from professionals then to create them within the organization. In the past, services did not receive the same attention as manufacturing. In recent years, however, there is a greater awareness of the need of having services and marketing them on account of increased competition. There has consequently been a vast change in the services sector. This is especially true for professional service scene also. Today, clients are better informed and more demanding than they used to be in the past. Their level of expectation is high. They engage in "shopping-around" while buying professional services. Long-term client loyalty must be nurtured and protected, not to be taken for granted. Along with these, shifts in economic, social, cultural, political and international environment calls forth the professional and professional firms to cope with these dynamic fundamental changes. The professional has adapted and need to continue to adapt to these changes by making use of the modern marketing practices that are used by the commercial firms. The application of the modern marketing management techniques to the professions shows the extension of marketing field, and is a natural evolutionary development in practice of management, which has been clearly brought out in the conceptual framework of the study. How product and services marketing differ, unique characteristics of services, what is marketing of professional services etc have been discussed at length in the first chapter of conceptual framework.

Marketing Myths most Professionals believe

Marketing Myth #1: "My marketing's most important purpose is to promote my services." False! The most important purpose of your marketing is to establish that you can be trusted. Most of us don't do business with people we don't trust. While your prospect is considering whether to hire your services, he is also trying to determine whether he trusts you.

Marketing Myth #2: "My prospects know the services I offer." Not true. If you believe prospects know the services you offer, you will start losing clients to professionals who make their offering of specific services crystal clear. Many professionals have had the experience where one of their clients has gone to another because he didn't know the first accountant provided the same service. Write a detailed list of your services and give a copy to all clients and prospects -- because if prospects don't see the service they want on your list, they may go to another professional.

Marketing Myth #3: "My referral sources will send me all the new clients I want." It won't happen. Certainly you're grateful to get referrals from time to time. But if you think all the new business you want and need will come from referrals, 99% of the time you're wrong. You must develop a marketing program that will attract clients directly to you so you don't rely solely on referrals. Also, this helps you avoid paying referral fees.

Marketing Myth #4: "When prospects or clients have questions, they will call me." Not true. People often hesitate to call unless they know their calls are welcome. This is particularly true of prospects that haven't yet established a relationship with you. In all of your communications, invite prospects and clients to call you with their questions or problems. Often, their questions lead to work you can perform on their behalf.

Marketing Myth #5: "It makes no difference whether my photo appears in my marketing materials." Not true. Your photograph is a key piece of your marketing puzzle. A warm, friendly, engaging photo with good eye contact can do wonders for your marketing. It helps establish a friendly, trusting relationship with your prospects and increases your reader's comfort. Prospects don't care what you look like, but they feel better when they know.

Marketing Myth #6: "Interacting with prospects is a waste of time." Wrong. Always look for new ways to get prospects to interact with you. The more prospects talk with you, the more opportunities you have to explain how you can help them. Your interaction can take place over the telephone, in your office, at your seminar, by e-mail -- almost anywhere. The nature of the interaction doesn't matter as long as you and your prospect carry on a meaningful dialogue.

Marketing Myth #7: "I have to be careful not to repeat myself when talking with prospects." Wrong. When people take in new information, they forget most of it. And unless prospects remember what you say, they won't likely hire you. It's good to repeat yourself when

Marketing Myth #8: "My prospects understand what I say because they know the legal vocabulary." Not true. When you assume your prospects have basic knowledge or understand simple terms, you're often wrong. Your message means nothing if your prospects don't understand what you're saying. Always go back to square one. Make sure you're not talking over your prospects' head. And if you must use a jargon of your profession, make sure you define it.

Marketing Myth #9: "Marketing methods don't work as well today as they once did." Not true. If your marketing doesn't work, it's probably due to a poor, inadequate or incomplete marketing message. Don't blame the method that delivers the message when it's really the message that's lacking. You should design your marketing message as carefully as you prepare a case for trial.

Marketing Myth #10: "The more complicated my message, the more prospects will understand the need for my services." Wrong. Every day, your prospects suffer from information overload. They screen out complicated messages. Keep your message simple because a simple message is the only message that has any chance of getting through to your target audience.

Marketing Myth #11: "How an advertisement looks is not as important as what the ad says." Not true. Graphics in print ads are critical, not only to your image, but also to make sure your ad seizes your prospect's attention. Yes, a powerful message is important. But without strong graphics, your prospect may never see your ad. Then you've wasted your money.

Marketing Myth #12: "Prospects and clients don't mind when I'm slow to return phone calls. They understand that I'm busy." In your dreams! Everybody's busy. Delays in returning phone calls are one of the biggest sources of complaints about professionals' services. They are a major hot button with clients and prospects. When you return phone calls promptly, you make a powerful, positive impression. When you don't, the impression you make is far more negative than you might imagine. Prospects cannot easily assess the depth of your knowledge or experience. But one thing they evaluate quickly is whether you return phone calls promptly.

Marketing Myth #13: "The articles our public relations firm generates will attract new clients." Maybe not. In most cases, p.r. programs bring exposure, but exposure does not always bring new clients. Attorneys routinely report, "We were happy with the number of articles about our firm, but we didn't get even one new client!" A good publicity program can be an important part of your marketing program. But whether your publicity program generates only exposure or solid-marketing results depends on the experience and know-how of the person conducting your program.

Marketing Myth #14: "The most effective time to deliver my marketing message is when my prospect is in my office." Wrong! The most effective time to deliver your marketing message is when your prospect first thinks about his problem and wants to know what solutions are available. You have a significant advantage over other professionals when you have a packet of materials you can mail to your prospect, regardless of his location. You can offer your information packet any number of ways, such as through your advertising, publicity, newsletters or mail. When your prospect thinks about his problem, he sees that you offer material on the subject. Then he calls or e-mails your office and requests your information. And you respond by sending your materials, as promised. In many cases, this puts your marketing message into his hands before he calls other professionals.

Marketing Myth #15: "My quarterly newsletter will prove to be an effective marketing tool." Not even close! In today's over-advertised society, you're fortunate indeed if you can create an impression in your prospect's mind. If you hope to make your impression stick, you should send your newsletter at least monthly. The more often you mail to prospects on your mailing list, the more new business you will likely attract. The frequency with which you deliver your newsletter is much more important than its size.

Marketing Myth #16: "By lowering my fees, I'll gain a stronger competitive position." Not true. When you lower your fees, (1) you undermine your credibility because prospects wonder why your services are no longer worth what you once charged, (2) you attract clients who know the price of everything and the value of nothing (people who are loyal to the dollar are never loyal to you!), and (3) you lose money because it is usually impossible to achieve the volume of cases you need to make up for the profits you lose. Instead of lowering your fees, raise them -- because it's easier to justify why you charge so much than to explain why you charge so little.

Marketing Myth #17: "If I invest enough dollars in marketing, I will eventually get the results I want." Not necessarily. Your results depend on the marketing methods you choose. If you don't get favorable results from a small investment, you won't likely get better results from a larger investment. The key element is the strategy you select, not the amount of money you invest.

Marketing Myth #18: "To attract new clients, I should promote my services." No! When you promote your services, you take on the role of a salesperson, which undermines your credibility. This is called selling-based marketing. Instead, promote your knowledge using Education-Based Marketing. This allows you to attract new clients, increase referrals, strengthen client loyalty and build your image as an authority without selling. Education-Based Marketing gives prospects what they want, information and advice -- and it removes what they don't want, a sales pitch.

Review of literature, on the marketing of services showed that several authors have concerned themselves with building the argument that services are different from products and that these differences necessitate special marketing considerations (Eiglier et al., 1977, judd, 1964: Rathmell, 1974; Ryans and Wittink, 1977).

Marketing of services being marketing of intangible offerings, so some studies have dealt with the need for and possible means of emphasizing the tangible aspects of services to professional services (Bloom, 1977; Shimp and Dyer, 1978; Smith and Myer, 1980; Uhl and Upah, 1980 (a); Wilson, 1972; Kotler and Bloom, 1984) Situational factors (eg. Physical surroundings and Atmospherics affecting quality of services have been dealt by other fews like Berry, 1975; Eiglier and langeard, 1977; Shostack, 1977). The importance of public contact personnel also has been stressed (Berry, 1975; George, 1977; Sasser and Arbeit, 1976, wheatley, 1983). Others dealt with need for and procedures used to more closely match supply and demand for services (Sasser, 1976: Lovelock and Young, 1977). Mechanization of service operations issues have been dealt with by Levitt, 1972 & 1976. The distribution-channel-related issues have been addressed by Donnelly, 1976; and Stern and E1-Ansary, 1977.

Review of literature further brought about that researches have been under taken in America and very few in Britain dealing with the particular marketing problems of and response to those problems by organizations providing professional services in general (Wilson, 1972; Kotler and Bloom 1984; Wheatley, 1983); Everett Turner (1969); accounting services (Mahon (1978), Kotler & Connor

(1977), Denney (1983); Legal services (Denney (1983), Deardan, Deardan & Kiser (1981) and the like. These studies have brought about the information services clients seek while selecting a professional; professional selection criteria's; types of services for which professionals are needed and the like, which if truly understood by professionals in their practice of management can lead to their overall growth and success. Review of literature further showed that the role of marketing in the professional services; and that these professional firms in their zeal to satisfy consumer needs, lacked true marketing orientation.

Professionals are using various marketing techniques unintentionally and without understanding their true marketing significance. But as the practice scene is changing, and competition is on the increase, greater realization has to be there on the part of the professionals especially Chartered Accountants in question to embrace the marketing concept in their working, which truly can ensure their future success and well-being. How to do it, has been brought out in step-by-step approach in the study.

The present study "Marketing of Professional Accounting Services" is basically exploratory in nature, and has made an in-depth analysis of need for marketing professional services of Chartered Accountants in Visakhapatnam. The study was aimed to bring out useful marketing strategies that professionals can adopt to remain client-centered rather than product-centered in terms of services offerings, target marketing selection, client review programme, client profiles, referrals as a source of business, importance of personal contact in promotion of professional services, importance of collateral appearance and atmospherics and need for hard, timely, accurate work by charging genuine fees and accessible location from the client's angle rather their own points of view. To project the client's angle, client survey covering-individual, institutional and other professionals were undertaken. Here, a study of attitudes of two types of clients' users and non-users was under taken to have useful cross validation.

Objectives

The specific objectives of this study are:

1. To find out if the CA's can be identified as having a production,

sales or consumer oriented marketing management orientation. To see whether services businesses (i.e. professionals firm's of CA) were opposed/or opposed to the idea of marketing, and whether they perceive themselves as producer of services Vs marketers of services.

2. To know whether the "Satisfaction of Client" was "Central" goal of CA. and to suggest a viable marketing strategy to practice development.
3. To identify the professional tactics used by most of the professionals while interacting with client and determine what were the potential areas for the CA in which they could do practice, to change over, or to diversify to what new areas of service product offerings.
4. Which types of service product offerings constituted the major chunk of business in case of professional services of practicing accountants? And to bring about if location, design and timing of service availability were considered important in marketing of professional service of CA's.
5. To find out the factors were considered important in practice development and client attraction, and the type of communication mix being used to inform prospective customers about the service and promote its use?
6. To know which information sources contributed maximum share of clienteles for the practicing CAs and to study the importance and type of referrals as a source of business.
7. To determine if these professionals feel change in the practicing environment:- Change in what respect, and their valuable suggestions for improvement.
8. To find out the type of client groups using CA services-their relationship with income, and category to which belonged and To know how the users and the non-users perceived, the different factors while choosing the CA firm.
9. To study how the user and non-users perceived, the necessity of a CA in different cases/service product offerings and to study among users, their sources of information about CA.

10. To find out the differences in service quality Expectations between users and non-users of all the categories of clients and service quality Perceptions of the professionals

Sample

The present study comprised of sample of 550, distributed as under:

Professional Chartered Accountants	= 150
Users of C.A. Services	= 200
Non-users of C.A. Services	= 200
Total Respondents	550

Professional Chartered Accountants were basically selected on a random basis, while users and non-users of a C.A. Services i.e. clients were mainly selected on the basis of convenience and judgment. But every care was taken to cover all possible segments of clients belonging to individual, Institutional and other Professionals category, in Visakhapatnam Area.

Research Tools

Two questionnaires, structured and undisguised, were developed based on pilot study to infer the responses from practicing Accountants, clients and non-users of accountancy services. Most of the questions were in the form of multiple choice or dichotomous questions and there were few open-ended questions also.

Chartered Accountants questionnaires covered such area as experience in Accountants profession, types of service offerings, whether activities like, segmentations targeting, client reviews, etc. are under taken, importance of referrals on a source of business, sources of clientele, their attitude towards the word " Marketing", ways of attracting of clients, and improving their images and the like.

Second and third questionnaire was related with the client survey part, one for user and other for non-user, where client's angle actual and potential one-was explored regarding for what services they need professional help, selection criteria's, source of information, etc.

Data Collection and Analysis:

The data collection was done by interviewing technique personally in view of the importance of the subject and the fact that the respondents were unlikely to return by mail the questionnaire posted to them because of their busy schedule. . The collected data from the respondents, Chartered Accountants, Clients and non-users with the help of research instrument were tabulated, analyzed and interpreted. Data analysis involved converting a series of recorded observations in proper descriptive statements and from this inferences were drawn. Most of the inferences have been drawn on the basis of the percentages, averages, weights, ranks, correlation techniques, chi^2 analysis and the like.

Conclusions and Implications

(1)Specialisation according to area of practice was being preferred rather than being a general practitioner. Auditing and taxation comprised the principal service offerings of al professionals irrespective of their experience. Newer areas of practice being adopted by professional with higher experience were those of management services, company and secretarial affairs, EDP and the like.

Implications

1. Rather than having only "Service" specialization, professionals should also develop market specialization Instead of thinking that auditing procedures can be standardized to apply to virtually any company in any industry, they should organize their practice by industry because of diversity of industry characteristics with specialists labels to accounting firms like bank men, brokerage men, retail specialists, construction company specialists and the like. This will enhance their scope of practice, as times have changed. Later on series of specialists can be further developed in many sub-areas of practice for experience in one area of tax practice; sub-areas can be reorganization, estate planning, state taxes and the other.

2. Mostly, professional accountancy firms were multi-service firms dealing in various service lines of Audit an Accounts, financial planning, Taxation, Secretarial and Company affairs, Internal

Audit, Management Services. Amongst these service offerings Audit and Accounts was the most opted for, and constituted the bread & butter for all professional accountants. How ever it was realised that as competition is on the increase, so the need to diversify to newer areas of service lines being those of management services, information system audit, Agricultural farm accounting, estate planning etc. was highlighted.

Implications

1. As the world becomes more complex and the knowledge revolution continues to accelerate, the breadth of professional services is constantly growing. At the same time, the depth of each single service increases. Such growth should be carefully monitored and adhered to as a source of new opportunities which if exploited will result in excitement, self-fulfillment and rewards.

2. Young members should try to diversify their professional work and explore new opportunities like the Management services, Agricultural farm accounting etc. rather than sticking to old and traditional audit work for the purpose of increasing the size of the cake.

3. Big firms having considerable knowledge, skill experience, maturity and expertise in the latest developments of modern techniques of management should try to develop new vistas of professional works such as management services and agricultural farm accounting and give up a portion of their traditional statutory audit work.

4. Majority of the professional accountants irrespective of whether new or established ones, were having a negative attitude towards the word "Marketing". Principally they equated marketing with "Selling", "Promotion" and advertising that according to them was banned in their profession by code of conduct. A very important finding here was that an overall commitment to the extent of 50% for the 22 marketing practices enumerated by the researcher was there among the professional firms of CA. How ever these activities were not performed in the formal manner and with an understanding of marketing significance. Because of this no approach to segmentation of market was used. No client profiles were maintained. No formal list of referrals as a source of

business was kept. Client review activities though performed were not done formally as knowledge of its true marketing significance were not there on their part. As such undifferentiated approach to target market selection was being practiced as opined by respondents.

Implications

1. Today, most professional firms need to realize that marketing plays an increasingly more important role in their overall success. "Selling, advertising etc." are only some of the elements of marketing and not marketing as such. Marketing is a more comprehensive term, which starts with the identification of needs and wants of the clients and ends with their satisfaction.

2. Increased competition for clients, greater consumer selectivity, and vast changes taking places both within the profession and in business in the last few years, have pointed that "Marketing" is a necessity and not a consideration on the part of professional firms which can only be included in the minds of professional accountants through constant education with changes in course curriculums of the Institute of Chartered Accountants of India.

3. "Recommendations of the existing clients "as opined by majority of professionals was the most important source of clientele contributing an average of 51% of the total work with personal/ business contacts as the next source accounting for 34.45% of the total work. Also client satisfaction was considered important by all professional firms. Factors like hard work, good, timely work; they considered perfect auditing; accuracy of work etc. important in bringing about desired satisfaction. But it was observed that in their zeal for client satisfaction, professional accountants lacked market-orientation, because services were performed by them posing " I am the Expert " and with better mousetrap fallacy in their minds.

Implications

1. Professional firms of Chartered Accountants in their zeal to bring about client satisfaction need to adopt the marketing concept - a consumer-oriented philosophy that views profits and client satisfaction as outgrowths of satisfying consumer wants

and needs. The marketing concept is important, since a lack of satisfied clients may eventually threaten the very life of a firm.

2. This external view, with a focus on client needs and wants should permeate all levels of a firm and guide it in marketing its services.

3. Services be rendered from client's angle, rather than the service provider angle, that is instead of taking the position that as a professional accountant he is capable of performing a service in a particular manner only, he should perform the service by uncovering clients objections.

(4) Majority of the professional accountant realized referrals as an important source of business without consciously realizing the marketing significance of keeping and developing referral sources. "Existing Clients" and "Other Professionals" at rank 1 & 2 were considered as a vital source of referrals by 100% and 53% of the respondents respectively.

Implications

The professional firms should take formal and concrete steps to cultivate key referral sources. Widening and deepening personal referral sources can be the most effective marketing strategy for a professional firm, as it is the best source for new business.

(6) Physical and abstract factors highlighted for client attraction/ retention in the light of self regulations in the profession, were "Professional Competence - in the form of hard work, good manners and good deeds " at rank 1; " Collateral appearance-human personality, dress etc." at rank 2; "Atmospherics-office décor, furnishings etc." at rank 3 and so on. Fee and location of office were considered relatively of minor importance. Relation with touts/dalals was considered a dirty practice.

Implications:

1. There is a need for conscious understanding of these factors, which are significant from marketing point of view on the part of these professionals. This is turn would result in understanding the significance of such factors like "Updating of knowledge", "Induction of qualified and knowledgeable staff" ---

and so on which will be helpful in building the successful practice.

(7) Regarding " advertising" permission, in India, majority 82% of public accountants were opposed to the idea and showed their negative bias towards Advertising. But unconsciously few of them were found to be issuing advertisements about them in newspapers as can be seen from the Appendix.

Implication

1. Merit of advertising as an economical means of disseminating information to reduce anxiety and consequent fear in buying of professional services needs to be carefully evaluated and understood, before giving opinion towards "Advertising Permission".

(8) "Personal Contact at rank 1: "Use of greeting" at rank 2; "Use of internal circulars to existing clients" at rank 3; "Personal Socialisation like joining in club etc. at rank 4; were few of the techniques commonly employed by the professionals to acquire the necessary quantum of work, but often used unintentionally, thus it can be said that ways open to the Chartered Accountants to make his existence known are not yet used fully. Other methods like contributing articles to journals, giving speeches at the meetings of the Regional Council and other places are also much in common.

Implications

1. Accounting firms need to constantly communicate with present and potential clients, with society at large and others, to keep the public and clients informed about their duties, responsibilities and effects for which massive public relation campaigns is a must. If members of the profession must not advertise, then why not the institute do it in a collective manner?

(9) It was interpreted that ethics of their professional were undergoing change. Financial rewards were becoming more important rather than rendering quality service. Also ethical & legal constraints imposed were not being adhered to by the fellow professionals as reported by majority of the professional accountants covered.

Implications

Ethical compromises to please client in the face of competition must be resisted on the part of professional service firms, as they are accountable to "Third Parties" - Share Holders, Government, and Banks etc. and not to their clients only. Professional service firm can take several steps to ensure that its marketing activities or "Practice developments activities" stay without ethical and legal boundaries. One such activity can be to educate clients about what constitutes acceptable professional behavior, and thus spend more time with their clients. Second is by becoming more selective in accepting customers- and weeding out unethical clients. So unethical compromises shouldn't be made at any cost to maintain the reputation/integrity of the profession.

(10) Many changes were reported having taken place in the practicing environment of the professionals. Some of these highlighted were like

1. Clients have become more demanding.
2. Clients engages in shopping around being better informed.
3. Tax Laws have changed.
4. Competition is on the increase and survival of the fittest principle will apply.
5. Work culture/Ethics have changed.
6. Sincerity towards profession has decreased and the like.

Implications

Keeping in view the above changes, suggestions aimed at both the institute side as well as towards their fellow professionals which could be helpful in improving the practicing scene in the country were given by professionals as:

Suggestions aimed at the institute side were

1. It should be ensured that government audit and other work be got uniformly distributed among the members of profession, rather being concentrated with select few.
2. Regular changes in the course curriculum of ICAI be there; Latest law changes be taught.

3. System of allowing part-time practice be abolished.

4. Monitoring of fees be there from institute side.

Other few aimed towards their fellow professionals were like

1. Unethical compromises and practice of undercutting by new entrants be avoided and rather resisted to maintain the image of the profession.
2. Only CA's with good family background should think of joining practice.
3. New CA. in practice, underemployed can take up other lines of business like 1. Financing 2. Consultancy.
4. Updation of knowledge on their part be a continuous affair, to maintain the sanctity of the profession.

(11)It can be concluded that attest function of accountants in India, constitute their bread & butter, and it is for this Official Business purposes of auditing and tax representation, CA are being hired by clients. If this audit work was not statutory, the existence of CA in India was under doubt. But simultaneously greater scope lies for professional accountants to diversify their practice keeping in tune with the need of clients-present ones as well as the future one's.

Implication

1. New fields of professional work have to be explored by these professionals to reduce their dependence on the traditional type of work-auditing and tax representation-where no professional work is undertaken, rather only liaison job is performed.

2. Usefulness of CA to clients for estate planning, real property handling etc. have to be demonstrated to further enlarge the scope of their operation, and to enable the clients to make increased use of CA's for such service in future, besides the traditional requirements of auditing and tax representation.

12. Importance of information sources consulted while selecting a service provider cannot be ruled out in case of professional accountants. Among the various sources of information consulted by various types of clients --- individual,

institutional and other professionals, "Personal Information Sources comprising of family members, self, friends, relatives etc. were ranked at no.1; with referral sources and daily contacts at rank 2. Thus it can be concluded that there is a fundamental shortage of consumer information sources to guide the choice process for professional service providers.

Implication

1. Client's "information gap" when selecting a professional accountant should be filled, as clients require substantially more data before selecting professional service providers. If advertising is banned in the profession, alternative information sources be developed like referrals etc. to guide the clients in their professional service provider choice.

(13) Considerable degree of consistency exists in the response pattern of two groups - Users and Non-users of CA with regards.

1. Selection Criteria's 2. Accountancy Service Needs:

As brought about in this study it further suggests that marketing strategy can be used successfully to allow for better distribution of accounting services irrespective of wheather we are dealing with traditional clients or future non-traditional clients. These two areas can be discussed separately as under.

(a) *Selection criteria*: Non-users rank overall reputation/ integrity of CA as more important selection criteria than do users.

However quality of work, technical competence, and experience of CA are other attributes considered important in selection of professional accountants both by users and non-users.

(b) *Accountancy service needs*:- Necessary of CA for auditing and business taxation was considered uniformly of paramount importance by both users and non-users; yet this study suggests that, for remaining thirteen area where CAs can render services, non users felt that services of CA are more important for attestation of financial reports for arranging bank loans, or preparing of project reports etc. i.e. for legal reasons rather than for such accountancy needs as consultation on tax matters advice on formation of new company and the like i.e. advisory functions.

Implications

In catering to accountancy service needs, an educational process directed at non-users would appear to be justified, as the non-users were found as having not recognized many situations where CA's could be of help (e.g. consultation, inventory management and the life).

(14) The study revealed that client loyality like brand loyality for product, existed in the professional setting of CAs . The reason for the same may be that the great uncertainity and consequent tension and anxiety-many client experience in buying professional services discourages "Shopping around" and encourages loyalty.

Implication

The professional's shouldn't stop working seeing the client loyalty, rather should continue to strive and work for increased client-satisfaction by showing hard, sincere, and timely work; since client loyalty can not be taken for granted irrespective of whether we are dealing with services or products.

9

Marketing Professional Services: Epilogue

"Some men succeed by what they know; some by what they do; and a few by what they are."

Though the service sector is growing at a very fast pace and is contributing to 55% of the India's GDP, and the changing environmental and legal conditions across the world are giving ample opportunities to India's professionals to expand their operations and their services to more than one nation. The only threat for the professional services in the future has been the short supply of talented pool of professionals while there are many contemporary professions are attracting the Indian youth like software, BPO's etc. The governing bodies of the professions and their associations have to take utmost care in promoting the profession as a lucrative opportunity to many and make sure that it continues to attract the intellectual diaspora.

Indian professionals have an upper hand during the interaction with their clients and this is no doubt true, which the research has also proved. As all the various types of clients have a full trust on their professional and will listen to anything they say. Improving the service quality and satisfaction level is to be made of a mandatory priority by the professional. What my research has made be understand throughout the process of my interaction with clients and professionals is that, there is a typical stereotyped view of professionals that the clients have, and this largely is influencing them to just have a minimum expectation towards the overall service quality, other than the "actual work" involved. Marketing has raised revolutionally the standards of performance in many sectors like Manufacturing; Retailing etc., it is now the time for professionals to adopt these tastefully beautiful concepts and mould it to their competitive advantage.

As noticed, professional service organizations have changed dramatically over the years. Therefore, Professionals have to cope with increasing competition, greater public dissatisfaction with professionals, rapidly changing technologies, and other changes in their external environments. One tool that they can turn to as a way to ensure their survival in this unpredictable environment is marketing. They are finding that marketing is not inherently unethical or manipulative nor is it defined by the field of advertising. Indeed, professional service firms should discover that marketing could be carried on with as much professionalism as the work of a lawyer, CPA, or doctor. The successful marketer of professional services is skilled at understanding, creating, and managing exchanges. He or she uses a marketing mix involving the right combination of service, price, place, promotion, physical evidence, processes, and people to achieve voluntary exchanges with target markets.

Professional services are intangible, inseparable, variable, and perishable. Professional service providers face some distinctive problems not faced by other types of service organizations and must deal with high levels of client uncertainty, limited service differentiability, quality control difficulties, and several other obstacles to mounting a successful marketing effort.

The development of a client orientation should be the very first mission of a professional service organization seeking to become proficient at marketing. Such an orientation involves having the entire organization give primary attention to serving the needs and wants of its clients.

Before concluding, researcher would like to point out the twelve keys to effective professional services marketing (Kotler, Bloom and Hayes, 2002).Marketing professional services successfully involves the right mix of various elements, including the following 12 keys.

Key 1: Quality Is King

Individuals belonging to the professions are likely to enjoy a

Managing service offerings at different stages of their life cycles requires different marketing strategies. Each stage presents new marketing challenges and requires adjustments in the target market and marketing mix.

Finally, as consumer and client needs and desires change, the firm must develop new services.

Key 7: Pricing for Success

Professional service firms must not only develop attractive service offerings but also price them appropriately. Customers evaluate pricing for services differently from goods. They often have inaccurate or limited references for prices for services. There are also non-monetary costs in obtaining a service. Furthermore, price is a key signal to quality in a client's mind. If a client believes that "you get what you pay for," a low fee structure can actually be a detriment to the client's perception of the firm's professional services.

Key 8: Accessibility, Accessibility, Accessibility

Although location, location, location is still important to the success of. the professional service firm, it is not the final consideration when determining client access and acceptability toward the service firm. Clients are increasingly demanding services based upon their needs and time schedules. Professional service firms may provide greater access to their organization through the use of the Internet, telephone system, expanded hours of operation, and the use of non-traditional points of access.

The physical evidence that a service firm presents to a client will affect the customer's ability to mentally access an organization. This holds true with both the physical location' and the Website.

Key 9: You Cannot Communicate

Everything the organization says, is, and does communicate. The challenge is to make sure that the communications are consistent, clear, and effective. Service professionals can use many different tools to communicate with their clients: advertising, personal selling, sales promotion, publicity, and direct marketing. The tools have different strengths and limitations. Furthermore, each tool may be controlled by different people within the organization. The professional service firm must work hard to ensure that everyone in the firm is "on the same page" when it comes to deciding what the firm wants to say, to whom, how, and with what intended effect. Given the many communication options, this can best be achieved by appointing a marketing communications manager who has responsibility for the overall communication efforts and who will coordinate the use, timing, expenditures, and effectiveness of the communication tools.

For most professional service organizations, personal selling through personal contact is probably the most important of all tools available within the promotional mix. Through personal contact, the professional can persuade and reassure existing and potential clients.

Key 10: Riding the E-Train

In the future the Internet will be viewed as just another communication improvement following the likes of language, the printing press, newspapers, mail, telegraph, telephone, television, and the fax machine. Today, it represents one of the most exciting and challenging opportunities facing professional service firms in their efforts to provide superior client based services. E-commerce and the Internet offer ever-expanding possibilities for serving clients, including the ability to expand from national to international markets; decrease the costs of creating, processing, distributing, storing, and retrieving paper-based information such as brochures or catalogs; improving the efficiencies of service systems; building brand awareness and brand equity, and even helping build stronger relationships with clients.

The Internet represents challenges to the professional service firm primarily because it is so new. It is still in its infancy and is very likely to undergo rapid and dramatic changes, requiring the professional service firm to continuously invest in newer software that will maximize its effectiveness.

Key 11: Building Meaningful Relationships

Most people take comfort and enjoyment in the presence of others and earn for the ability to connect with others and develop meaningful relationships. Meaningful relationships give us comfort and peace of mind and make our lives richer and simpler.

The desire for relationships in business is no different from what it is in people's personal lives. A strong business relationship between a professional service firm and a client is mutually rewarding and simplifies the lives of both parties. To the professional service firm, the relationship is rewarding both on a professional and financial basis. It is rewarding to the client because it provides peace of mind about that particular aspect of the client's life. Strong business relationships simplify both parties' lives by reducing the need or the desire to constantly seek out, evaluate, choose, and develop new relationships.

Key 12: The Future Is Now

Any student of military strategy understands that there are three essential components for winning the battle, and ultimately the war. First, one must be aware of history, because as George Santana once said, "He who does not know history is doomed to repeat it." By understanding the firm and its industry as well as the firm's relationship with its clients and being able to view it in a historical context, the professional service marketer will be better able to anticipate and respond to future events. Second, one must have a thorough understanding of the environment in which he finds himself. Members of the firm must understand the firm's external environment (competition, clients, economy, social/political shifts) as well as its internal environment (organizational strengths and weaknesses, expertise, capital needs, and financial resources).

Finally, to succeed one must create strategies that include multiple plans based upon multiple scenarios. Plan A rarely ever works perfectly. Clients change, competition changes, the environment changes, all potentially interfering with the organization's strategic initiatives. It is far better to develop Plans A, B, C, D, and so forth based upon scenarios that have a pre-determined probability of occurring. This will allow for seamless and smooth transitions as the environment in which the firm operates changes.

Bibliography

Anderson, Ralph E. (1973), "Consumer Dissatisfaction: The Effect of Disconfirmed Expectancy on Perceived Product Performance," *Journal of Marketing Research*, 10 (February), 38-44.

B.Van Looy, R.Van Dierdonck, and P. Gemmel, eds. Harlow, UK: Financial Times Prentice Hall, 3-23.38 JOURNAL OF SERVICE RESEARCH / August 2004

Babakus, E. and Boller, G.W. (1992), "An Empirical Assessment of the SERVQUAL Scale", *Journal of Business Research,* Vol. 24, May, pp. 253-68.

Bartels, R. (1988), *The History of Marketing Thought*, third edition, Publishing Horizons, Inc., Columbus, OH.

Bateson, J.E.G. (1979), "Why We Need Service Marketing", in Ferrell, O.C., Brown, S.W. and Lamb,C.W. (Eds), *Conceptual and Theoretical Developments in Marketing,* American Marketing Association, Chicago, IL, pp. 131-46.

Bateson, J.E.G. (1983), "The Self-Service Customer – Empirical Findings", in Berry L.L., Shostack,

Bateson, J.E.G. (1985), "Self-Service Consumer: An Exploratory Study", *Journal of Retailing,* Vol.61, Fall, pp. 49-76.

Bateson, J.E.G. (1989), *Managing Services Marketing: Text and Readings,* Dryden Press, Hinsdale, IL.

Bateson, J.E.G. (1992), *Managing Services Marketing: Text and Readings,* Second Edition, Dryden Press, Orlando, FL.

Bateson, J.E.G., Eiglier, P., Langeard, E. and Lovelock, C.H. (1978), *Testing a Conceptual Framework for Consumer Service Marketing*, Marketing Science Institute, Cambridge, MA.

Baum, S.H. (1990), "Making Your Service Blueprint Pay Off", *Journal of Services Marketing,* Vol.4, Summer, pp. 45-52.

Berry, L.L. (1980a), "Services Marketing Is Different", *Business,* Vol. 30, May-June, pp. 24-9.

Berry, L.L. (1980b), "The Time Buying Consumer", *Journal of Retailing*, Vol. 56, Winter, pp. 58-69.

Berry, L.L. (1981), "Perspectives on the Retailing of Services", in Stampfl, R.W. and Hirsch man, E.C. (Eds), *Theory in Retailing: Traditional and Non-traditional Sources*, American Marketing Association, Chicago, Ill, pp. 9-20.

Berry, L.L. (1983), "Relationship Marketing", in Berry, L., Shostack, L.G., and Upah, G.D. (Eds) *Emerging Perspectives on Services Marketing*, American Marketing Association, Chicago, Ill,pp. 25-8.

Berry, L.L. and Parasuraman, A. (1991), *Marketing Services: Competing Through Quality*, The Free Press, New York, NY.

Berry, L.L. and Parasuraman, A. (1993), "Building a New Academic Field— The Case of Services Marketing", *Journal of Retailing*, Vol. 69, Spring.

Berry, L.L., Shostack, G.L. and Upah, G.D. (Eds) (1983), *Emerging Perspectives on Services Marketing*, American Marketing Association, Chicago, Ill.

Bitner, M.J. (1990), "Evaluating Service Encounters: The Effects of Physical Surroundings and Employee Responses", *Journal of Marketing*, Vol. 54, April, pp. 69-82.

Bitner, M.J. (1992), "Servicescapes: The Impact of Physical Surroundings on Customers and Employees", *Journal of Marketing*, Vol. 56, April, pp. 57-71.

Bitner, M.J., Booms, B.H. and Tetreault, M.S. (1990), "The Service Encounter: Diagnosing Favorable and Unfavorable Incidents", *Journal of Marketing*, Vol. 54, January, pp. 71-84.

Bloch, T.M., Upah, G.D. and Zeithaml, V.A. (Eds) (1985), *Services Marketing in a Changing Environment*, American Marketing Association, Chicago, Ill.

Blois, K.J. (1974), "The Marketing of Services: An Approach", *European Journal of Marketing*, Vol.8, Summer, pp. 137-45.

Bolton, R.N. and Drew, J.H. (1991a), "A Longitudinal Analysis of the Impact of Service Changes on Consumer Attitudes", *Journal of Marketing*, Vol. 55, January, pp. 1-9.

Bolton, R.N. and Drew, J.H. (1991b), "A Multistage Model of Customers' Assessments of Service Quality and Value", *Journal of Consumer Research*, Vol. 17 No. 4, pp. 375-84.

Booms, B.H. and Bitner, M.J. (1981), "Marketing Strategies and Organizational Structures for Service Firms", in Donnelly, J.H. and George, W.R. (Eds), *Marketing of Services*, American Marketing Association, Chicago, IL, pp. 47-51.

Bowen, D.E. and Lawler, E.E. (1992), "The Empowerment of Service Workers: What, Why, How, and When", *Sloan Management Review*, Vol. 33, Spring, pp. 31-9.

Bowen, D.E., Chase, R.B. and Cummings, T.G. (Eds) (1990), *Service Management Effectiveness: Balancing Strategy, Organization and Human Resources, Operations and Marketing*, Jossey-Bass Inc., San Francisco, CA.

Bowen, David E. (2000), Pt. 3, in *Services Marketing Self-Portraits: Introspections, Reflections, and Glimpses from the Experts*, R. P. Fisk, S. J. Grove, and J. John, eds. Chicago: American Marketing Association, 37-51.

Bowen, John (1990), "Development of a Taxonomy of Services to GainStrategic Marketing Insights," *Journal of the Academy of Marketing Science*, 18 (Winter), 43-49.

Boyer, Kenneth K, Roger Hallowell, and Aleda V. Roth (2002), "EServices: Operating Strategy—A Case Study and a Method for AnalyzingOperational Benefits," *Journal of Operations Management*, 20, 175-88.

Brown, S.W. and Swartz, T.A. (1989), "A Gap Analysis of Professional Service Quality", *Journal of Marketing*, Vol. 53, April, pp. 92-8.

Brown, S.W., Gummesson, E., Edvardsson, B. and Gustafsson, B. (Eds) (1991), *Service Quality:Multidisciplinary and Multinational Perspectives*, Lexington Books, Lexington,

Brown, Stephen W. (2000), Pt. 4, in *Services Marketing Self-Portraits: Introspections, Reflections, and Glimpses from the Experts*, R. P. Fisk, S. J. Grove, and J. John, eds. Chicago: American Marketing Association, 53-69.

Butterfield, Herbert (1949), *The Origins of Modern Science, 1300-1800*. London: G. Bell & Sons.

Canton, I.D. (1984), "Learning to Love the Service Economy", *Harvard Business Review*, Vol. 62,May-June, pp. 89-97.

Cardozo, Richard N. (1965), "An Experimental Study of Customer Effort, Expectation, and Satisfaction," *Journal of Marketing Research*, 2 (August), 244-49.

Carlzon, J. (1987), *Moments of Truth*, Harper & Row, New York, NY.

Carlzon, Jan (1987), *Moments of Truth*. Cambridge, MA: Ballinger. Chamberlin, Edward Hastings ([1933] 1962), *and The Economics of Imperfect Competition*, 8th ed. Cambridge, MA: Harvard University Press.

Carman, J.M. (1990), "Consumer Perceptions of Service Quality: An Assessment of the SERVQUAL Dimensions", *Journal of Retailing*, Vol. 66, Spring, pp. 33-55.

Chase, Richard B. (1978), "Where Does the Customer Fit in a Service Operation?" *Harvard Business Review*, 56 (November), 137-42.

Cherlow, Jay R. (1981), "Measuring the Value of Travel Time Savings," *Journal of Consumer Research*, 7 (March), 360-71.

Christine Moorman, and Peter R. Dickson (2002), "Getting Return on Quality: Revenue Expansion, Cost Reduction, or Both?"

Converse, P.D. (1921), *Marketing: Methods and Policies*, Prentice-Hall, Inc, New York, NY.

Cooper, Robin and Robert S. Kaplan (1991), "Profit Priorities from Activity-Based Costing," *Harvard Business Review*, 69, (May-June),130-35.

Copulsky, J. R. and M. J. Wolf (1990), "Relationship Marketing: Positioning for the Future," *Journal of Business Strategy*, 11 (4), 16-20.

Cowell, D.W. (1985), *The Marketing of Services*. Heinemann Ltd, London.

Cronin Jr., J.J. and Taylor, S.A. (1992), "Measuring Service Quality: A Reexamination and Extension", *Journal of Marketing*, Vol. 56, July, pp. 55-68.

Crosby, L.A. and Stephens, N. (1987), "Effects of Relationship Marketing on Satisfaction, Retention, and Prices in the Life Insurance Industry", *Journal of Marketing Research*, Vol. 24,November, pp. 404-11.

Crosby, L.A., Evans, K.R. and Cowles, D. (1990), "Relationship Quality in Services Selling: An Interpersonal Influence Perspective", *Journal of Marketing*, Vol. 54, July, pp. 68-81.

Crosby, Lawrence A., Kenneth R. Evans, and Deborah Cowles (1990),"Relationship Quality in Services Selling: An Interpersonal Influence Perspective," *Journal of Marketing*, 54 (July), 68-81.

Czepiel, J.A. (1990), "Service Encounters and Service Relationships: Implications for Research", *Journal of Business Research*, Vol. 20, January, pp. 13-21.

Czepiel, J.A., Solomon, M.R. and Surprenant, C.F. (Eds) (1985), *The Service Encounter: Managing Employee/Customer Interaction in Service Businesses*, Lexington Books, Lexington, MA.

Czepiel, John A., Michael R. Solomon, and Carol F. Surprenant, Eds. (1985), *The Service Encounter*. Lexington, MA: Lexington Books.

D.E., and Brown, S.W. (Eds), *Advances in Services Marketing, and Management: Research and Practice*, Vol. 1, JAI Press Inc., Greenwich, CT, pp. 75-90.

Darby, M. E. and E. Karni (1973), "Free Competition and the Optimal Amount of Fraud," *Journal of Law and Economics*, 16 (April), 67-86

Deighton, John (1997), "Commentary on 'Exploring the Implications of the Internet for Consumer Marketing,'" *Journal of the Academy of Marketing Science*, 25 (Fall), 347-51.

Delaunay, Jean-Claude and Jean Gadrey (1992), *Services in Economic Thought*. Boston: Kluwer. Desmet, Steven, Bart Van Looy, and Roland Van Dierdonck (1998), "The Nature of Services," in *Service Management: An Integrated Approach*,

Donnelly, J.H. Jr. (1976), "Marketing Intermediaries in Channels of Distribution for Services", *Journal of Marketing*, Vol. 40, January, pp. 55-7.

Donnelly, J.H. Jr. and George, W.R. (Eds) (1981), *Marketing of Services*, American Marketing Association, Chicago, IL.

Durrande-Moreau, Agnes and Jean-Claude Usinier (1999), "Time Styles and theWaiting Experience," *Journal of Service Research*, 2 (November), 173-86.

Edgett, Scott and Stephen Parkinson (1993), "Marketing for Service Industries—A Review," *The Service Industries Journal*, 13 (July), 19-39.

Edvardsson, Bo, Anders Gustafsson, Michael D. Johnson, and Bodily Sanden (2000), *New Service Development and Innovation in the New Economy*. Lund, Sweden: Student Literature

Eiglier, P., Langeard, E., Lovelock, C.H., Bateson, J.E.G. and Young, R.F. (Eds) (1977), *Marketing Consumer Services: New Insights*, Marketing Science Institute, Cambridge, MA.

Enis, B.M. and Roering, K.J. (1981), "Services Marketing: Different Products, Similar Strategy", in Donnelly, J.H. and George, W.R. (Eds), *Marketing of Services,* American Marketing Association, Chicago, IL, pp. 1-4.

Enis, Ben M. and Kenneth J. Roering (1981), "Services Marketing: DifferentProducts, Similar Strategy," in *Marketing of Services*, J. H.Donnelly and W. R. George, eds. Chicago: American Marketing Association, 1-4.

European Journal of Marketing, 18 (4), 36-45.000), *Service Management and Marketing: A Customer RelationshipApproach*, 2nd ed. Chichester, UK: Wiley.

Firat, A. Fuat, Nikhiseh Dholakia, and Alladi Venkatesh (1995), "Marketing in a Postmodern World," *European Journal of Marketing*, 29 (1), 40-56.

Fisk, R.P. and Tansuhaj, P.S. (1985), *Services Marketing: An Annotated Bibliography*, : American Marketing Association, Chicago, IL.

Fisk, R.P., Tansuhaj, P.S. and Crosby, L.A. (1988), *SERVMARK: The Electronic Bibliography of Services Marketing Literature*, The First Interstate Center for Services Marketing, Arizona State University, Tempe, AZ.

Fisk, Raymond P., Stephen W. Brown, and Mary Jo Bitner, (1993), "Tracking the Evolution of the Services Marketing Literature," *Journal of Retailing,* 69 (Spring), 61-103.

Fitzsimmons, James A. and Mona J. Fitzsimmons (1998), *Service Management: Operations, Strategy, and Information Technology*, 2nd ed.New York: Irwin/McGraw-Hill.

George, W.R. (1972), "Marketing in the Service Industries", Ph.D. dissertation, University of Georgia.

George, W.R. (1977), "The Retailing of Services – A Challenging Future", *Journal of Retailing,* Vol. 53, pp. 85-98.

George, W.R. (1990), "Internal Marketing and Organizational Behavior: A Partnership in Developing Customer-Conscious

Employees at Every Level", *Journal of Business Research*, Vol. 20, January, pp. 63-70.

George, W.R. and Barksdale, H.C. (1974), "Marketing Activities in the Service Industries", *Journal of Marketing*, Vol. 38, October, pp. 65-70.

George, W.R. and Gibson, B.E. (1991), "Blueprinting: A Tool for Managing Quality in Service", in Brown, S.W., Gummesson, E., Edvardsson, B. and Gustavsson, B. (Eds), *Service Quality: Multidisciplinary and Multinational Perspectives*, Lexington Books, Lexington, MA, pp. 73-91.

George,William R. and Leonard L. Berry (1981), "Guidelines for the Advertising of Services," *Business Horizons*, 24 (July-August), 52-56.

Glaser, Barney G. (2001), *The Grounded Theory Perspective: Conceptualization Contrasted with Description*. Mill Valley, CA: Sociology Press. and Anselm L. Strauss (1967), *The Discovery of Grounded Theory.*

Goodwin, C.F. (1990), "I Can Do It Myself: Training the Service Consumer to Contribute to Service Productivity", *Journal of Services Marketing*, Vol. 2, pp. 71-8.

Greenfield, Harry I. (2002), "A Note on the Goods/Services Dichotomy,"*Service Industries Journal*, 22 (October), 19-21.

Grönroos, C. (1979), "Marketing of Services: A Study of the Marketing Function of Service Firms",

Grönroos, C. (1981), "Internal Marketing – An Integral Part of Marketing Theory", in Donnelly, Econ. D. dissertation, Swedish School of Economics (Finland).

Grönroos, C. (1983), *Strategic Management and Marketing in the Service Sector*, Marketing Science Institute, Cambridge, MA, (Also published by Swedish School of Economics and Business Administration, 1982).

Grönroos, C. (1990a), "Relationship Approach to Marketing in Service Contexts: The Marketing and Organizational Behaviour Interface", *Journal of Business Research*, Vol. 20, January,pp. 3-11.

Grönroos, C. (1990b), *Service Management and Marketing: Managing the Moments of Truth in Service Competition*, Lexington Books, Lexington, MA.

Grönroos, C. and Gummesson, E. (Eds) (1985), *Service Marketing – Nordic School Perspectives*, Swedish School of Economics, Stockholm, Sweden.

Grove, Stephen J., Raymond P. Fisk, and Joby John (2003), "The Futureof Services Marketing: Forecasts from Ten Services Experts," *Journal of Services Marketing*, 17, 106-19.

Gummesson, E. (1987), "Using Internal Marketing to Develop a New Culture – The Case of Ericsson Quality", *Journal of Business and Industrial Marketing*, Vol. 2, Summer, pp. 23-8.

Gummesson, Evert (1981), "The Marketing of Professional Services— 25 Propositions," in *Marketing of Services*, J. H. Donnelly andW. R.George, eds. Chicago: American Marketing Association, 108-12.

———(1968), "Similarities or Differences in Products and Service Retailing," *Journal of Retailing*, 43 (Winter), 1-9.

———(1993), *Quality Management in Service Organizations*. New York: International Service Quality Association.

———(1997), "Exploring the Implications of the Internet for Consumer Marketing," *Journal of the Academy of Marketing Science*, 25 (Fall), 329-46.

———1974), *Marketing in the Service Sector*. Cambridge, MA: Winthrop.

———1994), "Service Management: An Evaluation and the Future," *International Journal of Service IndustryManagement*, 5 (1), 77-96.

———2002a), "Practical Value of Adequate Marketing Management Theory," *European Journal of Marketing*, 36 (3), 325-49.

———2002b), *Total Relationship Marketing*, 2nd rev. ed. Oxford, UK: Butterworth-Heinemann. (forthcoming), "Qualitative Research in Marketing: Roadmapfor a Wilderness of Complexity and Unpredictability." *EuropeanJournal of Marketing*. Hart, Myra, Michael J. Roberts, and Julia D. Stevens (2003), *Zipcar: Refining the Business Model*, Case No. 9-803-096. Boston: Harvard Business School Press.

Hart, C.W.L. (1988), "The Power of Unconditional Service Guarantees", *Harvard Business Review*, July-August, pp. 54-62.

Hart, C.W.L., Heskett, J.L. and Sasser, W.E., Jr. (1990), "The Profitable Art of Service Recovery", *Harvard Business Review*, July-August, pp. 148-56.

Hawthorne, NY: Aldine.Gonçalves, Karen P. (1998), *Services Marketing: A Strategic Approach.*

Heskett, J.L. (1986), *Managing in the Service Economy*, Harvard Business School Press, Boston,MA.

Heskett, J.L., Sasser, W.E, Jr. and Hart, C.W.L. (1990), *Service Breakthroughs: Changing the Rules of the Game*, The Free Press, New York, NY.

Hill, Peter (1999), "Tangibles, Intangibles, and Services: A New Taxonomy for the Classification of Output," *Canadian Journal of Economics*, 32 (April): 426-46.

Hill, T. P. (1977), "On Goods and Services," *Review of Income and Wealth*, 20, 315-18.

Hoffman, K. Douglas, and John E. G. Bateson (2001), *Essentials of Services Marketing*, 2nd ed. New York: Dryden.

Hogan, John E., Katherine N. Lemon, and Roland T. Rust (2002), "Customer Equity Management: Charting New Directions for the Futureof Marketing," *Journal of Service Research*, 5 (August), 4-12.

Hui, M.K. and Bateson, J.E.G. (1991), "Perceived Control and the Effects of Music on High- and Low-Involvement Consumers' Processing of Ads", *Journal of Consumer Research*, Vol. 18,September, pp. 174-84.

Hunt, H.Keith, ed. (1977), "Conceptualization and Measurement of Consumer Satisfaction and Dissatisfaction," National Science Foundation Report NSF/RA 770003, Marketing Science Institute, Cambridge,

Hunt, Shelby D. (1976), *Marketing Theory: Conceptual Foundations of Research in Marketing*. Columbus, OH: Grid.

"If Everything Is Service, Why Is This Happening Now and What Difference Does It Make?" *Journal of Marketing*, 69 (January), 23-24.

Jinhong Xie (2000), "Advance Pricing of Services and Other Implications of Separating Purchase and Consumption," *Journal of Service Research*, 2 (February), 227-39.

Jochen Wirtz (2003), "Has Revenue Management Become Acceptable? Findings from an International Study on the Perceived Fairness of Rate Fences," *Journal of Service Research* 6 (November), 125-35.

Jochen Wirtz (2004), *Services Marketing: People, Technology, Strategy*, 5th ed. Upper Saddle Rover, NJ: Prentice Hall.???and Lauren Wright (2002), *Principles of Service Marketing and Management*, 2nd ed. Upper Saddle Rover, NJ: Prentice Hall.????and Robert F. Young (1979), "Look to Consumers to Increase Productivity," *Harvard Business Review*, 57 (May-June), 168-78.

Johnson, E.M. (1964), *An Introduction to Service Marketing Management*, University of Delaware, Newark, NJ.

Johnson, E.M. (1968), *Our Service Economy: Trends and Implications,* Marketing Science Institute, Philadelphia, PA.

Johnson, E.M. (1969), "Are Goods and Services Different? An Exercise in Marketing Theory", PhD dissertation, Washington University.

Johnson, E.M., Scheuing, E.E. and Gaida, K.A. (1986), *Profitable Services Marketing*, Dow Jones-Irwin, Inc., Homewood, IL.

Johnston, R. (1987), "A Framework for Developing a Quality Strategy in a Customer Processing Operation", *International Journal of Quality & Reliability Management*, Vol. 4 No. 4, pp. 35-44.

Jones, Peter and Emma Peppiatt (1996), "Managing Perceptions ofWaiting Times in Service Queues," *International Journal of Service IndustryManagement*, 7 (5), 47-61.

Journal of Marketing, 66 (October), 7-24.Sasser,W. Earl, Jr. (1976), "Match Supply and Demand in Service Industries," *Harvard Business Review*, 54 (November-December), 133-40.

Judd, R.C. (1964), "The Case for Redefining Services", *Journal of Marketing,* Vol. 28, January,pp. 58-9.

Judd, Robert C. (1964), "The Case for Redefining Services," *Journal of Marketing,* 28 (January), 59.

Kasper, Hans, Piet van Helsdingen, andWouter de Vries (1999), *Services Marketing Management: An International Perspective.* Chichester, UK: Wiley.

Katz, Kren L., Blaire M. Larson, and Richard C. Larson (1991), "Prescription for theWaiting-in-Line Blues: Entertain, Enlighten, and Engage," *Sloan Management Review*, 31 (Winter): 44-53.

Kelley, S.W., Donnelly, J.H. Jr. and Skinner, S.J. (1990), "Customer Participation in Service Production and Delivery", *Journal of Retailing*, Vol. 66, Fall, pp. 315-35.

Kelly, J.P. and George, W.R. (1982), "Strategic Management Issues for the Retailing of Services", *Journal of Retailing*, Vol. 58, Summer, pp. 26-43.

Kerin, Roger A., Eric N. Berkowitz, Steven W. Hartley, and William Rudelius (2003), *Marketing*, 7th ed. New York: McGraw-Hill.

Kimes, Sheryl E. (2003),"Revenue Management: ARetrospective," *Cornell Hotel and Restaurant Administration Quarterly*, (October-December), 131-38.

Kingman-Brundage, J. (1989), "The ABCs of Service System Blueprinting", in Bitner, M.J. and Crosby, L.A. (Eds), *Designing a Winning Service Strategy: 7th Annual Services Marketing Conference Proceedings*, American Marketing Association, Chicago, IL, pp. 30-3.

Kingman-Brundage, J. (1991), "Technology, Design and Service Quality", *International Journal of Service Industry Management*, Vol. 2 No. 3, pp. 47-59.

Kostecki, Michel (1996), "Waiting Lines as a Marketing Issue," *EuropeanManagement Journal*, 14 (3), 295-303.

Kotler, Philip (2003), *Marketing Management*, 11th ed. Upper Saddle River, NJ: Prentice Hall.

Kotter, John P. and James L. Heskett (1992), *Corporate Culture and Performance*, New York: Free Press.

Kuhn, Thomas S. (1970), *The Structure of Scientific Revolutions*, 2nd ed.Chicago: University of Chicago Press.

Kurtz, David L. and Kenneth L. Clow (1998), *Services Marketing*. New York: John Wiley.

L.G. and Upah, G.D. (Eds), *Emerging Perspectives on Services Marketing*, American Marketing Association, Chicago, IL, pp. 50-3.

LaLonde, Bernard J. and Paul H. Zinszer (1976), *Customer Service: Meaning and Measurement.* Chicago: National Council of PhysicalDistribution Management.

Laroche, Michel, Jasmine Bergeron, and Christine Goutaland (2001), "A Three-Dimensional Scale of Intangibility," *Journal of Service Research,*4 (August), 26-38.

Larsson, R. and Bowen, D.E. (1989), "Organization and Customer: Managing Design and Coordination of Services", *Academy of Management Review,* Vol. 14, April, pp. 213-33.

Lehtinen, J.R. and Lehtinen, U. (1982), "Service Quality: A Study of Quality Dimensions", Unpublished Working Paper, Service Management Institute, Helsinki.

Levitt, T. (1981), "Marketing Intangible Products and Product Intangibles", *Harvard Business Review,* Vol. 59, May-June, pp. 94-102.

Levitt, Theodore (1972), "Production Line Approach to Service," *Harvard Business Review,* 50 (September-October), 41-52.

Lewis, B.R. and Entwistle, T.W. (1990), "Managing the Service Encounter: A Focus on the Employee", *International Journal of Service Industry Management,* Vol. 1 No. 3, pp. 41-52.

Lovelock, C.H. (1979), "Theoretical Contributions from Services and Nonbusiness Marketing", in Ferrell, O.C., Brown, S.W. and Lamb, C.W. Jr. (Eds), *Conceptual and Theoretical Developments in Marketing,* American Marketing Association, Chicago, pp. 147-65.

Lovelock, C.H. (1983), "Classifying Services to Gain Strategic Marketing Insights", *Journal of Marketing,* Vol. 47, Summer, pp. 9-20.

Lovelock, C.H. (1984), *Services Marketing: Text, Cases, and Readings,* Prentice-Hall, Inc., Englewood Cliffs, NJ.

Lovelock, C.H. (1988), *Managing Services: Marketing, Operations, Human Resources,* : Prentice-Hall, Inc., Englewood Cliffs, NJ.

Lovelock, C.H. (1991), *Services Marketing,* second edition, Prentice-Hall, Inc., Englewood Cliffs, NJ.

Lovelock, C.H. (1992), *Managing Services: Marketing, Operations, Human Resources,* Second Edition, Prentice-Hall, Inc., Englewood Cliffs, NJ.

Lovelock, Christopher H. (1983a), "Classifying Services to Gain Strategic Marketing Insights," *Journal of Marketing* 47 (Summer), 9-20.

Maister, David H. (1985), "The Psychology of Waiting Lines," in *The Service Encounter*, J. A. Czepiel, M. R. Solomon, and C. F.Surprenant, eds. Lexington, MA: Lexington Books, 113-26.

Marshall, Alfred ([1890] 1962), *Principles of Economics*. London: Macmillan.

McDowell, W.J. (1953), "The Marketing of Consumer Services", PhD dissertation, University of Iowa.

McKenna, Regis (1997), *Real Time*. Boston: Harvard Business School Press.

Meuter, Maktthew L., Amy L. Ostrom, Robert I. Roundtree, and Mary Jo Bitner (2000), "Self-Service Technologies: Understanding CustomerSatisfaction with Technology-Based Service Encounters," *Journal of Marketing*, 64 (July), 50-64.

Miller, Danny (1990), *The IcarusParadox*.NewYork: Harper Business.

Mills, P.K. (1990), "On the Quality of Services in Encounters: An Agency Perspective", *Journal of Business Research*, Vol. 20, January, pp. 31-41.

Mittal, Banwari and Julie Baker (2002), "Advertising Strategies for Hospitality Services," *Cornell Hotel and Restaurant Administration Quarterly*, 43 (April), 51-63.

Morris, Barbara and Robert Johnson (1987), "Dealing with InherentVariability: The Difference between Manufacturing and Service?" *International Journal of Production Management*, 7 (4), 13-22.

Namisvayam, Karthik (2003), "The Consumer as Transient Employee: Consumer Satisfaction through the Lens of Job-Performance Models,"*International Journal of Service Industry Management*, 14 (4),420-35.

Nelson, Philip (1970), "Advertising as Information," *Journal of Political Economy*, 82(July-August), 729-54.

Nonaka, Ikujiro and Hirotaka Takeuchi, (1995), *The Knowledge-Creating Company*. New York: Oxford University Press.

Normann, R. (1984), *Service Management: Strategy and Leadership in Service Businesses*, Wiley, Chichester.

Norris, Ruby T. (1941), *The Theory of Consumer's Demand*.NewHaven,CT: Yale University Press.

Oliva, T.A., Oliver, R.L. and Macmillan, I.C. (1992), "A Catastrophe Model for Developing Service Satisfaction Strategies", *Journal of Marketing*, Vol. 56, July, pp. 83-95.

Oliver, R.L. (1980), "A Cognitive Model of the Antecedents and Consequences of Satisfaction Decisions", *Journal of Marketing Research*, Vol. 17, November, pp. 460-9.

P. K. Kannan, eds. (2002), *e-Service: New Directions in Theory and Practice*. Armonk, NY: M. E. Sharpe.

Parasuraman, A., Berry, L.L. and Zeithaml, V.A. (1991b), "Understanding, Measuring and Improving Service Quality: Findings from a Multiphase Research Program", in Brown, S.W ., Gummesson, E., Edvardsson, B. and Gustavsson, B. (Eds), *Service Quality: Multidisciplinary and Multinational Perspectives*, Lexington Books, Lexington, MA, pp. 253-68.

Parasuraman, A., Berry, L.L., and Zeithaml, V.A. (1991a), "Refinement and Reassessment of the SERVQUAL Scale", *Journal of Retailing*, Vol. 67, Winter, pp. 420-50.

Parasuraman, A., Zeithaml, V.A. and Berry, L.L. (1985), "A Conceptual Model of Service Quality and Its Implications for Future Research", *Journal of Marketing*, Vol. 49, pp. 41-50.

Parker, D.D. (1958), "The Marketing of Consumer Services", DBA dissertation, University of Washington.

Parker, Donald D. (1960), *The Marketing of Consumer Services*. Seattle: Bureau of Business Research, University of Washington.

Peppers, Don and Martha Rogers (1999), *The One to One Manager*. New York: Doubleday. Peterson, Robert A., Sridhar Balasubramanian, and Bart J. Bronnenberg

Pine, B. Joseph II (1993),*Mass Customization: The NewFrontier in Business Competition*. Boston: Harvard Business School Press.

Prahalad, C. K., and Allen Hammond (2002), "Serving theWorld's Poor, Profitably." *Harvard Business Review*, 80 (September), 48-57.

Pride, William M. and O. C. Ferrell (2003), *Marketing: Concepts and Strategies*, 12th ed. Boston: Houghton Mifflin.

Quinn, J.B. (1992), *Intelligent Enterprise*, The Free Press, New York, NY.

Quinn, J.B. and Paquette, P.C. (1990), "Technology in Services: Creating Organizational Revolutions", *Sloan Management Review*, Winter, pp. 67-78.

Quinn, J.B., Dooley, T.L. and Paquette P.C. (1990), "Beyond Products: Services-Based Strategy", *Harvard Business Review*, Vol. 68, March-April, pp. 58-68.

R. Paul Olson, and D. Daryl Wyckoff (1978), *Management of Service Operations*. Boston: Allyn & Bacon.

Rakowski, James P. (1982), "The Customer Service Concept," *Review of Business and Economic Research*, 18 (Winter), 55-86.

Rathmell, J.M. (1966), "What Is Meant By Services?", *Journal of Marketing*, Vol. 30, October,pp. 32-6.

Rathmell, J.M. (1974), *Marketing in the Service Sector*, Winthrop Publishers, Inc., Cambridge, MA.

Rathmell, John M. (1966), "What Is Meant by Services?" *Journal ofMarketing*, 30 (October), 32-36.

Regan, W.J. (1963), "The Service Revolution", *Journal of Marketing*, Vol. 27, July, pp. 57-62.

Regan,William J., (1963), "The Service Revolution," *Journal of Marketing*,47 (July), 57-62.

Reichheld, F.F. and Sasser, W.E., Jr. (1990), "Zero Defections: Quality Comes to Services", *Harvard Business Review*, Vol. 68, September-October, pp. 105-11.

Reichheld, Frederick F., and Phil Schefter (2000), "E-Loyalty: Your Secret Weapon on the Web," *Harvard Business Review*, 78 (July-August), 105-112.

Richard B. Chase (1998), "The Strategic Levers of Yield Management," *Journal of Service Research*, 1 (November), 156-66.

Riddle, Dorothy I. (1986), *Service-Led Growth*. New York: Praeger.

Robinson, Joan ([1933] 1969), *The Economics of Imperfect Competition*, 2nd ed. London: Macmillan.

Rossiter, Margaret (2003), "State-Based Management:AProcess for Reducing Customer Waiting in Over-the-Counter Service Transactions,"

Rust, R.T. and Oliver, R.L. (1993), "Frontiers in Service Quality" in Rust, R.T. and Oliver, R.L. (Eds), *Frontiers in Service Quality*, Sage Publications, Beverly Hills, CA.

Rust, Roland T. (1998), "What Is tho Domain of Service Research?" *Journal of Service Research*, 1 (November), 107.

Sasser, W.E., Jr., Christopher, W.L. and Heskett, J.L. (1991), *The Service Management Course*, The Free Press, New York, NY.

Say, Jean-Baptiste ([1803] 1964), *A Treatise on Political Economy*. Reprintsof Economic Classics. New York: Augustus M. Kelly.

Scheuing, E.E. and Johnson, E.M. (1989), "A Proposed Model for New Service Development", *Journal of Services Marketing*, Vol. 3, Spring, pp. 25-34.

Schlesinger, L.A. and Heskett, J.L. (1991), "Breaking the Cycle of Failure in Services", *Sloan Management Review*, Vol. 32, Spring, pp. 17-28.

Schlesinger, L.A. and Heskett, J.L. (1991), "Enfranchisement of Service Workers", *California Management Review*, Summer, pp. 83-100.

Schmenner, Roger W. (1986), "How Can Service Businesses Survive and Prosper?" *Sloan Management Review*, 27 (Spring), 21-32.

Schneider, Benjamin (2000), Pt. 9, in *Services Marketing Self-Portraits: Introspections, Reflections, and Glimpses from the Experts*, R. P. Fisk, S. J. Grove, and J. John, eds. Chicago: American Marketing Association, 173-187.

Schumpeter, Joseph A. (1950), *Capitalism, Socialism and Democracy*, 4th ed. New York: Harper & Row.

Shelp, Ronald Kent (1981), *Beyond Industrialization: Ascendancy of t he Global Service Economy*. New York: Praeger.

Shostack, G. Lynn (1977), "Breaking Free from Product Marketing,"*Journal of Marketing*, 44 (April), 73-80.

Shostack, G.L. (1977), "Breaking Free from Product Marketing", *Journal of Marketing*, Vol. 41, April, pp. 73-80.

Shostack, G.L. (1984), "Designing Services That Deliver", *Harvard Business Review*, 62 January-February, pp. 133-39.

Shostack, G.L. (1987), "Service Positioning through Structural Change", *Journal of Marketing,* Vol. 51, January, pp. 34-43.

Shugan, Steven M. (2004), "Finance, Operations and Marketing Conflicts in Service Firms," *Journal of Marketing,* 68 (January), 24-27.

Sidney J. Levy (1969), "Broadening the Concept of Marketing,"*Journal of Marketing,* 33 (January), 10-15.

Silvestro, Rhian, Lyn Fitzgerald, Robert Johnston, and Christopher Voss (1992), "Towards a Classification of Service Processes," *International Journal of Service Industry Management,* 3 (3), 62-75.

Smith, Adam ([1776] 1969), *The Wealth of Nations, Books I-III,* with an Introduction by A. Skinner. London: Penguin Books.

Soberson-Ferrer, H. and Dardis, R. (1991), "Determinants of Household Expenditures for Services", *Journal of Consumer Research,* Vol. 17, March, pp. 385-97.

Solomon, M.R., Surprenant, C., Czepiel, J.A. and Gutman, E.G. (1985), "A Role Theory Perspective on Dyadic Interactions: The Service Encounter", *Journal of Marketing,* Vol. 49, Winter, pp. 99-111.

Solomon, Michael R. and ElnoraW. Stuart (2003), *Marketing: Real Peo ple,Real Choices.* Upper Saddle River, NJ: Prentice Hall.

Soman, Dilip (2001), "The Mental Accounting of Sunk Time Costs:Why Time Is Not Like Money," *Journal of Behavioral Decision Making,* 14, 169-85.

Stephen J. Grove, and Joby John, eds. (2000), *Services Marketing Self-Portraits: Introspections, Reflections, and Glimpses from the Experts.* Chicago: American Marketing Association. eds. (2004), *Interactive Services Marketing,*2nd ed. New York: Houghton Mifflin.

"Strategies for Managing Demand in Capacity-Constrained Service Organizations," *Service Industries Journal,* 4 (November),12-30.????(2000), Pt. 7, in *Services Marketing Self-Portraits: Introspections,*

Stix, Gary (2002), "RealTime," *Scientific American,* (September), 36-39.

Sundbo, Jon (2002), "The Service Economy: Standardization or Customization?" *The Service Industries Journal*, 22 (October), 93-116.

Surprenant, C.F. and Solomon, M.R. (1987), "Predictability and Personalization in the Service Encounter", *Journal of Marketing*, Vol. 51, April, pp. 86-96.

Swartz, T.A., Bowen, D.E. and Brown, S.W. (1992b), "Fifteen Years After Breaking Free: Services Then, Now and Beyond", in Swartz, T.A., Bowen, D.E. and Brown, S.W. (Eds), *Advances in-Services Marketing and Management*, Vol. 1, JAI Press Inc., Greenwich, CT, pp. 1-21.

Swartz, T.A., Bowen, D.E., and Brown, S.W. (Eds) (1992a), *Advances in Services Marketing and Management,* Vol. 1, JAI Press, Greenwich, CT.

Takeuchi, H. and Quelch, J.A. (1983), "Quality is More than Making a Good Product", *Harvard Business Review,* Vol. 83, July-August, pp. 139-45.

Tansuhaj, P., Randall, D. and McCullough J. (1988), "A Services Marketing Management Model: Integrating Internal and External Marketing Functions", *Journal of Services Marketing*, Vol.2, Winter, pp. 31-8.

"The Co-Creation of Value," *Journal of Marketing*, 69 (January),

"The Servicescape," in T. A. Swartz and D. Iacobucci, eds. *Handbook of Services Marketing and Management*, Thousand Oaks, CA: Sage, 37-50.

Thomas, D.R.E. (1978), "Strategy is Different in Service Businesses", *Harvard Business Review*,Vol. 56, July-August, pp. 158-65.

Vargo, Stephen L. and Robert F. Lusch (2004a), "Evolving to a New Dominant Logic for Marketing," *Journal of Marketing*, 69 (January), 1-17.

Weinberger, M.G. (1976), "Services and Goods: A Laboratory Study of Informational Influences", PhD dissertation, Arizona State University, AZ.

Weinberger, M.G. and Brown, S.W. (1977), "A Difference in Informational Influences: Services vs. Goods", *Journal of the Academy of Marketing Science*, Vol. 5, Winter, pp. 389-407.

William T. Faranda, Amy R. Hubbert, and Valarie A. Zeithaml (1997), "Customer Contributions and Roles in Service Delivery," *International Journal of Service Industry Management*, 8 (3), 193-205.

Williams, M.R. and Mowen, J.C. (1990), "The Goods Versus Services Marketing Dichotomy: Factor Fiction?", in Parasuraman, A., Bearden, W., Deshpande, R., Folkes, V.S., Madden, T.J.,Stewart, D.W. Varadarajan, P.R. and Wilkie, W.L. (Eds), *1990 AMA Educators' Proceedings Enhancing Knowledge Development in Marketing*, American Marketing Association, Chicago,Ill, pp. 355-60.

Wilson, Aubrey (1972), *The Marketing of Professional Services.* London: McGraw-Hill.

Wyckham, R. G., P. T. Fitzroy, and G. D. Mandrey (1975), "Marketing of Services—An Evaluation of the Theory," *European Journal of Marketing*, 9 (Spring), 59-67.

Zeithaml, V.A. (1981), "How Consumer Evaluation Processes Differ between Goods and Services", Donnelly, J.H. and George, W.R. (Eds), *Marketing of Services,* American Marketing Association, Chicago, Ill, pp. 186-90.

Zeithaml, V.A., Berry, L.L. and Parasuraman, A. (1988), "Communication and Control Processes in the Delivery of Service Quality", *Journal of Marketing*, Vol. 52, April, pp. 35-48.

Zeithaml, V.A., Parasuraman, A. and Berry, L.L. (1985), "Problems and Strategies in Services Marketing", *Journal of Marketing*, Vol. 49, Spring, pp. 33-46.

Zeithaml, Valerie A. (1981), "How Consumer Evaluation Processes Differ Between Goods and Services," in J. H. Donnelly and. W.R. George, *Marketing of Services*, eds. Chicago: American Marketing Association,186-90.

Zeithaml, V.A., Parasuraman, A. and Berry, L.L. (1990), *Delivering Quality Service: Balancing Customer Perceptions and Expectations*, Free Press, New York, NY.

Index

***